VACCINE DRUG DELIVERY

PRINCIPLES AND APPLICATIONS

VEERAREDDY PRABHAKAR REDDY,
MURALIDHAR RAO AKKALADEVI

Contents

Vaccine Drug Delivery: Principles And Applications

Dr. Prabhakar Reddy Veerareddy
Head, University College of Pharmaceutical Sciences,
Palamuru University,
Mahabubnagar, Telangana, India
Dr. Muralidhar Rao Akkaladevi
Principal, St. Mary's College of Pharmacy,
Secunderabad, Telangana, India

Year of Publication: January 2025
Published by Notion Press
Notion Press, Inc.
800, West El Camino Real #180,
California, USA 94040
Notion Press Media Pvt Ltd
#7, Red Cross Road,
Egmore, Chennai, Tamil Nadu 600008
Email ID: publish@notionpress.com
Phone Number: +91 44 46315631

Preface

Vaccines have transformed global health, reducing the burden of infectious diseases and improving life expectancy across populations. From the first crude inoculations against smallpox to the sophisticated mRNA vaccines of today, vaccine development has continuously evolved, integrating advancements in immunology, molecular biology, and material science. Yet, the efficacy of vaccines is not determined solely by the antigen or the immune response it elicits—it is deeply influenced by how the vaccine is delivered. **Vaccine drug delivery systems** play a pivotal role in ensuring that antigens reach the right cells, at the right time, in the right way, to elicit robust and lasting immunity.

This book, **"Vaccine Drug Delivery: Principles and Applications,"** aims to provide a **comprehensive exploration of the science, technology, and innovation behind vaccine delivery systems**. By integrating principles of immunology, nanotechnology, biomaterials, and pharmaceutical sciences, we delve into how modern delivery platforms are designed, optimized, and applied in real-world immunization strategies.

Scope and Objectives

The primary goal of this book is to serve as a **foundational reference** for students, researchers, healthcare professionals, and industry experts seeking to understand vaccine delivery at an advanced level. Whether one is interested in **lipid nanoparticles for mRNA vaccines, polymeric carriers for controlled release, microneedles for transdermal immunization, or biomimetic delivery systems**, this book provides detailed insights into the mechanisms, challenges, and innovations shaping the future of vaccination.

Key themes explored include:

- **Historical Evolution of Vaccines and Delivery Systems** – Tracing vaccine delivery from **Pasteur's early discoveries** to modern nanotechnology-driven platforms.
- **Immunological Principles of Vaccine Delivery** – Understanding how vaccine formulations interact with **immune cells, antigen-presenting pathways, and adjuvants** to elicit effective responses.
- **Conventional and Next-Generation Delivery Systems** – Examining classic approaches such as **intramuscular injections** and **live-attenuated vaccines**, as well as advanced systems such as **lipid**

nanoparticles (LNPs), polymeric nanoparticles (PLGA), hybrid nanocarriers, and microneedles.
- **Challenges in Global Vaccine Distribution** – Addressing **cold chain dependency, vaccine stability, and accessibility issues**, especially in resource-limited settings.
- **Future Innovations and Personalized Vaccination** – Exploring next-generation vaccine strategies, including **self-amplifying RNA (saRNA), AI-driven antigen selection, and cell-membrane-coated nanoparticles**.

Why Focus on Vaccine Drug Delivery?

While the **antigenic component** of vaccines has always been the focal point of research, the **delivery mechanism** significantly impacts vaccine efficacy. Factors such as **dosage precision, immune cell targeting, thermostability, and patient compliance** are directly influenced by the delivery system used. The **rapid development of COVID-19 mRNA vaccines** highlighted the importance of delivery science, as **lipid nanoparticles** emerged as critical vehicles for protecting and transporting fragile nucleic acids. Beyond COVID-19, similar breakthroughs are shaping vaccines against **HIV, tuberculosis, malaria, and cancer**, making this an exciting and transformative field.

Target Audience

This book is designed to be **accessible yet rigorous**, catering to:

- **Undergraduate and postgraduate students** in pharmacy, biomedical sciences, biotechnology, and immunology.
- **Researchers and scientists** involved in vaccine development, nanotechnology, and pharmaceutical sciences.
- **Healthcare professionals** interested in understanding how vaccine formulations affect immunization strategies.
- **Regulatory professionals** overseeing vaccine formulation, approval, and global distribution.

Structure of the Book

This book is divided into **twelve chapters**, progressing from **fundamental principles to advanced innovations**:

- **Chapter 1** introduces **historical perspectives** on vaccine development and the emergence of novel delivery systems.

- **Chapter 2** discusses **immunological mechanisms**, including **antigen recognition, immune activation, and memory formation**.
- **Chapters 3 and 4** cover **conventional vaccine formulations** and **adjuvant systems**, detailing their roles in enhancing immunogenicity.
- **Chapters 5 and 6** focus on **nanotechnology-based delivery** and **microneedle-based vaccines**, highlighting key advantages in precision immunization.
- **Chapter 7** explores **nucleic acid vaccines** (DNA, mRNA, and saRNA) and their specialized delivery methods.
- **Chapter 8** addresses **stability and formulation strategies**, including lyophilization, spray drying, and the role of excipients in vaccine preservation.
- **Chapter 9** examines **biomimetic and cell-based delivery systems**, including artificial antigen-presenting cells (aAPCs) and membrane-coated nanoparticles.
- **Chapter 10** delves into **regulatory, ethical, and global considerations**, with discussions on harmonization, vaccine equity, and pandemic preparedness.
- **Chapter 11** highlights **cutting-edge innovations**, such as AI-driven vaccine development and tailored vaccines for specific populations.
- **Chapter 12** presents **case studies**, illustrating how novel delivery strategies have influenced real-world vaccines.

Final Thoughts

The field of vaccine drug delivery is at an inflection point. As we enter a **new era of vaccinology**, the convergence of **nanotechnology, bioengineering, and computational sciences** will redefine how vaccines are designed, delivered, and optimized for diverse populations. By compiling the latest knowledge, challenges, and innovations, this book serves as both a **scientific reference** and an **inspiration for future breakthroughs** in immunization science.

We hope that this book provides **valuable insights** and encourages further **exploration and research** into the fascinating world of vaccine drug delivery systems.

Acknowledgments

This book is the result of extensive research, collaborations, and insights from **experts in immunology, pharmacy, bioengineering, and nanotechnology**. We extend our gratitude to the **scientific community,**

vaccine developers, and healthcare professionals whose efforts continue to drive progress in global health.

Finally, we acknowledge the **millions of healthcare workers and vaccine researchers worldwide** who have played an instrumental role in combating **infectious diseases** and shaping the future of immunization.

Dr. Prabhakar Reddy Veerareddy
Dr. Muralidhar Rao Akkaladevi

Chapterwise Contents

ONE

INTRODUCTION TO VACCINE DRUG DELIVERY SYSTEMS

The development of **vaccine drug delivery systems** has revolutionized the prevention and control of infectious diseases, offering a precise, efficient, and targeted approach to immunization. While the primary function of vaccines remains to stimulate the immune system to recognize and combat pathogens, advancements in delivery systems have significantly enhanced the safety, efficacy, and accessibility of vaccines. This chapter provides a detailed exploration of the historical evolution of vaccines and the key milestones that have led to the sophisticated drug delivery technologies available today.

1.1 Historical Evolution of Vaccines

Vaccines have a fascinating history that mirrors humanity's persistent battle against infectious diseases. The journey from rudimentary inoculation methods to highly sophisticated delivery systems showcases a blend of empirical wisdom, scientific breakthroughs, and technological innovation.

1.1.1 Early Vaccines: Smallpox and Pasteur's Contributions

The history of vaccines begins with the fight against **smallpox**, a devastating disease that claimed millions of lives across centuries. The earliest documented vaccine practices date back to **variolation**, an ancient method practiced in China and the Middle East. Variolation involved introducing material from smallpox lesions into healthy individuals to induce immunity. Although risky, this method significantly reduced mortality rates.

The pivotal breakthrough came in **1796**, when **Edward Jenner**, an English physician, discovered that exposure to **cowpox** could confer immunity to smallpox. Jenner's use of cowpox material to vaccinate a young boy marked the beginning of modern vaccinology. His work demonstrated the potential of vaccines to provide targeted and long-lasting protection, laying the foundation for future research.

In the late 19th century, **Louis Pasteur** further revolutionized vaccine development. Known as the father of microbiology, Pasteur introduced the concept of **attenuation**, wherein pathogens were weakened in the laboratory to create safe and effective vaccines. His work on **rabies** and **anthrax vaccines** not only saved countless lives but also established scientific principles that continue to guide vaccine research today. Pasteur's contributions underscored the importance of controlled experimentation and opened new avenues for developing vaccines against a wide range of diseases.

1.1.2 Advancements in Vaccine Technology

The 20th century witnessed an explosion of advancements in vaccine development. The discovery of **inactivated and subunit vaccines** addressed safety concerns associated with live-attenuated vaccines. For instance, the **Salk polio vaccine**, introduced in the 1950s, utilized inactivated poliovirus to protect millions without the risk of causing the disease itself.

Concurrently, the advent of **adjuvants**—substances that enhance the immune response—marked a significant leap in vaccine efficacy. The inclusion of adjuvants such as **alum** in vaccines improved their ability to stimulate the immune system, reducing the required dosage and enabling mass immunization programs.

In the latter half of the century, breakthroughs in **recombinant DNA technology** facilitated the development of **genetically engineered vaccines**. The **hepatitis B vaccine**, produced using recombinant DNA techniques, was a pioneering example, offering both safety and efficacy. This era also saw the introduction of **conjugate vaccines**, which addressed the challenges posed by polysaccharide antigens in pathogens such as **Haemophilus influenzae type b** (Hib).

1.1.3 The Era of Novel Delivery Systems

The focus of vaccine research has gradually shifted towards enhancing delivery mechanisms to improve immune responses and patient compliance. Traditional delivery methods, such as intramuscular and subcutaneous injections, have given way to innovative technologies, including **needle-free systems**, **nanoparticles**, and **mucosal delivery platforms**.

For example, the development of **lipid nanoparticles (LNPs)** as carriers for **mRNA vaccines** was pivotal in the rapid creation and deployment of **COVID-19 vaccines**. These systems not only stabilized the fragile mRNA molecules but also ensured their efficient delivery to immune cells, maximizing efficacy. Similarly, the introduction of **microneedle patches** has made vaccine administration painless and accessible, particularly in resource-limited settings.

Furthermore, **oral vaccines** such as the **rotavirus vaccine** have demonstrated the feasibility of mucosal delivery, offering advantages such as ease of administration and reduced reliance on trained healthcare professionals. These advancements reflect the growing emphasis on patient-centric approaches in vaccine delivery.

1.1.4 Current Challenges and Future Directions

Despite remarkable progress, several challenges remain in vaccine delivery. Ensuring **cold chain stability** for temperature-sensitive vaccines, addressing the **global disparity in vaccine access**, and developing effective vaccines for rapidly mutating pathogens are key areas of focus.

Emerging technologies, such as **self-amplifying RNA vaccines, virus-like particles (VLPs)**, and **artificial intelligence (AI)-driven vaccine design**, hold promise for overcoming these challenges. Additionally, research on **universal vaccines** that target conserved regions of pathogens, such as the influenza virus, represents an ambitious goal with transformative potential.

The historical evolution of vaccines underscores the interplay of scientific innovation and public health imperatives. From the rudimentary practices of variolation to the cutting-edge technologies of the present day, each milestone reflects humanity's determination to combat infectious diseases. As we delve deeper into the principles and methods of vaccine drug delivery systems in subsequent sections, the historical context will provide valuable insights into the challenges and opportunities that lie ahead.

1.1.2 Development of Modern Vaccines: Polio, MMR, and Influenza

The development of **modern vaccines** marks a pivotal chapter in medical science, showcasing how systematic research and technological advancements have effectively combated some of the most pervasive diseases. Vaccines against **polio, measles, mumps, rubella (MMR)**, and

influenza exemplify how innovative approaches to immunization have transformed global health outcomes.

Polio Vaccines: From Paralysis to Eradication

Poliomyelitis, a crippling disease caused by the poliovirus, was a global scourge throughout much of the 20th century, leaving millions of children paralyzed or dead. The journey to an effective vaccine began in earnest in the 1950s, culminating in two groundbreaking vaccines: the **inactivated polio vaccine (IPV)** and the **oral polio vaccine (OPV)**.

The **IPV**, developed by **Jonas Salk** in 1955, was the first successful polio vaccine. Using inactivated (killed) poliovirus, Salk's vaccine provided robust immunity while eliminating the risk of causing the disease. Administered via injection, IPV dramatically reduced polio cases in the developed world.

Shortly thereafter, **Albert Sabin** introduced the **OPV** in 1961. This oral vaccine, based on a live-attenuated poliovirus, was easier to administer and cheaper to produce, making it ideal for large-scale immunization campaigns in resource-limited settings. The OPV's ability to generate both systemic and mucosal immunity further strengthened its effectiveness.

Global vaccination efforts, spearheaded by the **Global Polio Eradication Initiative (GPEI)**, have brought the world closer than ever to eradicating polio. Today, IPV and OPV continue to complement each other, with IPV serving as the cornerstone of immunization in polio-free regions and OPV playing a crucial role in outbreak response.

MMR Vaccine: A Triple Shield Against Childhood Diseases

The **MMR vaccine**, introduced in 1971, was a revolutionary advancement in preventing **measles**, **mumps**, and **rubella**—three highly contagious viral infections that posed severe risks to children. Developed by **Maurice Hilleman**, the MMR vaccine combined live-attenuated strains of the three viruses into a single shot, simplifying administration and enhancing vaccine coverage.

- **Measles**, caused by the measles virus, is one of the most infectious diseases known. The introduction of the MMR vaccine reduced global measles mortality by over 80% between 2000 and 2020.
- **Mumps**, characterized by painful swelling of the salivary glands, can lead to complications such as deafness and infertility. The MMR vaccine has significantly reduced the incidence of mumps in vaccinated populations.

- **Rubella**, also known as German measles, poses particular risks to pregnant women, potentially causing congenital rubella syndrome (CRS) in newborns. By reducing rubella circulation, the MMR vaccine has played a critical role in preventing CRS.

The MMR vaccine's combination approach exemplifies how modern vaccines can address multiple diseases simultaneously, maximizing public health impact while minimizing logistical challenges.

Influenza Vaccines: Adapting to an Evolving Threat

Influenza, caused by rapidly mutating influenza viruses, presents a unique challenge to vaccine development. Unlike most vaccines, which provide long-lasting immunity, influenza vaccines must be updated annually to match the circulating strains.

The first influenza vaccines were developed in the 1940s using inactivated virus technology. These vaccines targeted specific viral proteins, such as **hemagglutinin (HA)** and **neuraminidase (NA)**, which play key roles in viral entry and replication.

Modern influenza vaccines fall into three main categories:

1. **Inactivated influenza vaccines (IIVs):** Containing killed viruses, these vaccines are the most widely used and are administered intramuscularly.
2. **Live-attenuated influenza vaccines (LAIVs):** Delivered via nasal spray, these vaccines mimic natural infection, generating strong mucosal and systemic immunity.
3. **Recombinant influenza vaccines (RIVs):** Using recombinant DNA technology, these vaccines offer flexibility in production and eliminate the need for egg-based manufacturing, making them suitable for individuals with egg allergies.

Despite their effectiveness, influenza vaccines face challenges such as **antigenic drift** and **antigenic shift**, which allow the virus to evade immunity. To address these issues, researchers are exploring **universal influenza vaccines** that target conserved regions of the virus, potentially providing broad and long-lasting protection against multiple strains.

The Legacy of Modern Vaccines

The development of vaccines for polio, MMR, and influenza highlights the adaptability of vaccine science in addressing diverse public health challenges. These vaccines have not only saved millions of lives but have also provided critical insights into immune system behavior, paving the way for innovations in vaccine design and delivery. The success of these vaccines underscores the importance of continuous research, global cooperation, and equitable distribution to achieve universal immunization goals.

1.1.3 Milestones in Drug Delivery Systems for Vaccines

The evolution of **drug delivery systems for vaccines** has played a pivotal role in enhancing their efficacy, safety, and accessibility. From traditional needle-and-syringe methods to cutting-edge nanotechnology, each innovation in vaccine delivery reflects advancements in science and a deeper understanding of immunology. This section explores key milestones in vaccine drug delivery systems, emphasizing their impact on global immunization efforts and public health.

Traditional Needle-and-Syringe Administration

For much of the 20th century, vaccines were administered using standard **needle-and-syringe techniques**, a reliable and straightforward method. Despite its simplicity, this delivery system faced challenges such as pain, needle-stick injuries, and the risk of infection from reused or improperly sterilized needles.

The needle-and-syringe method laid the groundwork for mass immunization campaigns, such as the eradication of **smallpox**, where millions of doses were delivered efficiently. However, the limitations of this method, particularly in low-resource settings, spurred the development of alternative delivery technologies.

Jet Injectors: Needle-Free Revolution

Jet injectors, introduced in the mid-20th century, represented a **needle-free vaccine delivery system** that used high-pressure streams of liquid to penetrate the skin. These devices offered several advantages, including the elimination of needle-stick injuries and reduced reliance on disposable needles.

Jet injectors were extensively used during smallpox eradication campaigns, delivering vaccines to millions of people quickly and safely. However, concerns about **cross-contamination** between patients led to their decline in favor of safer, disposable alternatives. Recent advancements in jet injector technology, such as **single-use nozzle designs**, have addressed these issues, rekindling interest in this method.

Microneedle Arrays: Painless Precision

The advent of **microneedle arrays** marked a breakthrough in vaccine delivery, offering a minimally invasive, painless alternative to traditional injections. Microneedles, ranging from 50 to 900 microns in length, are designed to penetrate the skin's outer layer without reaching pain receptors or blood vessels.

This technology allows vaccines to be delivered directly to **antigen-presenting cells (APCs)** in the dermis, enhancing the immune response. Microneedle patches are particularly promising for **self-administration** and **mass vaccination campaigns**, as they require minimal training and do not generate sharps waste.

Examples of microneedle technology in vaccines include:

- **Influenza microneedle patches**, which have demonstrated efficacy comparable to traditional injections.
- **COVID-19 microneedle vaccines**, currently under development, aiming to improve distribution in low-resource settings.

Liposomes and Lipid Nanoparticles (LNPs): Targeted Delivery Systems

The introduction of **liposomes** and **lipid nanoparticles (LNPs)** has revolutionized vaccine delivery by enabling the encapsulation and stabilization of delicate molecules such as **mRNA** and **proteins**.

Liposomes, spherical vesicles composed of lipid bilayers, were among the first nanocarriers to be used in vaccine formulations. They protect antigens from degradation, enhance uptake by immune cells, and allow for **controlled release**, improving the overall immune response.

LNPs, a more advanced nanocarrier system, gained global attention during the **COVID-19 pandemic** as the delivery vehicle for mRNA vaccines developed by Pfizer-BioNTech and Moderna. These nanoparticles:

1. Protect mRNA from enzymatic degradation.
2. Facilitate cellular uptake through endocytosis.
3. Deliver mRNA to the cytoplasm, enabling protein synthesis and subsequent immune activation.

LNP technology has set the stage for future nucleic acid-based vaccines, with applications extending beyond infectious diseases to include cancer immunotherapy.

Mucosal Delivery Systems: Targeting Natural Entry Points

Vaccines delivered via **mucosal routes**, such as oral or intranasal administration, mimic natural infection pathways, generating both systemic and local immunity.

- **Oral vaccines**, such as the **rotavirus vaccine**, have proven effective in reducing child mortality in developing countries. These vaccines are easy to administer and do not require trained healthcare professionals.
- **Intranasal vaccines**, like the **live-attenuated influenza vaccine (FluMist)**, target the respiratory mucosa, offering strong immunity at the site of viral entry.

Mucosal delivery systems address the challenges of **cold chain logistics** and improve patient compliance, making them ideal for resource-limited settings.

Controlled Release Systems: Sustained Immunity

Controlled release systems, such as **biodegradable polymer microspheres**, allow for the gradual release of antigens over time, reducing the need for multiple doses.

For example, **poly(lactic-co-glycolic acid) (PLGA)** microspheres have been investigated for their ability to release vaccine antigens in a sustained manner, ensuring prolonged immune stimulation. Such systems are particularly beneficial for vaccines targeting **chronic diseases** or **latent infections**.

DNA and RNA Vaccines: A Paradigm Shift

The emergence of **DNA** and **RNA vaccines** has redefined vaccine delivery, shifting the focus from traditional antigen-based approaches to genetic instructions for antigen production. These vaccines rely on advanced delivery systems to ensure stability and efficient cellular uptake.

Key innovations include:

- **Electroporation devices** for DNA vaccines, which use electrical pulses to enhance cell membrane permeability.
- **Lipid nanoparticle (LNP) platforms** for RNA vaccines, optimizing stability and delivery efficiency.

The success of RNA vaccines during the COVID-19 pandemic has validated this approach, opening new possibilities for personalized and universal vaccines.

Future Directions: Innovations on the Horizon

The field of vaccine delivery continues to evolve, with ongoing research into:

- **Virus-like particles (VLPs):** Synthetic particles that mimic the structure of viruses, enhancing immune recognition.
- **Bioprinted vaccines:** Personalized vaccines produced using 3D bioprinting technology.
- **Transdermal patches:** Combining microneedles and adhesive technologies for prolonged vaccine delivery.

The milestones in vaccine drug delivery systems reflect a commitment to improving immunization outcomes through innovation. These advancements not only address existing challenges but also pave the way for equitable and efficient global vaccination strategies.

1.2 Importance of Drug Delivery in Immunization

Drug delivery systems play an essential role in the success of immunization programs by ensuring that vaccines are administered in a manner that maximizes their safety, efficacy, and accessibility. While the primary goal of immunization remains the stimulation of a robust immune response, the method of vaccine delivery significantly influences its effectiveness. Innovative drug delivery technologies address several critical challenges, such as stability, patient compliance, and access, while paving the way for broader immunization coverage.

1.2.1 Challenges Addressed by Drug Delivery Systems

Modern drug delivery systems have emerged as solutions to overcome the myriad challenges associated with traditional vaccine administration. Each challenge, if unaddressed, can hinder the success of immunization programs and compromise public health. Below, we explore these challenges and the corresponding advancements in vaccine delivery systems.

1. Stability and Cold Chain Requirements

Vaccines, especially those based on live-attenuated or inactivated viruses, are highly sensitive to temperature fluctuations. Maintaining a strict **cold chain** is crucial to preserving their efficacy. This dependency poses significant logistical challenges, particularly in resource-limited settings where refrigeration infrastructure is inadequate.

Solutions Provided by Drug Delivery Systems:

- **Lipid nanoparticles (LNPs):** These carriers protect fragile mRNA vaccines from degradation and improve their stability, reducing the need for ultra-cold storage. For instance, mRNA vaccines for COVID-19 have demonstrated stability at moderately low temperatures with the aid of LNPs.
- **Thermostable formulations:** Advances in vaccine formulation, such as freeze-dried (lyophilized) powders, eliminate the need for cold storage. These formulations can be reconstituted just before administration, making them ideal for remote regions.
- **Encapsulation techniques:** Microspheres and nanoparticles shield antigens from environmental degradation, extending vaccine shelf life without refrigeration.

2. Patient Compliance and Acceptance

Traditional needle-based administration can cause pain, fear, and anxiety, particularly in children. These factors contribute to vaccine hesitancy, which remains a significant barrier to achieving herd immunity.

Solutions Provided by Drug Delivery Systems:

- **Microneedle patches:** These painless and minimally invasive devices are gaining popularity for their ability to deliver vaccines through the skin without triggering fear of needles. They are user-friendly and suitable for self-administration.
- **Mucosal delivery systems:** Oral and intranasal vaccines eliminate the need for injections, increasing acceptance among needle-phobic individuals. For example, the oral rotavirus vaccine has been widely adopted in pediatric immunization programs.
- **Jet injectors:** Modern jet injectors provide a needle-free alternative that administers vaccines through high-pressure liquid streams, reducing patient discomfort and the risk of needle-related injuries.

3. Controlled Antigen Release and Immunogenicity

The immune response to vaccines depends on the controlled presentation of antigens to the immune system. Traditional vaccines often require booster doses to sustain immunity, which can complicate immunization schedules and reduce adherence.

Solutions Provided by Drug Delivery Systems:

- **Controlled-release systems:** Biodegradable polymers, such as PLGA microspheres, enable the gradual release of antigens, mimicking natural infections and prolonging immune stimulation. These systems can eliminate the need for multiple booster doses.
- **Adjuvant delivery platforms:** Advanced adjuvants, encapsulated within nanoparticles, enhance immune responses while reducing the antigen dose required. This approach improves vaccine efficacy and minimizes side effects.

4. Global Accessibility and Equity

Achieving equitable access to vaccines is a persistent challenge, particularly in low-income and remote regions. Barriers such as high costs, limited infrastructure, and logistical complexities often delay or prevent vaccine delivery in these areas.

Solutions Provided by Drug Delivery Systems:

- **Self-administrable systems:** Technologies like microneedle patches and transdermal patches enable individuals to administer vaccines at home, reducing the reliance on healthcare workers and clinics.
- **Scalable production technologies:** Recombinant DNA and RNA vaccine platforms allow for rapid and cost-effective vaccine production, ensuring timely distribution during outbreaks.
- **Compact, portable designs:** Innovations such as thermostable formulations and prefilled syringes simplify transportation and storage, improving accessibility in under-resourced settings.

5. Reducing Wastage and Improving Efficiency

Traditional delivery methods are prone to wastage due to issues like multi-dose vial contamination, incorrect handling, or expiration. In mass immunization campaigns, even minor wastage can translate into significant losses.

Solutions Provided by Drug Delivery Systems:

- **Single-dose systems:** Prefilled syringes and single-dose vials reduce wastage by eliminating the need to draw doses manually.

- **Dose-sparing technologies**: Advanced delivery systems, such as nanoparticle carriers and intradermal injectors, ensure precise dosing, maximizing the number of individuals immunized with a given vaccine supply.

6. Immunization Against Complex Pathogens

Emerging infectious diseases and pathogens with complex life cycles, such as HIV and malaria, pose unique challenges to vaccine development and delivery. These diseases often require vaccines capable of eliciting both humoral and cellular immune responses.

Solutions Provided by Drug Delivery Systems:

- **Multicomponent delivery systems**: Polyvalent vaccines that incorporate multiple antigens within a single platform can address complex pathogens.
- **Targeted delivery**: Nanoparticles and viral vectors can deliver antigens directly to antigen-presenting cells (APCs), optimizing immune responses against difficult-to-treat pathogens.
- **Nucleic acid-based vaccines**: RNA and DNA vaccines allow for rapid iteration and customization to target evolving pathogens, such as the constantly mutating influenza virus or SARS-CoV-2 variants.

7. Emergency Preparedness and Rapid Deployment

In pandemics or sudden outbreaks, the speed of vaccine delivery can determine the course of the crisis. Traditional vaccine production and distribution models often fall short in responding to such emergencies.

Solutions Provided by Drug Delivery Systems:

- **mRNA platforms**: These systems enable rapid vaccine development and large-scale production, as demonstrated during the COVID-19 pandemic.
- **Thermostable oral vaccines**: Easily transportable and administrable vaccines reduce the time required to vaccinate populations in emergencies.

The Transformative Role of Drug Delivery in Immunization

By addressing these challenges, drug delivery systems have not only expanded the scope of vaccine technology but also ensured that immunization efforts are more efficient, inclusive, and sustainable. The integration of innovative delivery platforms into routine immunization programs has led to improved patient outcomes, reduced disease burden, and enhanced global health security.

1.2.2 Enhancing Efficacy and Patient Compliance

Efficacy and **patient compliance** are two critical factors in the success of immunization programs. While efficacy determines the ability of a vaccine to elicit a robust and lasting immune response, compliance ensures the vaccine reaches a sufficient portion of the population to achieve **herd immunity**. Drug delivery systems play a transformative role in addressing these aspects, bridging gaps in traditional vaccination methods and paving the way for broader immunization coverage.

Enhancing Efficacy Through Advanced Delivery Systems

Efficacy in vaccines is determined by how well they stimulate the immune system to recognize and respond to a pathogen. Innovative drug delivery systems ensure precise and efficient antigen delivery, optimizing immune activation while minimizing side effects.

1. Improved Antigen Presentation

Modern delivery systems focus on targeting **antigen-presenting cells (APCs)** such as dendritic cells and macrophages, which are critical for initiating immune responses. Traditional vaccines often fail to efficiently direct antigens to these cells, reducing their potency.

Examples of Enhancements:

- **Nanoparticle-based systems**, such as lipid nanoparticles (LNPs), encapsulate antigens and deliver them directly to APCs, significantly boosting vaccine efficacy. For instance, LNPs have been instrumental in the success of mRNA vaccines for COVID-19.
- **Microneedle patches** deliver antigens into the skin, which is rich in APCs, ensuring rapid and robust immune activation.

2. Sustained Immune Stimulation

The immune system benefits from prolonged exposure to antigens, which enhances both primary and memory immune responses. Traditional vaccines often require booster doses to achieve sustained immunity, which can reduce patient adherence.

Solutions Through Controlled Release Systems:

- **Polymer-based microspheres**, such as those made of poly(lactic-co-glycolic acid) (PLGA), release antigens over an extended period, mimicking the gradual exposure seen in natural infections.
- **Adjuvant integration**, such as aluminum salts or squalene-based emulsions, amplifies immune responses while reducing the required antigen dose.

3. Enhanced Immunogenicity for Complex Pathogens

Some pathogens, like HIV or malaria, require vaccines capable of eliciting both humoral (antibody-mediated) and cellular (T-cell-mediated) immune responses. Traditional delivery methods often fail to achieve this balance.

Innovative Approaches:

- **DNA and RNA vaccines** use genetic material to instruct cells to produce antigens, ensuring simultaneous activation of B-cells (antibody production) and T-cells (cell-mediated immunity).
- **Viral vector platforms**, such as adenovirus-based vaccines, efficiently deliver antigens to cells, inducing strong cellular immunity.

Improving Patient Compliance Through Patient-Centric Solutions

Compliance is often influenced by factors such as pain, fear, convenience, and accessibility. Addressing these aspects ensures that vaccines are not only effective but also widely accepted and used.

1. Needle-Free and Painless Administration

One of the most significant barriers to vaccine compliance is the fear of needles, particularly among children.

Innovative Delivery Systems:

- **Microneedle arrays** provide a painless alternative, as they do not penetrate deep enough to reach pain receptors. This approach has shown high acceptability among patients, particularly in pediatric and needle-phobic populations.
- **Jet injectors** eliminate needles entirely, using high-pressure liquid streams to deliver vaccines intradermally or subcutaneously.

2. Simplified Vaccine Schedules

Multiple doses and booster schedules can reduce compliance due to logistical challenges and patient forgetfulness.

Solutions:

- **Single-dose controlled-release formulations**, such as polymer-based systems, eliminate the need for boosters by providing prolonged antigen exposure in a single administration.
- **Combination vaccines**, like the MMR vaccine (measles, mumps, rubella), reduce the number of injections required while protecting against multiple diseases.

3. Convenient Self-Administration

Access to healthcare providers can be a significant barrier in remote or underserved areas.

Patient-Centric Technologies:

- **Microneedle patches**, designed for self-application, allow individuals to administer vaccines at home without the need for trained personnel.
- **Oral vaccines**, such as those for rotavirus or cholera, provide a needle-free and easily administered alternative.

4. Improved Accessibility in Low-Resource Settings

In regions with limited healthcare infrastructure, traditional vaccine delivery methods often fail to reach all populations.

Technological Interventions:

- **Thermostable vaccines**, which do not require refrigeration, simplify logistics and ensure potency even in extreme climates.
- **Prefilled syringes** and ready-to-use delivery systems reduce preparation errors and facilitate rapid deployment in mass immunization campaigns.

Real-World Applications: Balancing Efficacy and Compliance

The practical impact of these innovations is evident in real-world scenarios:

- **COVID-19 Vaccines**: The use of LNPs in mRNA vaccines addressed both efficacy (through precise antigen delivery) and compliance (by reducing the antigen dose and number of injections).
- **Polio Vaccination Campaigns**: The oral polio vaccine (OPV) overcame compliance challenges by enabling mass immunization without needles, particularly in low-resource settings.
- **HPV Vaccines**: Single-dose regimens, combined with adjuvant systems, have improved compliance in adolescent vaccination programs, particularly in school-based settings.

The Dual Imperative: Efficacy and Compliance in Global Immunization

The interplay between vaccine efficacy and patient compliance highlights the importance of holistic approaches to immunization. Drug delivery systems that address both aspects ensure that vaccines not only work but also reach the people who need them most. As vaccine technologies continue to evolve, the integration of patient-centric delivery methods will be instrumental in achieving universal immunization coverage and eradicating preventable diseases.

1.3 Global Challenges in Vaccination

Despite remarkable advancements in vaccine development and delivery, significant **global challenges** persist in achieving widespread immunization. These challenges, rooted in disparities in **accessibility, equity, infrastructure**, and **policy frameworks**, pose obstacles to the goal of universal vaccination coverage. Understanding these issues is essential to devising strategies that bridge gaps and ensure that vaccines reach the populations that need them most.

1.3.1 Vaccine Accessibility and Equity

Vaccine accessibility and equity remain two of the most pressing issues in global public health. While vaccines have proven to be one of the most effective tools in preventing infectious diseases, their distribution is often hindered by socioeconomic, political, and logistical barriers.

1. Unequal Distribution of Vaccines

A striking manifestation of inequity in vaccination is the disparity between **high-income** and **low- and middle-income countries (LMICs).** Wealthier nations often secure large quantities of vaccines through **advance purchase agreements**, leaving fewer doses available for resource-limited regions. This imbalance became starkly evident during the **COVID-19**

pandemic, where high-income countries rapidly vaccinated their populations while many LMICs struggled to access even the first doses.

Key Factors Contributing to Unequal Distribution:

- **Economic disparities:** The high cost of vaccines, especially newer technologies like mRNA vaccines, often places them out of reach for LMICs.
- **Geopolitical factors:** Vaccine nationalism, where countries prioritize their own populations over global needs, exacerbates inequity.
- **Production capacity:** Limited manufacturing capabilities in LMICs create dependence on imports, which are often insufficient to meet demand.

2. Infrastructure and Cold Chain Limitations

Vaccine delivery relies heavily on robust infrastructure, including transportation networks and cold chain systems to maintain temperature-sensitive vaccines. In many regions, particularly rural and remote areas, these systems are inadequate or entirely absent, leading to vaccine spoilage and reduced efficacy.

Challenges:

- **Cold chain requirements:** Vaccines such as those for **polio** and mRNA-based COVID-19 vaccines require storage at ultra-low temperatures, making distribution challenging in regions with unreliable electricity or refrigeration.
- **Transportation barriers:** Poor road networks, geographic isolation, and political instability hinder vaccine delivery to remote areas.

3. Social and Cultural Barriers

Vaccine hesitancy, fueled by misinformation, distrust in healthcare systems, and cultural beliefs, is a significant barrier to achieving high vaccination coverage.

Examples of Social and Cultural Barriers:

- **Misinformation:** The spread of myths about vaccine safety and efficacy through social media and other channels undermines public confidence.
- **Religious beliefs:** In some communities, religious doctrines oppose vaccination, viewing it as unnatural or harmful.

- **Distrust in healthcare systems:** Historical injustices, such as unethical medical experiments, contribute to skepticism about vaccination campaigns, particularly among marginalized populations.

4. Policy and Funding Gaps

In many LMICs, limited government funding and poorly coordinated health policies restrict access to vaccines. Dependence on international aid and donor organizations further complicates long-term planning and sustainability.

Policy Challenges:

- **Inconsistent immunization schedules:** A lack of standardized schedules across regions leads to missed vaccinations and gaps in immunity.
- **Inadequate investment in healthcare:** Low prioritization of public health funding limits the resources available for vaccination programs.
- **Fragmented international support:** While initiatives like Gavi, the Vaccine Alliance, aim to improve access, insufficient funding and political hurdles often delay implementation.

5. Gender and Socioeconomic Disparities

Equity in vaccination is also affected by gender and socioeconomic status. Women and children in impoverished or marginalized communities often face additional barriers to accessing vaccines.

Gender-Specific Challenges:

- In some cultures, women's healthcare is deprioritized, leading to lower vaccination rates among girls and women.
- Mothers in rural areas may face challenges traveling to clinics to vaccinate their children due to societal expectations or economic constraints.

Addressing Accessibility and Equity: The Path Forward

Tackling vaccine accessibility and equity requires a multifaceted approach, combining innovative solutions, international cooperation, and community engagement.

1. Strengthening Manufacturing and Distribution

Investments in regional vaccine manufacturing facilities can reduce dependency on imports and improve access in LMICs. For example, initiatives like **Africa CDC's plan for local production hubs** aim to enhance the continent's self-reliance in vaccine production.

2. Leveraging Technology

Innovations such as **thermostable vaccines** and **digital tracking systems** can address logistical barriers. Thermostable formulations reduce the need for cold chains, while digital platforms monitor supply chains and vaccination coverage in real time.

3. Community Engagement

Building trust within communities is vital to overcoming vaccine hesitancy. Collaboration with local leaders, religious figures, and influencers can help dispel myths and encourage acceptance of vaccines.

4. International Cooperation

Global partnerships, such as the **COVAX initiative**, aim to ensure equitable vaccine distribution by pooling resources and securing doses for underserved regions. Strengthening such collaborations is essential for bridging the access gap.

5. Policy Reform and Advocacy

Governments must prioritize healthcare funding and create comprehensive immunization policies that address the unique needs of vulnerable populations. Advocacy for global health equity can mobilize resources and political will to support these reforms.

The Global Imperative for Equity

Achieving vaccine accessibility and equity is not just a moral imperative—it is a critical factor in global health security. Infectious diseases do not respect borders; ensuring that everyone has access to life-saving vaccines protects the world from future pandemics and outbreaks. By addressing the systemic barriers that limit vaccine distribution, we can create a future where immunization truly benefits all of humanity.

1.3.2 Cold Chain Dependency and Costs

The **cold chain**—a temperature-controlled supply chain—is a critical component in the storage, transport, and distribution of most vaccines. Maintaining the required temperature ensures the stability and potency of vaccines, preventing degradation that can render them ineffective or even unsafe. However, this dependency introduces significant challenges, particularly in terms of logistics and cost, and poses a considerable barrier to equitable vaccine distribution, especially in low-resource settings.

Understanding the Cold Chain Requirements

Most vaccines are biological products that require storage within a specific temperature range to maintain their efficacy. Common temperature requirements include:

- **Refrigerated (2–8°C):** Vaccines such as those for polio (IPV), measles, and MMR fall into this category.
- **Frozen (-15 to -50°C):** Some vaccines, such as the varicella vaccine, require deep freezing for stability.
- **Ultra-cold (-60 to -90°C):** Recent advancements in mRNA-based vaccines, such as the Pfizer-BioNTech COVID-19 vaccine, necessitate storage at ultra-cold temperatures to preserve the fragile lipid nanoparticles and mRNA strands.

Any deviation from these temperature ranges during storage or transport can lead to vaccine spoilage. The **World Health Organization (WHO)** estimates that nearly **50% of vaccines are wasted globally**, partly due to inadequate cold chain infrastructure.

Challenges of Cold Chain Dependency

1. High Costs of Infrastructure and Maintenance

Maintaining a reliable cold chain involves significant investment in specialized equipment, facilities, and processes. These include:

- **Refrigeration units:** Costly equipment designed for temperature control across the storage and distribution chain.
- **Monitoring systems:** Devices to track and log temperature data in real time, ensuring that vaccines remain within the required range.
- **Energy requirements:** Cold chain systems are energy-intensive, relying heavily on uninterrupted electricity, which may be scarce in rural or resource-poor regions.

For vaccines requiring ultra-cold storage, the costs are exponentially higher. For instance, the distribution of mRNA vaccines during the COVID-19 pandemic required ultra-cold freezers and specialized dry ice packaging, driving up logistical expenses.

2. Inadequate Infrastructure in Low-Resource Settings

In many low- and middle-income countries (LMICs), cold chain infrastructure is either non-existent or insufficient to meet the demands of large-scale vaccination programs.

- **Rural areas:** Limited access to electricity, poor road networks, and a lack of refrigerated transport vehicles hinder vaccine distribution.
- **Urban settings in LMICs:** Overcrowded storage facilities and outdated equipment result in frequent temperature breaches.

3. Vaccine Wastage

Cold chain failures, such as power outages or equipment malfunctions, can lead to vaccine spoilage and significant financial losses. In LMICs, where resources are already constrained, such wastage undermines immunization programs and public trust.

4. Increased Costs of End-to-End Logistics

Cold chain logistics require specialized handling at every stage of the supply chain, including:

- **Cold boxes and insulated containers** for transport.
- **Specialized training** for healthcare workers to handle temperature-sensitive vaccines.
- **Real-time temperature monitoring systems**, such as **loggers** and **radio-frequency identification (RFID) tags**, to prevent temperature excursions.

These additional layers of logistics inflate the overall cost of vaccine distribution, often making it economically unfeasible for LMICs without substantial external funding.

5. Environmental Impact

Cold chain logistics contribute to environmental challenges due to the reliance on energy-intensive refrigeration systems and non-recyclable packaging materials such as dry ice and plastic containers.

Addressing Cold Chain Dependency and Costs

Innovations in vaccine technology and supply chain management are helping to reduce reliance on cold chains and lower associated costs.

1. Development of Thermostable Vaccines

Thermostable vaccines are designed to remain effective even outside traditional cold chain conditions.

- **Heat-stable formulations:** Certain vaccines, such as the thermostable rotavirus vaccine, can withstand higher temperatures for extended periods, reducing the need for refrigeration.
- **Freeze-dried (lyophilized) vaccines:** These vaccines are more stable and can be reconstituted at the point of use. For example, the freeze-dried measles vaccine has been widely adopted in immunization campaigns.

2. Advancements in Packaging Technology

Innovative packaging solutions, such as **phase-change materials (PCMs)**, maintain stable temperatures during transport without the need for constant refrigeration.

- **Insulated containers:** Lightweight and reusable containers minimize energy use while preserving vaccine potency.
- **Passive cooling systems:** These systems use non-electric cooling materials, making them ideal for remote and off-grid locations.

3. Alternative Delivery Methods

New delivery technologies can bypass traditional cold chain requirements entirely.

- **Microneedle patches:** Stable at room temperature, these patches eliminate the need for refrigeration and simplify vaccine administration.
- **Oral vaccines:** Many oral formulations, such as the oral polio vaccine, are less reliant on cold chains and easier to transport.

4. Strengthening Infrastructure in LMICs

Global health initiatives, such as **Gavi, the Vaccine Alliance**, and the **WHO Expanded Programme on Immunization (EPI)**, are investing in improving cold chain infrastructure in LMICs. Efforts include:

- Deployment of **solar-powered refrigerators** in rural areas.
- Training programs for healthcare workers in cold chain management.

5. Digital Monitoring Systems

Real-time tracking technologies, such as **IoT-enabled sensors** and **blockchain platforms**, ensure vaccine quality by providing continuous temperature monitoring across the supply chain.

Balancing Costs and Accessibility: The Global Perspective

While cold chain dependency has long been a barrier to equitable vaccination, advancements in technology and infrastructure are creating new possibilities for overcoming these challenges. The successful deployment of thermostable vaccines and innovative delivery systems offers hope for reducing costs and improving access, particularly in resource-limited settings.

The global health community must continue to prioritize investments in sustainable cold chain solutions and the development of robust, temperature-independent vaccines to ensure that lifesaving immunizations reach every corner of the world.

1.3.3 Lessons from Pandemics (SARS, MERS, COVID-19)

Pandemics such as **SARS** (Severe Acute Respiratory Syndrome), **MERS** (Middle East Respiratory Syndrome), and **COVID-19** (Coronavirus Disease 2019) have underscored the critical role of vaccines in global health security. Each of these outbreaks revealed vulnerabilities in healthcare systems, supply chains, and research infrastructures while providing invaluable lessons that have shaped modern approaches to vaccine development, manufacturing, and distribution. By examining these pandemics, we gain insights into overcoming challenges and preparing for future public health emergencies.

The SARS Pandemic: A Wake-Up Call for Preparedness

The **SARS pandemic of 2002-2003** was caused by the **SARS-CoV** coronavirus, which emerged in Guangdong, China, and quickly spread to over 30 countries. Although SARS was contained relatively quickly, its high case fatality rate (~10%) and the economic disruption it caused were alarming.

Key Challenges and Lessons

1. **Delayed Response and Containment**

   The global response to SARS was initially slow due to inadequate surveillance and communication. This highlighted the importance of rapid pathogen identification and transparent reporting systems.

   - **Lesson Learned:** Establishing global networks for disease surveillance, such as the **WHO's Global Outbreak Alert and Response Network (GOARN),** became a priority.

2. **The Need for Vaccines**

   Vaccine development for SARS started but was never completed due to the decline of the outbreak. This demonstrated the challenges of sustaining vaccine research in the absence of immediate threats.

   - **Lesson Learned:** Investment in **pandemic preparedness platforms** and technologies, such as mRNA vaccines, gained traction post-SARS.

3. **Zoonotic Spillover Risks**

   SARS underscored the risks posed by zoonotic diseases, emphasizing the need for surveillance at the animal-human interface.

   - **Lesson Learned:** Programs like **One Health**, which integrate human, animal, and environmental health, became central to pandemic prevention strategies.

The MERS Pandemic: The Role of Regional Preparedness

In 2012, **MERS-CoV**, another coronavirus, emerged in Saudi Arabia, with dromedary camels identified as the primary source of zoonotic transmission. MERS had a higher case fatality rate (~34%) than SARS but was less transmissible, leading to sporadic outbreaks rather than a global pandemic.

Key Challenges and Lessons

1. **Regional Containment**

   MERS highlighted the importance of regional responses to disease outbreaks. Saudi Arabia and neighboring countries implemented stringent measures to control its spread.

   - **Lesson Learned:** Regional cooperation, particularly in areas with shared zoonotic risks, is critical for containment.

2. **Vaccine Development Gaps**

   Despite ongoing outbreaks, no licensed vaccine for MERS exists due to limited global interest and funding.

   - **Lesson Learned:** The concept of **vaccine platforms**, allowing rapid customization for related pathogens, became a focal point for future preparedness.

3. **Hospital-Associated Transmission**
   MERS outbreaks were often linked to healthcare settings, emphasizing the need for robust infection control measures.

   - **Lesson Learned:** Enhanced **hospital protocols** and **healthcare worker training** became essential components of pandemic preparedness.

The COVID-19 Pandemic: A Global Turning Point

The **COVID-19 pandemic**, caused by **SARS-CoV-2**, has been the most disruptive global health crisis in over a century, resulting in millions of deaths and unprecedented economic and social consequences. Unlike SARS and MERS, COVID-19's high transmissibility and ability to spread asymptomatically posed unique challenges.

Key Challenges and Lessons

1. **Accelerated Vaccine Development**
   The rapid development of COVID-19 vaccines, with several authorized within a year of the pandemic's onset, was an extraordinary achievement.

   - **Lesson Learned:** Investments in platforms such as **mRNA technology** and **adenoviral vectors** paid off, enabling swift vaccine production. This validated the utility of flexible and scalable vaccine platforms.

2. **Global Inequities in Vaccine Distribution**
   Vaccine nationalism and unequal distribution left many LMICs without adequate supplies. The disparity underscored the need for equitable access mechanisms.

   - **Lesson Learned:** Initiatives like **COVAX**, aimed at equitable vaccine distribution, became a cornerstone of global health policy.

3. **Supply Chain Vulnerabilities**
   The reliance on global supply chains for raw materials and components led to significant bottlenecks in vaccine production and distribution.

- ○ **Lesson Learned:** Building **regional manufacturing hubs** and stockpiling critical supplies are essential for pandemic resilience.

4. **Vaccine Hesitancy**
   Despite the availability of vaccines, misinformation and mistrust hindered uptake in many communities.

   - ○ **Lesson Learned:** Proactive public health communication and community engagement are vital to counter vaccine hesitancy.

5. **The Role of Technology**
   Technologies such as **artificial intelligence (AI)** and **big data analytics** were used to track virus spread, predict outbreaks, and optimize vaccine distribution.

   - ○ **Lesson Learned:** Leveraging technology for real-time surveillance and decision-making is crucial in managing pandemics.

Common Threads and Takeaways
While each pandemic was unique in its challenges and scope, several overarching lessons emerge:

1. **Preparedness Saves Lives**
   Investment in surveillance, diagnostics, and vaccine platforms prior to pandemics enables rapid responses and minimizes impact.
2. **Global Cooperation is Key**
   Pathogens do not respect borders; effective containment requires international collaboration and equitable resource distribution.
3. **Flexibility in Vaccine Development**
   Universal vaccine platforms and adaptive trial designs allow for faster responses to emerging threats.
4. **Focus on Equity**
   Addressing disparities in vaccine access and healthcare infrastructure is essential for global health security.

Towards a Resilient Future
The experiences of SARS, MERS, and COVID-19 have transformed the global health landscape, fostering innovations in vaccine science,

strengthening public health systems, and catalyzing international cooperation. However, the ongoing threat of pandemics necessitates continuous vigilance and investment in pandemic preparedness. By learning from these crises, the world can build a more resilient and equitable framework for combating future health emergencies.

TWO

IMMUNOLOGICAL FOUNDATIONS OF VACCINES

The success of vaccines is deeply rooted in their ability to leverage the **immune system** to recognize and combat pathogens effectively. Understanding the **mechanisms of the immune response** is critical for designing vaccines that are safe, effective, and capable of providing long-lasting protection. This chapter delves into the intricate interplay between antigens, immune cells, and signaling pathways that form the backbone of vaccine-induced immunity.

2.1 Mechanisms of the Immune Response

The immune response is a highly coordinated process designed to identify, neutralize, and eliminate foreign invaders such as bacteria, viruses, and toxins. It involves two main arms: **innate immunity** and **adaptive immunity**. While innate immunity provides the first line of defense, adaptive immunity offers specificity and memory, making it essential for vaccine efficacy.

2.1.1 Antigen Recognition: APCs, MHC, and TCRs

Antigen recognition is the cornerstone of the adaptive immune response, initiating the activation of T and B lymphocytes. This process involves a complex interaction between **antigen-presenting cells (APCs)**, **major histocompatibility complex (MHC)** molecules, and **T-cell receptors (TCRs)**

Antigen-Presenting Cells (APCs)

APCs are specialized immune cells responsible for capturing, processing, and presenting antigens to T cells, thereby bridging innate and adaptive immunity. The primary APCs include:

- **Dendritic cells (DCs):** These are the most potent APCs, strategically located at sites of pathogen entry such as the skin and mucosal surfaces. Dendritic cells excel in capturing antigens through **phagocytosis** or **endocytosis** and migrating to lymph nodes to activate T cells.
- **Macrophages:** Found in tissues, macrophages are versatile APCs that engulf pathogens and cellular debris while producing cytokines to recruit other immune cells.
- **B cells:** Although primarily involved in antibody production, B cells can act as APCs by presenting antigens to helper T cells, amplifying the immune response.

Mechanism of Antigen Uptake:

1. **Pathogen Capture:** APCs use receptors such as **pattern recognition receptors (PRRs)** to identify pathogen-associated molecular patterns (PAMPs) on microbes.
2. **Antigen Processing:** Internalized antigens are degraded into peptide fragments within endosomes or lysosomes.
3. **Antigen Presentation:** The peptide fragments are loaded onto MHC molecules and transported to the cell surface for presentation to T cells.

Major Histocompatibility Complex (MHC)

The **MHC molecules** are integral to antigen presentation, determining the type of immune response elicited. There are two primary classes:

1. **MHC Class I:**

   - Found on all nucleated cells, these molecules present endogenous antigens (e.g., viral peptides) to **CD8+ cytotoxic T cells.**
   - This pathway is crucial for identifying and eliminating infected or cancerous cells.

Processing Pathway:

- Antigens are processed in the cytoplasm by the **proteasome**.
- Peptides are transported into the endoplasmic reticulum via **TAP (transporter associated with antigen processing)** and loaded onto MHC Class I molecules before being displayed on the cell surface.

2. **MHC Class II:**

- Expressed only on professional APCs, these molecules present exogenous antigens (e.g., bacterial toxins) to **CD4+ helper T cells**.
- This pathway activates helper T cells to coordinate immune responses, including antibody production and cytokine release.

Processing Pathway:

- Antigens are internalized into endosomes, where they are degraded into peptides.
- Peptides are loaded onto MHC Class II molecules in the late endosome before transport to the cell surface.

T-Cell Receptors (TCRs)

TCRs are found on the surface of T cells and are responsible for recognizing antigen-MHC complexes. Each T cell expresses a unique TCR, enabling the immune system to recognize a vast array of antigens.

Structure of TCRs:

- The TCR is composed of two chains, α **and** β, which form a heterodimer.
- The variable regions of these chains bind to specific peptide-MHC complexes, while the constant regions anchor the receptor to the cell membrane.

Mechanism of TCR Recognition:

1. **Signal Initiation:** When a TCR binds to an antigen-MHC complex, it triggers intracellular signaling cascades through associated molecules like **CD3**.

2. **Co-Stimulation:** Additional signals from co-stimulatory molecules, such as **CD28 binding to B7** on APCs, are required for full T cell activation.
3. **Differentiation and Proliferation:** Activated T cells differentiate into effector cells (e.g., cytotoxic T cells or helper T cells) and proliferate to mount an effective immune response.

Key Interactions and Outcomes in Antigen Recognition

1. **Activation of CD4+ Helper T Cells:**

   ◦ MHC Class II–peptide complexes activate CD4+ helper T cells, which produce cytokines to enhance macrophage activity, stimulate B cell antibody production, and recruit other immune cells.

2. **Activation of CD8+ Cytotoxic T Cells:**

   ◦ MHC Class I–peptide complexes activate CD8+ T cells, which release perforin and granzymes to kill infected or abnormal cells.

3. **Memory Formation:**

   ◦ Some activated T cells differentiate into memory T cells, providing long-lasting immunity and rapid responses upon re-exposure to the same antigen.

Significance for Vaccines

Understanding the mechanisms of antigen recognition has profound implications for vaccine design:

- **Targeting APCs:** Vaccines are increasingly designed to optimize antigen delivery to dendritic cells, enhancing immunogenicity. For example, adjuvants like **alum** and **CpG oligodeoxynucleotides** improve antigen uptake by APCs.
- **Mimicking Natural Infection:** Live-attenuated vaccines and viral vector platforms mimic natural antigen presentation pathways, eliciting robust T cell responses.
- **Precision Design:** mRNA and protein subunit vaccines utilize epitopes known to bind effectively to MHC molecules, ensuring specific and

strong immune activation.

Future Directions

Advancements in immunology continue to refine our understanding of antigen recognition. Emerging technologies, such as **artificial antigen-presenting cells (aAPCs)** and **nanoparticle-based delivery systems**, aim to enhance the efficiency and precision of immune activation, paving the way for next-generation vaccines capable of combating complex diseases like cancer and HIV.

2.1.2 Activation of T Cells and B Cells

The activation of **T cells** and **B cells** is a pivotal event in the adaptive immune response, driving the production of pathogen-specific antibodies and the elimination of infected or abnormal cells. This process is a complex interplay of cellular interactions, molecular signals, and environmental cues that culminate in a robust and tailored immune defense. Understanding these mechanisms is essential for designing effective vaccines, as they aim to mimic natural immune activation.

Activation of T Cells

T cells play a central role in the immune system, with two main subsets:

- **CD4+ Helper T Cells:** These cells orchestrate the immune response by producing cytokines and supporting other immune cells.
- **CD8+ Cytotoxic T Cells:** These cells directly kill infected or cancerous cells by releasing cytotoxic molecules.

1. Signal Requirements for T Cell Activation

Activation of T cells requires three key signals delivered by **antigen-presenting cells (APCs):**

1. **Signal 1: Antigen Recognition**

   - **T cell receptor (TCR)** binds to the antigen presented by **MHC molecules** on the APC.

     - **MHC Class I:** Presents endogenous antigens to CD8+ T cells.
     - **MHC Class II:** Presents exogenous antigens to CD4+ T cells.

- This interaction provides specificity, ensuring T cells are activated only by their cognate antigen.

2. **Signal 2: Co-Stimulation**

   - Co-stimulatory molecules on the APC, such as **B7-1 (CD80)** or **B7-2 (CD86)**, bind to **CD28** on T cells.
   - This signal ensures that T cells are not activated by self-antigens, preventing autoimmune reactions.

3. **Signal 3: Cytokine Environment**

   - APCs secrete cytokines such as **IL-12**, **IL-4**, or **TGF-β**, shaping the differentiation of T cells into specific effector subsets.

2. Differentiation of T Cells

Once activated, T cells proliferate and differentiate into distinct subsets based on the cytokine milieu:

- **CD4+ T Cell Subsets:**

  - **Th1 Cells:** Produce **IFN-γ**, supporting macrophage activation and cytotoxic responses.
  - **Th2 Cells:** Secrete **IL-4** and **IL-5**, driving B cell activation and antibody production.
  - **Th17 Cells:** Release **IL-17**, promoting inflammation and defense against extracellular pathogens.
  - **Tregs (Regulatory T Cells):** Suppress excessive immune responses to maintain homeostasis.

- **CD8+ Cytotoxic T Cells:**

  - These cells acquire cytolytic capabilities, releasing **perforin** and **granzymes** to induce apoptosis in infected or malignant cells.

Activation of B Cells

B cells are responsible for the production of **antibodies**, providing humoral immunity that neutralizes pathogens and facilitates their clearance.

1. Signal Requirements for B Cell Activation

B cells are activated through two pathways:

1. **T Cell-Dependent Activation**

    - **Signal 1:** The **B cell receptor (BCR)** binds to an antigen, internalizing it and presenting it on MHC Class II molecules.
    - **Signal 2:** Helper T cells recognize the antigen-MHC complex on the B cell and provide co-stimulatory signals through **CD40L-CD40 interaction.**
    - **Signal 3:** Helper T cells secrete cytokines such as **IL-4** and **IL-21**, driving B cell proliferation and differentiation.

2. **T Cell-Independent Activation**

    - Some antigens, such as polysaccharides, activate B cells without T cell help.
    - These antigens cross-link multiple BCRs, triggering a weaker and short-lived immune response.

2. Differentiation of B Cells

Activated B cells differentiate into two main types:

- **Plasma Cells:** Specialized in producing antibodies, these cells migrate to the bone marrow and secrete large quantities of antigen-specific antibodies.
- **Memory B Cells:** Long-lived cells that remain dormant until re-exposure to the same antigen, enabling a rapid and robust secondary response.

Effector Functions of T Cells and B Cells

The activation of T and B cells leads to specific effector functions that eliminate pathogens and prevent reinfection:

1. **Cytotoxic T Cell Effector Function:**

    - Release of **perforin** forms pores in the target cell membrane.

- **Granzymes** enter the target cell through these pores, triggering apoptosis.

2. **Helper T Cell Effector Function:**

- Cytokine secretion enhances macrophage activity, supports B cell maturation, and recruits other immune cells.

3. **Antibody-Mediated Functions by B Cells:**

- **Neutralization:** Antibodies bind to pathogens, preventing their attachment to host cells.
- **Opsonization:** Antibodies coat pathogens, facilitating their uptake by phagocytes.
- **Complement Activation:** Antibodies trigger the complement cascade, leading to pathogen lysis.

Significance for Vaccine Design

The activation of T and B cells underpins the mechanisms by which vaccines confer protection:

1. **Live-Attenuated Vaccines:** Mimic natural infections, eliciting robust T and B cell responses.
2. **Subunit Vaccines:** Focus on specific epitopes that are highly effective at activating B cells and helper T cells.
3. **mRNA Vaccines:** Deliver genetic instructions for antigens, activating both cytotoxic T cells and B cells.

Future Directions in Vaccine Strategies

Emerging approaches aim to optimize T and B cell activation through:

- **Adjuvants:** Enhancing antigen uptake and presentation by APCs to improve T cell priming.
- **Nanoparticles:** Delivering antigens directly to lymphoid tissues where T and B cell activation occurs.
- **Personalized Vaccines:** Using neoantigens specific to individual patients to elicit targeted T cell responses, especially in cancer immunotherapy.

2.1.3 Role of Cytokines in Immune Signaling

Cytokines are small **signaling proteins** that play a crucial role in regulating the immune response. Produced by a variety of immune and non-immune cells, they act as chemical messengers that coordinate the activity of different immune cells during an immune response. In the context of vaccination, cytokines are essential for shaping the magnitude and type of immunity, influencing the effectiveness of vaccines.

What Are Cytokines?

Cytokines are a broad category of proteins, including **interleukins (ILs)**, **interferons (IFNs)**, **tumor necrosis factors (TNFs)**, and **chemokines**, each with distinct roles in immune regulation. They are secreted in response to stimuli such as infection, inflammation, or tissue damage and function by binding to specific cytokine receptors on target cells.

Cytokines in Immune Signaling

Cytokines regulate various stages of the immune response, from the activation of innate immunity to the development of adaptive immunity.

1. Initiation of the Immune Response

During an infection or vaccination, **antigen-presenting cells (APCs)** such as dendritic cells and macrophages release pro-inflammatory cytokines to initiate the immune response.

- **IL-1, IL-6, and TNF-α:** Promote inflammation and recruit immune cells to the site of infection or vaccination.
- **Type I Interferons (IFN-α and IFN-β):** Produced in response to viral infections, these cytokines activate natural killer (NK) cells and enhance the antiviral state of nearby cells.

2. T Cell Differentiation

Cytokines are pivotal in determining the differentiation of naive **CD4+ helper T cells** into specific subsets, each tailored to combat different types of pathogens.

- **IL-12:** Promotes the differentiation of **Th1 cells**, which produce **IFN-γ** to activate macrophages and cytotoxic T cells, essential for intracellular pathogens like viruses.
- **IL-4:** Drives the formation of **Th2 cells**, which stimulate B cells to produce antibodies, particularly important for extracellular pathogens like bacteria and parasites.

- **IL-6 and TGF-β:** Induce **Th17 cell** differentiation, which plays a role in defending against fungi and extracellular bacteria by recruiting neutrophils.
- **IL-10 and TGF-β:** Support the generation of **regulatory T cells (Tregs)**, which suppress excessive immune responses and maintain tolerance.

3. Activation of Cytotoxic T Cells (CD8+ T Cells)

For cytotoxic T cells to effectively eliminate infected or malignant cells, cytokines play a dual role in priming and sustaining their activity.

- **IL-2:** Produced by activated CD4+ T cells, it promotes the proliferation and survival of CD8+ T cells.
- **IFN-γ:** Enhances the cytotoxic function of CD8+ T cells and increases MHC Class I expression on infected cells, improving antigen presentation.

4. B Cell Activation and Antibody Production

Cytokines also regulate B cell activation, isotype switching, and antibody production.

- **IL-4:** Encourages B cell proliferation and the production of IgE, crucial for combating parasitic infections.
- **IL-5:** Supports IgA production, which is important for mucosal immunity.
- **IFN-γ:** Stimulates IgG production, enhancing opsonization and complement activation.

5. Resolution of the Immune Response

After the pathogen is cleared, cytokines ensure that the immune response subsides, preventing chronic inflammation or autoimmune reactions.

- **IL-10:** Suppresses pro-inflammatory cytokines and dampens T cell activity.
- **TGF-β:** Promotes tissue repair and the resolution of inflammation.

Cytokines in Vaccine Responses

Vaccines rely on cytokine signaling to mimic the immune response triggered by natural infections, ensuring the development of protective immunity. The type and intensity of cytokine responses induced by a vaccine determine its effectiveness.

1. Role of Adjuvants

Adjuvants, substances added to vaccines to enhance their immunogenicity, often work by stimulating cytokine production.

- **Alum (aluminum salts):** Induces IL-1β and IL-18, promoting Th2 responses and antibody production.
- **MF59 and AS03:** Squalene-based adjuvants that recruit APCs and stimulate IL-6 and TNF-α production.
- **CpG Oligodeoxynucleotides:** Trigger strong IFN-α responses through Toll-like receptor 9 (TLR9), favoring Th1 responses.

2. Cytokine Profiles and Vaccine Types

Different vaccine platforms elicit distinct cytokine profiles:

- **Live-Attenuated Vaccines:** Induce robust IL-12 and IFN-γ responses, promoting Th1 and cytotoxic T cell activation.
- **Protein Subunit Vaccines:** Rely heavily on adjuvants to stimulate cytokines like IL-4 and IL-6, enhancing antibody responses.
- **mRNA Vaccines:** Trigger Type I interferons and IL-6, ensuring strong T cell and antibody-mediated immunity.

Challenges and Considerations

While cytokines are indispensable for immune signaling, dysregulated cytokine production can lead to adverse effects:

- **Cytokine Storms:** An overproduction of pro-inflammatory cytokines, such as IL-6 and TNF-α, can cause severe tissue damage, as seen in cases of severe COVID-19.
- **Autoimmune Risks:** Overactivation of cytokines like IFN-γ may lead to autoimmune conditions in susceptible individuals.

Harnessing Cytokines for Next-Generation Vaccines

Advances in immunology are enabling the strategic use of cytokines to design more effective and safer vaccines:

- **Cytokine-Loaded Nanoparticles:** Delivering cytokines alongside antigens ensures localized and sustained immune activation.
- **Cytokine Modulators:** Engineered cytokines or cytokine inhibitors can fine-tune immune responses, reducing side effects while maximizing efficacy.
- **Personalized Cytokine Profiles:** Vaccines tailored to an individual's immune environment could optimize protection in populations with diverse immune backgrounds.

2.2 Long-Term Immunity

The hallmark of effective vaccines lies in their ability to induce **long-term immunity**, a state where the immune system is primed to respond swiftly and effectively upon re-exposure to the same pathogen. This immunity is largely mediated by **memory cells**, specialized immune cells that persist long after the initial infection or vaccination. These cells form the foundation of adaptive immunity and are pivotal for sustaining protection against infectious diseases.

2.2.1 Memory Cells: Mechanisms and Lifespan

Memory cells are differentiated immune cells derived from **T cells** and **B cells** during the primary immune response. Unlike their short-lived effector counterparts, memory cells are long-lasting and can mount a rapid and robust secondary immune response. Understanding the mechanisms by which these cells are generated, maintained, and activated is crucial for designing vaccines that provide durable protection.

Mechanisms of Memory Cell Formation

Memory cells are formed during the resolution phase of the immune response when most effector cells die off through apoptosis. The remaining population of memory cells is retained for long-term surveillance and rapid response to future encounters with the same antigen.

1. T Memory Cells

T memory cells are derived from activated T cells during an immune response and are categorized into two main types:

1. **Central Memory T Cells (Tcm):**

   - Reside in secondary lymphoid organs such as lymph nodes and spleen.
   - Express high levels of **CCR7** and **CD62L**, which allow them to home to lymphoid tissues.
   - Respond by rapidly proliferating and differentiating into effector T cells upon re-exposure to antigens.

2. **Effector Memory T Cells (Tem):**

   - Circulate in peripheral tissues and blood.
   - Lack CCR7 but express markers such as **CD44**.
   - Provide immediate effector functions, including cytokine release and cytotoxic activity, upon encountering antigens.

3. **Tissue-Resident Memory T Cells (Trm):**

   - Reside in barrier tissues, such as the skin, lungs, and gut.
   - Do not circulate but provide localized immunity against reinfections at sites of pathogen entry.

Formation Pathway:

- Following antigen presentation, naive T cells are activated and differentiate into effector T cells.
- A subset of these effector T cells transitions into memory T cells during the contraction phase, influenced by cytokines such as **IL-7** and **IL-15**, which support their survival and maintenance.

2. B Memory Cells

B memory cells are derived from activated B cells that have undergone **somatic hypermutation** and **affinity maturation** in the germinal centers of lymphoid tissues.

Characteristics:

- Express high-affinity B cell receptors (BCRs) specific to the encountered antigen.

- Reside in secondary lymphoid organs and the bone marrow.
- Rapidly differentiate into plasma cells upon re-exposure to antigens, producing large quantities of antibodies.

Formation Pathway:

- During the primary response, naive B cells are activated and interact with helper T cells.
- In the germinal center, B cells undergo somatic hypermutation, leading to the selection of high-affinity clones.
- Some of these clones differentiate into memory B cells, while others become antibody-secreting plasma cells.

Lifespan of Memory Cells

Memory cells are remarkably long-lived, persisting for years or even decades in the absence of antigen stimulation.

1. T Memory Cell Lifespan

- Central memory T cells can survive for decades, continually patrolling lymphoid tissues for antigens.
- Effector memory T cells have shorter lifespans but are replenished through homeostatic proliferation driven by cytokines like **IL-7** and **IL-15**.

2. B Memory Cell Lifespan

- Memory B cells can persist for decades, even in the absence of antigen, supported by survival signals in the bone marrow niche.
- Long-lived plasma cells, a subset of memory B cells, continue to secrete low levels of antibodies, providing baseline immunity.

Mechanisms of Activation During Secondary Response

Memory cells are reactivated upon re-exposure to their specific antigen, leading to a faster and stronger immune response compared to the primary response.

1. **T Memory Cell Activation**

    - Antigen-presenting cells (APCs) present the antigen to memory T cells via MHC molecules.
    - Memory T cells proliferate and differentiate into effector T cells, releasing cytokines (e.g., **IFN-γ**) and exerting cytotoxic effects.

2. **B Memory Cell Activation**

    - Memory B cells bind the antigen through their high-affinity BCRs and internalize it for processing and presentation to helper T cells.
    - Helper T cells provide co-stimulatory signals, driving the rapid proliferation and differentiation of memory B cells into plasma cells.

Significance of Memory Cells in Vaccine-Induced Immunity
Vaccines aim to generate robust memory T and B cell populations that provide durable protection.

1. **Role in Long-Term Protection**

    - Memory cells enable the immune system to respond rapidly to subsequent exposures to the pathogen, preventing illness or reducing disease severity.

2. **Reduction of Booster Requirements**

    - Vaccines that induce long-lived memory cells, such as live-attenuated vaccines, often require fewer booster doses.

3. **Improved Secondary Responses**

    - Vaccines that optimize germinal center reactions enhance the quality of memory B cells, leading to more effective antibody responses during secondary infections.

Challenges and Research Directions

While memory cells are central to long-term immunity, several challenges remain in understanding and optimizing their role in vaccine design:

1. **Aging and Immune Senescence**

   ◦ Memory cell function declines with age, reducing vaccine efficacy in elderly populations. Strategies such as adjuvant optimization are being explored to address this.

2. **Variability Across Individuals**

   ◦ Genetic and environmental factors influence memory cell formation and longevity, leading to variability in vaccine responses.

3. **Pathogens That Evade Immunity**

   ◦ Some pathogens, such as influenza and HIV, mutate rapidly, evading recognition by memory cells. Research on universal vaccines targeting conserved regions of these pathogens is ongoing.

Future Directions in Vaccine Design

- **Adjuvants and Cytokine Modulation:** Enhancing the production and survival of memory cells by incorporating adjuvants that mimic cytokines like IL-7 and IL-15.
- **Nanoparticle Delivery Systems:** Targeting lymphoid tissues to optimize memory cell formation.
- **Single-Dose Vaccines:** Leveraging controlled-release systems to provide prolonged antigen exposure, enhancing memory cell generation.

2.2.2 Boosters and Their Role in Maintaining Immunity

Booster doses are a critical component of many vaccination regimens, ensuring the maintenance of immunity over time. While the initial vaccine dose generates a primary immune response and establishes **immunological memory**, boosters serve to re-expose the immune system to the antigen, amplifying and sustaining the immune response. This section delves into the immunological principles behind boosters, their role in long-term protection, and the challenges associated with booster vaccination.

Why Are Boosters Needed?

Despite the generation of memory cells during the primary immune response, immunity against certain pathogens may decline over time due to several factors:

1. **Natural Waning of Immunity**:

   - Memory T and B cells, though long-lived, do not remain active indefinitely. Their numbers may decline, reducing the speed and magnitude of secondary responses.
   - Antibody levels produced by plasma cells may decrease, lowering the body's immediate protective capability.

2. **Pathogen Characteristics**:

   - Some pathogens, such as **influenza**, undergo frequent mutations (antigenic drift), leading to the emergence of new strains that evade existing immunity.
   - Pathogens like **tetanus** produce toxins rather than replicating in large quantities, requiring high antibody titers for neutralization.

3. **Suboptimal Initial Response**:

   - Certain populations, such as young children, the elderly, or immunocompromised individuals, may generate weaker primary immune responses, necessitating boosters to achieve protective immunity.

Immunological Effects of Boosters

Boosters elicit a **secondary immune response**, which is faster, stronger, and more specific than the primary response. This is due to the reactivation and expansion of memory cells generated during the initial vaccination.

1. Enhanced Memory T and B Cell Pools

- **Memory T Cells**: Boosters stimulate the proliferation of memory T cells, replenishing their numbers and maintaining their readiness to respond.

- **Memory B Cells**: Boosters promote the survival and further affinity maturation of memory B cells, leading to the production of higher-quality antibodies.

2. Increased Antibody Production

- Boosters drive the differentiation of memory B cells into plasma cells, significantly increasing antibody titers.
- The antibodies produced during the secondary response have higher affinity due to **somatic hypermutation**, improving their effectiveness in neutralizing pathogens.

3. Long-Term Protection

- Boosters enhance the longevity of immunity by sustaining memory cell populations and stimulating **long-lived plasma cells** in the bone marrow.

Types of Boosters
The choice of booster vaccine depends on the pathogen, vaccine platform, and population being targeted.

1. Homologous Boosters

- Use the same vaccine as the primary dose.
- Example: **Tetanus-diphtheria (Td) boosters** are given every 10 years to maintain immunity against these bacterial toxins.

2. Heterologous Boosters (Mix-and-Match)

- Use a different vaccine platform for the booster dose.
- Example: For COVID-19, mRNA vaccines like **Pfizer-BioNTech** have been used as boosters for individuals initially vaccinated with adenoviral vector vaccines like **AstraZeneca.**
- **Advantages**: Heterologous boosters often broaden the immune response by activating different arms of the immune system.

Examples of Booster Vaccination Regimens

1. **Tetanus and Diphtheria Vaccines:**

- Primary series includes three doses, followed by boosters every 10 years.
- Boosters are essential to maintain high antibody titers capable of neutralizing the toxins produced by these bacteria.

2. **Measles, Mumps, and Rubella (MMR) Vaccine:**

- A two-dose schedule is recommended, with the second dose acting as a booster to ensure long-term immunity, especially in cases where the initial dose failed to produce adequate protection.

3. **COVID-19 Vaccines:**

- Initial two-dose regimens have been supplemented with booster doses to combat waning immunity and emerging variants like **Delta** and **Omicron.**

4. **Pertussis (Whooping Cough) Vaccine:**

- Boosters are given in adolescence and adulthood to address the rapid waning of immunity observed with acellular pertussis vaccines.

Challenges and Considerations in Booster Vaccination
1. Waning Public Compliance

- Individuals may not perceive the need for boosters, especially if the primary vaccine effectively prevents severe disease in the short term.
- Misinformation and vaccine hesitancy further complicate booster uptake.

2. Global Access and Equity

- In resource-limited settings, primary immunization coverage remains a challenge, making booster programs less feasible.
- Initiatives like **COVAX** aim to address inequities in booster access, especially during pandemics.

3. Logistics and Cost

- Repeated booster programs place a strain on healthcare systems, particularly in terms of vaccine storage, distribution, and administration.

4. Immune Exhaustion Concerns

- While rare, repeated stimulation of the immune system through frequent boosters could potentially lead to **immune exhaustion**, reducing the efficacy of subsequent doses.

Future Directions in Booster Development

1. **Universal Vaccines**

- Vaccines targeting conserved regions of pathogens (e.g., universal influenza vaccines) could reduce or eliminate the need for boosters.

1. **Adjuvant Optimization**

- Improved adjuvants that enhance memory cell longevity may extend the duration of immunity provided by the primary series.

3. **Controlled-Release Systems**

- Technologies such as **biodegradable microspheres** could deliver antigens over time, mimicking the effect of multiple doses and reducing the need for separate boosters.

4. **Personalized Booster Strategies**

- Advances in immunogenetics could enable tailored booster schedules based on individual immune profiles and risk factors.

2.3 Role of Adjuvants in Immune Activation

Adjuvants are critical components of many vaccines, designed to enhance their **immunogenicity** by stimulating a stronger and more sustained immune response. While vaccines containing live-attenuated pathogens can elicit robust immune activation without additional components, subunit, inactivated, and mRNA vaccines often require adjuvants to compensate for their lower intrinsic immunogenicity. This section explores the mechanisms by which adjuvants enhance immune responses, focusing on the action of commonly used adjuvants in vaccine formulations.

2.3.1 Mechanisms of Action for Common Adjuvants

Adjuvants work through a variety of mechanisms, which can be broadly categorized into three key functions:

1. **Antigen Presentation Enhancement**: Improving the uptake and processing of antigens by antigen-presenting cells (APCs).
2. **Innate Immune Activation**: Stimulating innate immune pathways to create a pro-inflammatory environment conducive to adaptive immunity.
3. **Prolonged Antigen Release**: Acting as a depot to slowly release antigens, extending their interaction with the immune system.

Each adjuvant operates uniquely, leveraging one or more of these mechanisms to amplify the immune response.

1. Aluminum-Based Adjuvants (Alum)

Aluminum salts (e.g., aluminum hydroxide, aluminum phosphate) are among the oldest and most widely used adjuvants in human vaccines. They are particularly effective in enhancing humoral (antibody-mediated) immunity.

Mechanism of Action:

- **Antigen Adsorption**: Alum binds to vaccine antigens, facilitating their uptake by APCs.
- **Inflammasome Activation**: Alum triggers the **NLRP3 inflammasome**, leading to the production of pro-inflammatory cytokines like **IL-1β** and **IL-18**, which enhance T and B cell activation.
- **Depot Effect**: Alum forms a gel-like structure at the injection site, providing sustained antigen release over time.

Applications:

- Used in vaccines for **hepatitis B, diphtheria-tetanus-pertussis (DTP),** and **human papillomavirus (HPV)**.

2. Oil-in-Water Emulsions (MF59 and AS03)

These adjuvants are composed of squalene oil droplets stabilized in water and are primarily used to enhance responses to influenza vaccines.

Mechanism of Action:

- **Recruitment of Immune Cells**: MF59 and AS03 promote the recruitment of monocytes, macrophages, and dendritic cells to the injection site.
- **Cytokine Induction**: They stimulate the production of cytokines like **IL-6**, which drives the activation and maturation of APCs.
- **Enhanced Antigen Uptake**: The emulsions facilitate antigen delivery to lymphoid tissues where immune activation occurs.

Applications:

- MF59 is used in the **seasonal influenza vaccine** for elderly populations.
- AS03 was included in the **H1N1 influenza vaccine** during the 2009 pandemic.

3. CpG Oligodeoxynucleotides

CpG adjuvants are synthetic DNA molecules containing unmethylated **CpG motifs**, which mimic bacterial DNA and stimulate innate immune pathways through **Toll-like receptor 9 (TLR9)**.

Mechanism of Action:

- **TLR9 Activation**: CpG motifs bind to TLR9 on dendritic cells and B cells, inducing the production of **Type I interferons** and **pro-inflammatory cytokines**.
- **Th1 Response Enhancement**: CpG adjuvants skew the immune response toward a Th1 profile, promoting cytotoxic T cell activation and IgG2a antibody production.

Applications:

- CpG adjuvants are used in the **Hepatitis B vaccine (Heplisav-B)** and are under investigation for cancer immunotherapies.

4. Monophosphoryl Lipid A (MPL)

MPL is a detoxified derivative of **lipopolysaccharide (LPS)**, a component of Gram-negative bacterial cell walls. It acts through **Toll-like receptor 4 (TLR4)**.
Mechanism of Action:

- **TLR4 Activation**: MPL triggers innate immune activation by engaging TLR4 on dendritic cells and macrophages, inducing the production of cytokines like **TNF-α** and **IL-12**.
- **Balanced Immune Response**: MPL enhances both humoral and cellular immunity, making it suitable for vaccines requiring broad protection.

Applications:

- MPL is a component of **AS04**, an adjuvant used in the **Cervarix (HPV vaccine)**.

5. QS-21 (Saponin-Based Adjuvant)

QS-21 is a purified extract from the bark of the **Quillaja saponaria** tree. It is used in vaccines targeting difficult pathogens, such as malaria and herpes zoster.
Mechanism of Action:

- **APC Stimulation**: QS-21 enhances the activation and migration of dendritic cells.
- **Th1 and Th2 Immune Responses**: It promotes both antibody production and cytotoxic T cell responses.
- **Synergistic Effects**: QS-21 is often combined with other adjuvants, such as MPL, for enhanced efficacy.

Applications:

- Included in the **Shingrix vaccine** for shingles and investigational malaria vaccines.

6. Adjuvants for RNA-Based Vaccines

mRNA vaccines, such as those for COVID-19, rely on lipid nanoparticles (LNPs) for delivery and adjuvanticity.
Mechanism of Action:

- **Innate Immune Activation**: LNPs stimulate **Toll-like receptors (TLRs)** and **retinoic acid-inducible gene I (RIG-I)** pathways, leading to Type I interferon production.
- **Efficient Delivery**: LNPs protect mRNA from degradation and facilitate its uptake by APCs, ensuring effective antigen presentation.

Applications:

- Used in **Pfizer-BioNTech** and **Moderna COVID-19 vaccines.**

Challenges and Considerations in Adjuvant Use

While adjuvants enhance vaccine efficacy, they also present challenges that must be addressed during vaccine development:

1. **Safety Concerns**:

   - Overstimulation of the immune system by potent adjuvants can lead to excessive inflammation or autoimmune reactions.

2. **Population-Specific Responses**:

   - Adjuvant efficacy may vary across age groups or individuals with differing immune profiles.

3. **Complex Manufacturing**:

   - The addition of adjuvants increases production costs and complexity, particularly for novel adjuvant systems.

Future Directions in Adjuvant Research

1. **Tailored Adjuvants**:

   - Development of adjuvants that target specific immune pathways, allowing for fine-tuned immune responses based on the pathogen and population.

2. **Nanoparticle-Based Systems**:

- ○ Nanoparticles that combine antigen delivery and adjuvanticity are being explored to enhance both safety and efficacy.

3. **Adjuvant Combinations**:

- ○ Combining adjuvants with complementary mechanisms (e.g., QS-21 and MPL) can enhance immune responses while minimizing side effects.

4. **Personalized Adjuvants**:

- ○ Advances in immunogenomics could enable the development of adjuvants tailored to individual genetic and immune profiles.

2.3.2 Impact on Cellular and Humoral Immunity

Adjuvants profoundly influence the **cellular** and **humoral** arms of the immune system, enhancing the effectiveness of vaccines by directing immune responses toward specific outcomes. These outcomes are essential for combating different pathogens and ensuring robust, long-lasting immunity. The ability of adjuvants to shape immunity is determined by their interaction with immune cells, cytokine signaling pathways, and antigen-presenting cells (APCs). This section explores how adjuvants impact cellular and humoral immunity and their significance in vaccine efficacy.

Cellular Immunity and the Role of Adjuvants

Cellular immunity, mediated by **T cells**, is crucial for combating intracellular pathogens such as viruses, bacteria, and cancer cells. Adjuvants enhance cellular immunity by activating dendritic cells (DCs), influencing T cell differentiation, and creating a cytokine environment that promotes cytotoxic and helper T cell responses.

1. Enhancement of Antigen Presentation

- Adjuvants stimulate APCs, particularly **dendritic cells (DCs)**, to upregulate **MHC molecules, costimulatory proteins (CD80, CD86)**, and **cytokine production**.
- Enhanced antigen presentation leads to more efficient activation of **CD4+ helper T cells** and **CD8+ cytotoxic T cells**.

Example:

- **CpG Oligodeoxynucleotides**, through **TLR9 activation**, drive robust dendritic cell maturation, enhancing the priming of Th1 and cytotoxic T cell responses.

2. Promotion of Th1 and Th17 Responses

- Adjuvants such as **monophosphoryl lipid A (MPL)** and **QS-21** skew the immune response toward a **Th1 phenotype**, characterized by the production of **IFN-γ**, which activates macrophages and promotes cytotoxic T cell activity.
- Certain adjuvants also stimulate **Th17 cells**, producing **IL-17**, which recruits neutrophils and is effective against fungal and bacterial infections.

Example:

- **MPL**, used in the HPV vaccine **Cervarix**, enhances Th1 responses, providing cellular immunity essential for clearing viral infections.

3. Cytotoxic T Cell Activation

- Cytotoxic T cells (CTLs) are essential for targeting virus-infected or cancerous cells. Adjuvants like **poly(I:C)**, a synthetic analog of double-stranded RNA, mimic viral infections and stimulate **Type I interferons (IFN-α/β)**, driving robust CTL responses.

Humoral Immunity and the Role of Adjuvants

Humoral immunity, mediated by **B cells** and **antibodies**, is critical for neutralizing extracellular pathogens, toxins, and preventing pathogen entry into cells. Adjuvants enhance humoral immunity by supporting B cell activation, antibody production, and isotype switching.

1. Increased Antibody Titers

- Adjuvants enhance the magnitude of antibody responses by facilitating B cell activation and plasma cell differentiation.
- Aluminum-based adjuvants (e.g., alum) are particularly effective at increasing **IgG** levels, providing strong neutralizing activity against pathogens.

Example:

- In the **hepatitis B vaccine**, alum significantly boosts antibody titers, ensuring effective and durable protection.

2. Induction of Isotype Switching

- Adjuvants influence the cytokine environment to promote isotype switching in B cells, tailoring antibody responses to the specific pathogen.

  - **IL-4 (Th2-driven):** Promotes IgG1 and IgE, effective against extracellular pathogens.
  - **IFN-γ (Th1-driven):** Promotes IgG2a/IgG2c, critical for intracellular pathogens.

Example:

- **AS03**, an oil-in-water emulsion, supports both IgG1 and IgG2a responses, providing broad-spectrum protection in influenza vaccines.

3. Germinal Center Formation and Affinity Maturation

- Adjuvants enhance germinal center formation in secondary lymphoid organs, where B cells undergo somatic hypermutation and affinity maturation. This process leads to the production of high-affinity antibodies.

Example:

- **MF59**, used in seasonal influenza vaccines, promotes robust germinal center reactions, improving antibody quality and durability.

Balancing Cellular and Humoral Responses

The choice of adjuvant determines whether a vaccine skews the immune response toward cellular or humoral immunity, depending on the pathogen and desired outcome.

Pathogens Requiring Cellular Immunity

- Intracellular pathogens, such as **viruses (e.g., HIV, influenza)** and **intracellular bacteria (e.g., Mycobacterium tuberculosis)**, require strong Th1 and cytotoxic T cell responses.
- Adjuvants like MPL and CpG favor Th1 polarization, supporting cellular immunity.

Pathogens Requiring Humoral Immunity

- Extracellular pathogens, such as **bacteria (e.g., Streptococcus pneumoniae)** and **toxins (e.g., diphtheria, tetanus)**, require robust antibody production.
- Adjuvants like alum and oil-in-water emulsions favor Th2 responses, enhancing humoral immunity.

Pathogens Requiring Both Arms of Immunity

- Complex pathogens, such as **malaria** or **COVID-19**, benefit from balanced cellular and humoral responses.
- Combination adjuvants, such as **AS01** (MPL and QS-21), provide synergistic activation of both arms of the immune system.

Adjuvants in Vaccine Development: Case Studies

1. **COVID-19 Vaccines**

   - mRNA vaccines (e.g., Pfizer-BioNTech, Moderna) utilize lipid nanoparticles (LNPs) that enhance both cellular (T cell activation) and humoral (antibody) immunity by stimulating innate immune pathways.

2. **Shingrix Vaccine (Herpes Zoster)**

   - Combines QS-21 and MPL to provide robust Th1 responses and long-lasting humoral immunity, protecting against shingles in older adults.

3. **Malaria Vaccine (RTS,S/AS01)**

- ○ Utilizes AS01, a combination of MPL and QS-21, to generate balanced cellular and humoral immunity against Plasmodium falciparum.

Challenges and Future Directions

1. **Safety Concerns**

   - ○ Overactivation of cellular immunity by potent adjuvants may lead to excessive inflammation or autoimmunity.

2. **Personalized Adjuvants**

   - ○ Developing adjuvants tailored to individual immune profiles could optimize the balance between cellular and humoral immunity.

3. **Adjuvant Innovations**

   - ○ Nanoparticle-based adjuvants and cytokine delivery systems are being developed to fine-tune immune activation and improve vaccine efficacy.

4. **Emerging Pathogens**

   - ○ Novel adjuvants that activate broad-spectrum immune responses are critical for combating emerging pathogens, such as SARS-CoV-2 variants and antimicrobial-resistant bacteria.

THREE

Conventional Vaccine Delivery Systems

Vaccines have historically relied on a variety of **delivery systems** to introduce antigens to the immune system effectively. These conventional systems, rooted in immunological and technological advancements, have been pivotal in controlling and eradicating several infectious diseases. This chapter explores the foundational types of vaccine delivery systems, beginning with **live-attenuated vaccines**, which have demonstrated exceptional efficacy in inducing robust and long-lasting immune responses.

3.1 Traditional Vaccine Types

Conventional vaccines can be broadly categorized based on the nature of the antigens they contain and the mechanisms by which they stimulate the immune response. Among these, **live-attenuated vaccines** stand out as one of the earliest and most effective strategies, leveraging weakened pathogens to mimic natural infections.

3.1.1 Live-Attenuated Vaccines: Strengths and Weaknesses

Live-attenuated vaccines (LAVs) use pathogens that have been weakened, or "attenuated," so they cannot cause disease in healthy individuals but still elicit strong immune responses. These vaccines are highly effective in generating both humoral and cellular immunity, making them an essential tool in global immunization efforts.

Mechanism of Action

The attenuation process involves altering the pathogen's genetic makeup or culture conditions to reduce its virulence while maintaining its ability to replicate and present antigens. Once administered, the attenuated pathogen:

1. **Replicates in the host** at a reduced level, closely mimicking a natural infection.
2. Stimulates **antigen-presenting cells (APCs)** such as dendritic cells to process and present antigens via **MHC molecules**.
3. Triggers robust activation of both **T cells** (cellular immunity) and **B cells** (humoral immunity).
4. Leads to the generation of **memory T and B cells**, providing long-lasting protection against the disease.

Examples of Live-Attenuated Vaccines

- **Measles, Mumps, and Rubella (MMR) Vaccine**: Protects against three highly contagious viral infections with lifelong immunity in most individuals after two doses.
- **Oral Polio Vaccine (OPV)**: Has been instrumental in the global effort to eradicate poliomyelitis.
- **Varicella (Chickenpox) Vaccine**: Provides protection against varicella-zoster virus, reducing disease severity and complications.
- **Yellow Fever Vaccine**: Offers nearly lifelong immunity with a single dose, essential for controlling outbreaks in endemic regions.

Strengths of Live-Attenuated Vaccines
1. Strong Immune Response

- **Cellular and Humoral Immunity**: LAVs stimulate both arms of the immune system, providing comprehensive protection.
- **Memory Formation**: Mimicking natural infection ensures the generation of long-lived memory cells, reducing the need for booster doses in most cases.

2. Long-Lasting Immunity

- Many live-attenuated vaccines provide immunity that lasts for decades, making them cost-effective and practical for large-scale immunization programs.

3. Rapid Onset of Protection

- Due to their ability to replicate in the host, LAVs can induce immunity quickly, which is beneficial during outbreaks.

4. Reduced Antigen Dosage

- Because live pathogens replicate and amplify their antigens within the host, lower doses of the vaccine are required compared to inactivated or subunit vaccines.

5. Induction of Mucosal Immunity

- Certain LAVs, such as OPV, stimulate **mucosal immunity** (IgA production), providing localized protection at the site of pathogen entry.

Weaknesses of Live-Attenuated Vaccines
1. Risk of Reversion to Virulence

- In rare cases, the attenuated pathogen may regain its virulence through genetic mutations, potentially causing disease.

    - Example: OPV has been associated with **vaccine-derived poliovirus (VDPV)** in under-immunized populations.

2. Contraindications in Immunocompromised Individuals

- LAVs can cause severe disease in individuals with weakened immune systems, such as those undergoing chemotherapy or living with HIV/ AIDS.

3. Complex Storage Requirements

- Many LAVs require **cold chain logistics**, as they are sensitive to heat and light. This dependency complicates distribution in low-resource settings.

4. Limited Shelf Life

- Live-attenuated vaccines often have shorter shelf lives than other vaccine types, necessitating efficient production and distribution systems.

5. Potential for Side Effects

- While generally safe, LAVs may cause mild reactions such as fever, rash, or localized swelling at the injection site.

Advancements and Innovations

Despite their limitations, research continues to improve the safety and efficacy of live-attenuated vaccines:

1. **Genetic Engineering**

   - Advances in **reverse genetics** allow for precise attenuation of pathogens, minimizing the risk of reversion to virulence.
   - Example: Genetically stabilized OPV strains are being developed to address the issue of VDPV.

2. **Thermostable Formulations**

   - Efforts are underway to create thermostable live-attenuated vaccines that can withstand higher temperatures, reducing cold chain dependency.

3. **Combination Vaccines**

   - LAVs are often combined with other vaccine types to protect against multiple diseases with a single administration.
   - Example: The **MMRV vaccine** (measles, mumps, rubella, and varicella) reduces the number of injections required.

4. **Reduced-Dose Strategies**

   ○ Research on fractional dosing aims to extend vaccine supplies during outbreaks, ensuring wider coverage without compromising efficacy.

Public Health Impact of Live-Attenuated Vaccines
Live-attenuated vaccines have been instrumental in controlling and eradicating infectious diseases:

- **Polio Eradication**: The OPV has reduced global polio cases by over 99% since 1988.
- **Smallpox Eradication**: Although not strictly a live-attenuated vaccine, the smallpox vaccine employed a live virus and contributed to the disease's eradication in 1980.
- **Measles Control**: Widespread use of the MMR vaccine has drastically reduced measles-related deaths worldwide.

Challenges in Global Use

1. **Access and Equity**

   ○ Cold chain requirements limit vaccine availability in low-resource regions.
   ○ International initiatives, such as **Gavi, the Vaccine Alliance**, aim to address these disparities.

2. **Public Perception and Vaccine Hesitancy**

   ○ Concerns about safety and side effects contribute to hesitancy in some communities. Proactive education and transparent communication are crucial for addressing these concerns.

3.1.2 Inactivated Vaccines: Preparation and Applications
Inactivated vaccines are a cornerstone of modern immunization, leveraging pathogens that have been rendered non-infectious while retaining their ability to stimulate an immune response. These vaccines are widely used for their safety and stability, offering a viable alternative to live-attenuated vaccines, particularly for immunocompromised individuals.

This section examines the preparation methods, mechanisms, and applications of inactivated vaccines, as well as their advantages and limitations in preventing infectious diseases.

Preparation of Inactivated Vaccines

The production of inactivated vaccines involves killing or inactivating the pathogen in a way that preserves its antigenic properties. These antigens are critical for eliciting an immune response while ensuring the pathogen cannot replicate or cause disease.

1. Pathogen Inactivation Methods

1. **Chemical Inactivation**

   - Chemicals such as **formaldehyde**, **β-propiolactone**, or **glutaraldehyde** are commonly used to inactivate viruses and bacteria.
   - These agents disrupt the nucleic acids and essential proteins of the pathogen while preserving surface antigens critical for immune recognition.
   - Example: The **Salk polio vaccine** employs formaldehyde to inactivate poliovirus.

2. **Physical Inactivation**

   - Heat or radiation (e.g., gamma rays) can also be used to kill pathogens.
   - Care must be taken to avoid denaturing antigens, as this can reduce vaccine efficacy.
   - Example: Heat-inactivated influenza vaccines have been developed for certain populations.

2. Antigen Preservation and Purification

- Once inactivated, pathogens are purified to remove contaminants and ensure vaccine safety.
- Stabilizers (e.g., sugars or proteins) may be added to preserve antigen integrity during storage and transportation.

Mechanism of Immune Activation

Inactivated vaccines primarily stimulate **humoral immunity** by eliciting antibody production.

1. **Antigen Uptake**:

   - APCs such as dendritic cells internalize inactivated pathogens and process their antigens for presentation on **MHC Class II molecules**.

2. **Helper T Cell Activation**:

   - CD4+ helper T cells recognize antigen-MHC complexes and secrete cytokines to activate B cells.

3. **Antibody Production**:

   - Activated B cells differentiate into plasma cells, producing high-affinity antibodies that neutralize pathogens.

Applications of Inactivated Vaccines

Inactivated vaccines are used to prevent a wide range of infectious diseases and are especially suited for populations where live-attenuated vaccines may pose risks.

1. Viral Diseases

1. **Polio (Salk Vaccine)**

   - The inactivated polio vaccine (IPV) provides effective immunity without the risk of vaccine-derived poliovirus (VDPV), making it a preferred choice in polio eradication campaigns in certain regions.

2. **Hepatitis A**

   - Inactivated hepatitis A vaccines are highly effective in preventing this foodborne and waterborne viral infection.

3. **Influenza**

- Inactivated influenza vaccines are widely used in annual vaccination campaigns, particularly for high-risk groups such as the elderly and healthcare workers.

4. **Rabies**

- Inactivated rabies vaccines are critical for pre- and post-exposure prophylaxis, offering near-complete protection when administered promptly.

2. Bacterial Diseases

1. **Pertussis (Whole-Cell Vaccine)**

- Early pertussis vaccines used inactivated Bordetella pertussis bacteria to provide immunity against whooping cough. Although effective, these have largely been replaced by acellular vaccines due to side effects.

2. **Cholera**

- Inactivated oral cholera vaccines, such as Dukoral, are used to prevent cholera in endemic regions or during outbreaks.

3. **Typhoid Fever**

- Inactivated typhoid vaccines are available as an alternative to live-attenuated vaccines for individuals who cannot tolerate live vaccines.

Advantages of Inactivated Vaccines

1. **Safety**

- Inactivated vaccines cannot replicate, making them safer for immunocompromised individuals and pregnant women.

2. **Stability**

- They are more stable than live-attenuated vaccines, often requiring less stringent cold chain logistics.

3. **Wide Applicability**

- Suitable for a broad range of populations, including those with weakened immune systems.

4. **No Risk of Reversion**

- Unlike live-attenuated vaccines, inactivated vaccines cannot revert to a virulent form, eliminating the risk of vaccine-derived infections.

Limitations of Inactivated Vaccines

1. **Weaker Immune Response**

- Inactivated vaccines often induce a weaker immune response compared to live-attenuated vaccines, primarily limited to humoral immunity.

2. **Need for Adjuvants**

- Adjuvants, such as aluminum salts, are often required to boost immunogenicity.

3. **Multiple Doses and Boosters**

- Repeated doses are typically required to achieve and maintain protective immunity.

4. **Limited Mucosal Immunity**

- Most inactivated vaccines do not stimulate robust mucosal immunity, reducing their effectiveness against pathogens entering through mucosal surfaces.

Advancements in Inactivated Vaccine Technology

Research and innovation have addressed many of the limitations of traditional inactivated vaccines:

1. **Adjuvant Development**

   - Advanced adjuvants, such as MF59 and AS03, enhance immune responses to inactivated vaccines by promoting antigen presentation and cytokine production.

2. **Molecular Tools for Antigen Integrity**

   - Novel inactivation methods, such as **ethyleneimine treatment**, better preserve antigen structure and immunogenicity.

3. **Combination Vaccines**

   - Inactivated vaccines are increasingly being incorporated into combination formulations, reducing the number of injections required for immunization.

4. **Nanoparticle Delivery Systems**

   - Encapsulating inactivated antigens in nanoparticles improves stability, antigen presentation, and immune activation.

Global Impact of Inactivated Vaccines

1. **Polio Eradication Efforts**

   - IPV has played a significant role in transitioning from live-attenuated oral polio vaccines to safer inactivated alternatives.

2. **Control of Zoonotic Diseases**

   - Inactivated rabies vaccines are essential for reducing human cases of rabies, particularly in regions with high rates of dog-to-human transmission.

3. **Pandemic Preparedness**

   ○ Inactivated vaccines have been developed for diseases such as H5N1 and H1N1 influenza, providing a critical tool for pandemic response.

Challenges and Future Directions

1. **Scaling Production**

   ○ Producing large quantities of pathogens for inactivation requires stringent biosafety measures, increasing costs.

2. **Cold Chain Dependence**

   ○ While more stable than live-attenuated vaccines, many inactivated vaccines still require refrigeration, posing challenges in low-resource settings.

3. **Optimizing Durability**

   ○ Research is focused on improving the duration of immunity provided by inactivated vaccines to reduce the need for boosters.

3.1.3 Toxoid and Subunit Vaccines

Toxoid and **subunit vaccines** represent key advancements in vaccine development, offering highly targeted approaches to immunization. Unlike live-attenuated or inactivated vaccines, these types focus on specific components of a pathogen—such as toxins or protein subunits—designed to elicit an immune response without introducing the whole pathogen. Their precision and safety have made them invaluable in the fight against numerous infectious diseases.

Toxoid Vaccines

Toxoid vaccines are based on **detoxified bacterial toxins**, known as **toxoids,** which retain their ability to stimulate an immune response but are no longer harmful. These vaccines are particularly effective against diseases where bacterial toxins are the primary cause of illness.

Mechanism of Action

1. **Detoxification of Toxins**:

   - Toxins produced by bacteria are inactivated using chemical agents such as **formaldehyde** or **glutaraldehyde** while preserving their antigenic structure.
   - These detoxified toxins, or toxoids, are then used as antigens in the vaccine.

2. **Immune Response**:

   - Upon administration, the immune system recognizes the toxoid as foreign and mounts a response, primarily involving B cells and antibody production.
   - Memory B cells are generated, ensuring rapid neutralization of the toxin upon future exposure.

Examples of Toxoid Vaccines

1. **Tetanus Vaccine**:

   - Protects against **Clostridium tetani**, which produces a neurotoxin causing muscle rigidity and spasms.
   - Administered as part of the **DTP** (diphtheria, tetanus, pertussis) combination vaccine.

2. **Diphtheria Vaccine**:

   - Targets the toxin produced by **Corynebacterium diphtheriae**, which can cause severe respiratory and systemic complications.

3. **Botulism Vaccine**:

   - Used primarily in high-risk populations to neutralize the toxin from **Clostridium botulinum**.

Advantages of Toxoid Vaccines

- **Safety**: Contain no live components, eliminating the risk of infection.

- **Targeted Immunity**: Focus on neutralizing toxins rather than the bacteria itself.
- **Stability**: Easier to store and transport than some other vaccine types.

Limitations of Toxoid Vaccines

- **Limited Immunogenicity**: Often require adjuvants (e.g., aluminum salts) to enhance the immune response.
- **Multiple Doses**: Booster doses are necessary to maintain immunity.
- **Pathogen-Specific**: Effective only against toxin-mediated diseases.

Subunit Vaccines

Subunit vaccines use **specific components** of a pathogen, such as proteins, polysaccharides, or surface antigens, to trigger an immune response. These vaccines avoid using the whole pathogen, significantly improving safety profiles while still eliciting effective immunity.

Mechanism of Action

1. **Isolation of Subunits**:

   - Pathogen components are identified, isolated, and purified for use in vaccines.
   - Common subunits include **capsular polysaccharides**, **viral surface proteins**, and **recombinant proteins** produced via genetic engineering.

2. **Immune Response**:

   - Subunits are recognized by antigen-presenting cells (APCs) and presented to T cells via MHC molecules.
   - Helper T cells activate B cells to produce antibodies specific to the subunit antigen.

Examples of Subunit Vaccines

1. **Hepatitis B Vaccine**:

- ◦ Contains the **hepatitis B surface antigen (HBsAg)**, produced using recombinant DNA technology in yeast cells.
- ◦ Highly effective in preventing hepatitis B and its complications, including liver cancer.

2. **Human Papillomavirus (HPV) Vaccine**:

- ◦ Includes **L1 proteins** from various HPV types, assembled into virus-like particles (VLPs).
- ◦ Protects against cervical cancer and other HPV-associated diseases.

3. **Pertussis (Whooping Cough) Vaccine**:

- ◦ The acellular pertussis vaccine uses purified pertussis toxins and other bacterial components.
- ◦ Safer and less reactogenic than whole-cell pertussis vaccines.

4. **Meningococcal and Pneumococcal Vaccines**:

- ◦ Based on capsular polysaccharides conjugated to carrier proteins to enhance immunogenicity.

Advantages of Subunit Vaccines

- **Safety**: No risk of infection, as they do not contain live pathogens.
- **Fewer Side Effects**: Reduced reactogenicity compared to whole-cell vaccines.
- **Customizable**: Specific antigens can be selected to target particular immune responses.

Limitations of Subunit Vaccines

- **Weaker Immune Response**: Generally less immunogenic than live-attenuated vaccines, requiring adjuvants and booster doses.
- **Complex Manufacturing**: Recombinant and purified antigens require advanced production methods.
- **Limited Antigen Presentation**: May not stimulate cellular immunity as robustly as whole-pathogen vaccines.

Applications of Toxoid and Subunit Vaccines
1. Routine Immunization Programs

- Toxoid and subunit vaccines form the backbone of global vaccination efforts against diseases like tetanus, diphtheria, hepatitis B, and pertussis.

2. Cancer Prevention

- Subunit vaccines such as the HPV vaccine provide effective protection against cancers caused by oncogenic viruses.

3. Outbreak Response

- Subunit vaccines for meningitis and pneumococcal diseases are critical in managing outbreaks in high-risk regions.

Advancements in Toxoid and Subunit Vaccine Technology

1. **Conjugate Vaccines**

   - Combine polysaccharides with carrier proteins to improve immunogenicity, especially in young children.
   - Example: **Haemophilus influenzae type b (Hib) vaccine.**

2. **Recombinant Subunit Vaccines**

   - Use genetic engineering to produce antigens in yeast, bacterial, or mammalian cells.
   - Example: Recombinant hepatitis B and HPV vaccines.

3. **Virus-Like Particles (VLPs)**

   - Mimic the structure of viruses without containing genetic material, enhancing immunogenicity.
   - Example: **HPV vaccines Gardasil and Cervarix.**

4. **Adjuvant Optimization**

- ○ Advanced adjuvants such as MF59 and AS01 improve the immune response to subunit antigens.

Public Health Impact of Toxoid and Subunit Vaccines

- **Global Eradication Efforts**: Tetanus and diphtheria vaccines have drastically reduced morbidity and mortality worldwide.
- **Cancer Prevention**: HPV vaccines are reducing the global burden of cervical and other HPV-related cancers.
- **Pandemic Preparedness**: Subunit vaccines for emerging infectious diseases, such as COVID-19, are being developed using cutting-edge technologies.

Challenges and Future Directions

1. **Accessibility**

   - ○ The high cost and complexity of manufacturing recombinant subunit vaccines limit their availability in low-resource settings.

2. **Enhancing Immunogenicity**

   - ○ Research on adjuvants and delivery systems aims to improve the efficacy of subunit and toxoid vaccines.

3. **Next-Generation Platforms**

   - ○ Innovations such as nanoparticle-based delivery and mRNA technologies are paving the way for more effective vaccines.

3.2 Routes of Administration

The **route of vaccine administration** is a critical factor in determining the efficacy, safety, and practicality of immunization. Each route has unique benefits and challenges, influencing how the vaccine interacts with the immune system and how it is distributed globally. Among the most common methods, **intramuscular (IM)** and **subcutaneous (SC)** delivery stand out for their reliability, safety, and widespread use in conventional vaccine programs.

3.2.1 Intramuscular and Subcutaneous Delivery

Intramuscular (IM) and **subcutaneous (SC)** routes are widely used for administering vaccines. These methods allow vaccines to reach immune cells efficiently while minimizing risks associated with other routes, such as oral or intradermal administration.

Intramuscular (IM) Delivery

IM delivery involves injecting the vaccine into a muscle, usually in the **deltoid muscle** (upper arm) or the **vastus lateralis muscle** (thigh). The muscle tissue provides a robust and consistent environment for antigen absorption, making this route ideal for many vaccines.

Mechanism of Immune Activation

1. **Depot Formation**:

   - Upon injection, the vaccine forms a depot in the muscle tissue, allowing for slow antigen release and prolonged interaction with antigen-presenting cells (APCs).

2. **Recruitment of Immune Cells**:

   - Muscle tissue is well-vascularized, promoting the recruitment of dendritic cells and macrophages to the injection site.

3. **Antigen Presentation**:

   - APCs migrate to nearby lymph nodes, where they present the vaccine antigens to T cells, initiating adaptive immunity.

Advantages of IM Delivery

- **Efficient Absorption**: Muscle tissue has a rich blood supply, ensuring rapid and efficient antigen uptake.
- **Reduced Reactogenicity**: Compared to subcutaneous or intradermal routes, IM delivery is less likely to cause localized inflammation or irritation.
- **Broad Application**: IM delivery is suitable for a wide range of vaccines, including inactivated, subunit, and mRNA vaccines.

Examples of IM Vaccines

- **Hepatitis B Vaccine**
- **Human Papillomavirus (HPV) Vaccine**
- **Influenza Vaccine (Inactivated)**
- **COVID-19 Vaccines (e.g., Pfizer-BioNTech, Moderna)**

Challenges of IM Delivery

- **Pain at the Injection Site**: IM injections can be painful due to needle depth and tissue penetration.
- **Not Ideal for All Populations**: In individuals with reduced muscle mass, such as infants or the elderly, administration may be less effective or require alternative sites.

Subcutaneous (SC) Delivery

SC delivery involves injecting the vaccine into the **subcutaneous fat layer**, located between the dermis and muscle. Common injection sites include the **outer upper arm**, **thigh**, or **abdomen**. This route is particularly effective for vaccines that require slower antigen absorption and reduced reactogenicity.

Mechanism of Immune Activation

1. **Gradual Antigen Release**:

   - The subcutaneous fat layer has a lower vascular density than muscle, resulting in slower antigen release and a more sustained immune response.

2. **Localized Immune Activation**:

   - The SC layer contains immune cells such as mast cells and dendritic cells, which capture antigens and initiate immune responses.

3. **Lymphatic Drainage**:

   - Antigens are transported via the lymphatic system to regional lymph nodes, where they are presented to T cells.

Advantages of SC Delivery

- **Lower Risk of Adverse Reactions**: SC delivery is associated with fewer side effects, such as pain and inflammation, compared to IM injections.
- **Ease of Administration**: SC injections are simpler to administer and less invasive, making them ideal for mass immunization campaigns.
- **Suitability for Certain Populations**: Preferred for individuals with conditions that contraindicate IM injections, such as clotting disorders.

Examples of SC Vaccines

- **Measles, Mumps, and Rubella (MMR) Vaccine**
- **Varicella (Chickenpox) Vaccine**
- **Yellow Fever Vaccine**

Challenges of SC Delivery

- **Variable Absorption**: Slower and less consistent absorption compared to IM delivery can affect vaccine efficacy.
- **Localized Reactions**: SC injections may cause swelling, redness, or irritation at the injection site.

Feature	Intramuscular (IM)	Subcutaneous (SC)
Injection Depth	Deep into muscle	Into subcutaneous fat
Absorption Speed	Faster	Slower
Common Vaccines	Hepatitis B, COVID-19	MMR, Varicella
Adverse Reactions	Pain, soreness	Swelling, redness
Ease of Administration	Moderate	High

Comparison of IM and SC Delivery

Public Health Applications

1. **Routine Immunization Programs**

   ◦ IM and SC routes are used globally for administering childhood vaccines, ensuring consistent immunization coverage.

2. **Mass Vaccination Campaigns**

   ◦ SC vaccines like MMR are ideal for rapid deployment during outbreaks due to their ease of administration.

3. **Pandemic Preparedness**

   ◦ IM delivery systems have been critical in administering COVID-19 vaccines at scale, leveraging existing healthcare infrastructure.

Advancements in Delivery Systems

1. **Needle-Free Injectors**

   ◦ Devices such as **jet injectors** deliver vaccines via high-pressure streams, eliminating the need for needles.

2. **Pre-Filled Syringes**

   ◦ These syringes enhance the safety and accuracy of vaccine delivery, reducing wastage and contamination risks.

3. **Microneedle Patches**

   ◦ Emerging technologies like microneedle patches offer painless, user-friendly alternatives for IM and SC administration.

3.2.2 Oral and Nasal Vaccines

Oral and **nasal vaccine delivery** systems represent innovative approaches to immunization, leveraging the natural routes of pathogen entry to stimulate robust immune responses. These non-invasive methods offer several advantages, such as ease of administration, enhanced patient compliance, and the potential to induce mucosal immunity. This section explores the mechanisms, examples, and applications of oral and nasal vaccines, highlighting their transformative impact on vaccination strategies.

Oral Vaccines

Oral vaccines are designed to be ingested, delivering antigens to the gut-associated lymphoid tissue (GALT), a critical component of the mucosal immune system. This route mimics the natural infection process of many enteric pathogens, promoting immunity at the site of pathogen entry.

Mechanism of Action

1. **Antigen Uptake:**

   - After ingestion, the vaccine antigen is transported to the small intestine, where specialized cells known as **M cells** capture and deliver it to underlying immune tissues.
   - The GALT, which includes **Peyer's patches**, processes the antigen and activates immune cells.

2. **Immune Activation:**

   - Dendritic cells present the antigen to **T cells** and **B cells**, initiating adaptive immunity.
   - Activated B cells produce **IgA antibodies**, which provide mucosal immunity by neutralizing pathogens at the mucosal surface.

3. **Systemic Immunity:**

   - In addition to mucosal immunity, oral vaccines often generate systemic immunity, including IgG production, protecting against systemic spread.

Examples of Oral Vaccines

1. **Oral Polio Vaccine (OPV):**

- Contains live-attenuated poliovirus strains and has been instrumental in the global fight against polio.
- Induces both mucosal (IgA) and systemic (IgG) immunity, preventing viral replication in the gut and reducing transmission.

2. **Rotavirus Vaccine**:

- Protects against severe diarrhea caused by rotavirus, particularly in infants and young children.
- Delivered as an oral liquid, the vaccine directly targets the gastrointestinal tract.

3. **Cholera Vaccine**:

- Vaccines like **Dukoral** and **Shanchol** contain inactivated Vibrio cholerae or its components to protect against cholera in endemic regions.

4. **Typhoid Vaccine**:

- **Vivotif**, a live-attenuated oral vaccine, protects against Salmonella typhi.

Advantages of Oral Vaccines

- **Ease of Administration**: No needles or trained personnel are required, facilitating mass immunization campaigns.
- **Induction of Mucosal Immunity**: Provides protection at mucosal surfaces, where many pathogens first invade.
- **Patient Compliance**: Non-invasive delivery improves acceptance, especially in children.
- **Reduced Risk of Needle-Stick Injuries**: Eliminates the need for syringes, enhancing safety in healthcare settings.

Limitations of Oral Vaccines

- **Stability Issues**: Oral vaccines are sensitive to degradation by stomach acid and digestive enzymes, requiring stabilizers or encapsulation technologies.

- **Cold Chain Requirements**: Many oral vaccines require refrigeration, complicating distribution in resource-limited settings.
- **Inconsistent Absorption**: Factors such as gastrointestinal health and age can affect vaccine efficacy.

Nasal Vaccines

Nasal vaccines are delivered as a spray or droplets into the nasal cavity, targeting the nasopharyngeal-associated lymphoid tissue (NALT), a key site for initiating immune responses against respiratory pathogens.

Mechanism of Action

1. **Antigen Uptake**:

   - Antigens are absorbed by epithelial cells and captured by dendritic cells in the nasal mucosa.

2. **Immune Activation**:

   - Dendritic cells process and present the antigens to T cells and B cells in nearby lymphoid tissues.
   - IgA production in the nasal mucosa provides localized immunity, while systemic IgG antibodies offer additional protection.

3. **Broad Protection**:

   - Nasal vaccines stimulate both mucosal and systemic immunity, preventing infection at the site of entry and reducing disease severity.

Examples of Nasal Vaccines

1. **Influenza Vaccine (FluMist)**:

   - A live-attenuated vaccine delivered intranasally, providing immunity against seasonal influenza.
   - Particularly effective in children, offering both mucosal and systemic protection.

2. **COVID-19 Nasal Vaccines (Under Development):**

   - Several intranasal vaccines are being developed to target SARS-CoV-2, aiming to block viral entry at the respiratory mucosa and reduce transmission.

3. **RSV Vaccines:**

   - Research is ongoing for nasal vaccines against **respiratory syncytial virus (RSV),** a major cause of respiratory infections in infants and the elderly.

Advantages of Nasal Vaccines

- **Non-Invasive Delivery:** Eliminates the need for needles, improving patient compliance.
- **Targeted Mucosal Immunity:** Provides protection at the respiratory mucosa, the primary site of entry for many airborne pathogens.
- **Ease of Administration:** Suitable for self-administration or mass immunization during pandemics.
- **Rapid Onset of Action:** Quickly generates localized immunity, ideal for controlling respiratory infections.

Limitations of Nasal Vaccines

- **Limited Stability:** Nasal vaccines may require advanced formulations to prevent degradation in the nasal environment.
- **Shorter Duration of Immunity:** Booster doses may be needed to maintain long-term protection.
- **Risk of Local Reactions:** Nasal irritation or congestion may occur following administration.

Feature	Oral Vaccines	Nasal Vaccines
Targeted Tissue	Gut-associated lymphoid tissue	Nasopharyngeal-associated lymphoid tissue
Induces Mucosal Immunity	Yes	Yes
Ease of Administration	High	High
Examples	OPV, Rotavirus, Cholera	FluMist, RSV, COVID-19 (under development)

Comparison of Oral and Nasal Vaccines

Public Health Applications

1. **Eradication Campaigns**

   ◦ Oral vaccines like OPV have been critical in the near-eradication of polio.

2. **Pandemic Preparedness**

   ◦ Nasal vaccines for influenza and COVID-19 aim to curb respiratory virus transmission during pandemics.

3. **Mass Immunization**

   ◦ Non-invasive delivery systems are ideal for large-scale campaigns, particularly in low-resource settings.

Advancements in Oral and Nasal Vaccine Technologies

1. **Encapsulation and Stabilization**

   ◦ Advanced encapsulation techniques protect oral vaccines from stomach acid and digestive enzymes, improving efficacy.
   ◦ Example: Enteric-coated capsules for typhoid vaccines.

2. **Nanoformulations**

   ◦ Nanoparticles and lipid-based carriers enhance antigen stability and delivery for both oral and nasal vaccines.

3. **Thermostable Formulations**

   ◦ Thermostable vaccines reduce reliance on cold chains, improving accessibility in remote areas.

4. **Broad-Spectrum Mucosal Adjuvants**

   ◦ Adjuvants specifically designed for mucosal vaccines, such as **LT (heat-labile toxin)** and **CTB (cholera toxin B subunit)**, enhance immune responses.

Challenges and Future Directions

1. **Addressing Efficacy Variability**

   ◦ Research is needed to optimize vaccine delivery for populations with differing immune responses.

2. **Expanding Applications**

   ◦ Developing oral and nasal vaccines for non-mucosal pathogens, such as malaria or HIV, remains a challenge.

3. **Global Accessibility**

   ◦ Ensuring affordable, stable formulations for widespread use in low-resource settings is a priority.

3.2.3 Comparison of Administration Methods

The choice of **vaccine administration method** plays a critical role in determining the vaccine's efficacy, safety, and practicality. Different routes of administration—**intramuscular (IM)**, **subcutaneous (SC)**, **oral**, and **nasal**—offer distinct advantages and limitations based on the target pathogen, the type of vaccine, and the population being immunized. This section provides a comparative analysis of these administration methods, exploring their immunological mechanisms, practical considerations, and suitability for various vaccine types.

Key Parameters for Comparison

1. **Targeted Immune Response**: The route of administration influences the type of immunity generated, such as systemic versus mucosal immunity.
2. **Ease of Administration**: Practicality and accessibility are essential for large-scale immunization programs.
3. **Safety Profile**: The risk of side effects and adverse reactions varies with the method of delivery.
4. **Stability and Storage**: Different routes require specific formulations, affecting cold chain logistics and vaccine stability.
5. **Cost and Scalability**: Cost-effectiveness and scalability are critical for global vaccination efforts.

Parameter	Intramuscular (IM)	Subcutaneous (SC)	Oral	Nasal
Targeted Tissue	Muscle	Subcutaneous fat	Gut-associated lymphoid tissue	Nasopharyngeal-associated lymphoid tissue
Immune Response	Systemic (IgG)	Systemic (IgG)	Mucosal (IgA) and systemic (IgG)	Mucosal (IgA) and systemic (IgG)
Ease of Administration	Moderate	Easy	Very easy (no needles)	Very easy (no needles)
Pain and Discomfort	Moderate	Low	None	Minimal
Examples	Hepatitis B, COVID-19, Influenza	MMR, Varicella, Yellow Fever	Polio (OPV), Rotavirus, Cholera	Influenza (FluMist), RSV
Stability	Moderate	Moderate	Sensitive to stomach acid	Sensitive to environmental factors
Cold Chain Dependence	High	High	High	High
Suitability for Mass Campaigns	Moderate	High	Very High	High
Adverse Reactions	Injection site soreness	Swelling, redness	Rare gastrointestinal side effects	Nasal irritation or congestion

Comparison of Administration Methods

Intramuscular (IM) Delivery

Strengths:

Consistent antigen absorption and immune activation.

Suitable for a wide range of vaccines, including inactivated, subunit, and mRNA vaccines.

Limitations:

Requires trained personnel and needles.

Pain at the injection site may reduce compliance, particularly in children.

Subcutaneous (SC) Delivery

Strengths:

Easier to administer than IM, with fewer localized side effects.

Ideal for live-attenuated vaccines requiring slower antigen absorption.

Limitations:

Slower and less consistent absorption compared to IM delivery.

Oral Delivery

Strengths:

Non-invasive, needle-free method enhances compliance.

Induces both mucosal (IgA) and systemic (IgG) immunity, crucial for enteric pathogens.

Limitations:

Antigen degradation in the gastrointestinal tract may reduce efficacy.

Requires stabilizers or encapsulation technologies for effective delivery.

Nasal Delivery

Strengths:

Targets mucosal immunity at the respiratory tract, the primary site of entry for many pathogens.

Painless and easily administered, suitable for self-administration.

Limitations:

Risk of nasal irritation or mild adverse reactions.

Limited to vaccines designed for respiratory or systemic infections.

Factors Influencing Route Selection

Type of Vaccine:

Live-Attenuated Vaccines: Often administered orally (e.g., OPV) or subcutaneously (e.g., MMR) to mimic natural infection.

Inactivated Vaccines: Typically delivered via IM injection for optimal systemic immunity.

Subunit and mRNA Vaccines: Prefer IM delivery for consistent absorption and immune activation.

Target Population:

Children and infants may benefit from oral vaccines due to ease of administration.

Nasal vaccines are well-suited for individuals with needle phobia.

Disease Characteristics:

Enteric diseases (e.g., cholera, rotavirus) benefit from oral vaccines that induce gut immunity.

Respiratory diseases (e.g., influenza, RSV) are ideal candidates for nasal vaccines.

Logistical Considerations:

Mass campaigns in resource-limited settings favor oral vaccines due to ease of administration and scalability.

Advancements in Administration Methods

Needle-Free Technologies

Jet injectors and **microneedle patches** reduce pain and improve accessibility for IM and SC vaccines.

Thermostable Formulations

Innovations in vaccine stability are expanding the applicability of oral and nasal routes by reducing cold chain dependence.

Combination Approaches

Multi-route strategies (e.g., priming with IM and boosting with oral or nasal vaccines) are being explored to maximize immune responses.

Public Health Impact

Polio Eradication: Oral polio vaccines have been instrumental in eliminating poliovirus from most regions.

Influenza Control: Nasal influenza vaccines have enhanced coverage, particularly in pediatric populations.

Childhood Immunization: SC administration remains a mainstay for delivering MMR and varicella vaccines globally.

3.3 Limitations of Conventional Methods

While conventional vaccine delivery systems have been instrumental in combating infectious diseases globally, they are not without limitations. One of the most significant challenges associated with traditional vaccine delivery is ensuring **stability and proper storage** throughout the supply chain. These issues have profound implications for vaccine efficacy, distribution logistics, and equitable access, particularly in resource-limited settings.

3.3.1 Stability and Storage Challenges

Vaccine stability refers to the ability of a vaccine to retain its potency, purity, and safety over time under specific storage conditions. Conventional vaccines often require stringent temperature controls to maintain their efficacy, making stability and storage a critical aspect of global immunization efforts.

The Cold Chain System

The **cold chain** is a temperature-controlled supply chain used to store and transport vaccines from manufacturers to end-users. Most conventional vaccines require storage at **2°C to 8°C**, with some requiring ultra-cold conditions (e.g., -70°C for certain mRNA vaccines). Breaks in the cold chain can compromise vaccine quality, leading to reduced efficacy or complete loss of potency.

Factors Influencing Vaccine Stability

1. **Temperature Sensitivity**:

    - Many vaccines, particularly live-attenuated and protein-based formulations, are highly sensitive to heat and freezing.
    - Exposure to temperatures outside the recommended range can denature proteins, degrade antigens, or kill attenuated pathogens.

2. **Moisture and Humidity**:

    - Vaccines in lyophilized (freeze-dried) form are stable at ambient temperatures but require careful reconstitution with sterile diluents.
    - Improper handling during reconstitution can introduce moisture, leading to contamination or reduced stability.

3. **Light Sensitivity**:

    - Certain vaccines, such as the **measles vaccine**, are sensitive to light, which can degrade their active components.

4. **Adjuvant Stability**:

- Adjuvants like aluminum salts may precipitate or degrade under improper storage conditions, affecting vaccine immunogenicity.

5. **Examples of Stability-Dependent Vaccines**
6. **Live-Attenuated Vaccines**:

   - Examples: **Oral Polio Vaccine (OPV), MMR vaccine.**
   - Require strict cold chain maintenance as their viability is highly temperature-dependent.

7. **mRNA Vaccines**:

   - Examples: **Pfizer-BioNTech (Comirnaty), Moderna (Spikevax).**
   - Require ultra-cold storage (-70°C for Pfizer-BioNTech and -20°C for Moderna), making distribution challenging in low-resource settings.

8. **Reconstituted Vaccines**:

   - Examples: **BCG vaccine, Yellow Fever vaccine.**
   - Stability post-reconstitution is limited, necessitating immediate use.

Challenges in Resource-Limited Settings

1. **Infrastructure Gaps**:

   - Inadequate cold chain infrastructure in remote and underserved areas leads to vaccine spoilage during storage and transportation.

2. **High Costs**:

   - Maintaining cold chain systems requires significant financial investment in refrigeration equipment, power supply, and monitoring devices.

3. **Logistical Complexity**:

   - Transporting ultra-cold vaccines involves specialized containers and dry ice, which are logistically demanding and environmentally taxing.

4. **Temperature Excursions**:

   - Power outages, human error, or equipment failures can lead to breaks in the cold chain, rendering vaccines unusable.

Strategies to Overcome Stability Challenges

1. **Development of Thermostable Vaccines**

   - Researchers are exploring formulations that remain stable at ambient temperatures.
   - Example: **Thermostable rotavirus and measles vaccines** have been developed for use in tropical climates.

2. **Lyophilization (Freeze-Drying)**

   - Converts liquid vaccines into a dry powder form, increasing stability and shelf life.
   - Requires reconstitution before use, with careful handling of diluents.

3. **Innovative Packaging Solutions**

   - **Vial monitors**: Heat-sensitive labels that change color to indicate exposure to damaging temperatures.
   - **Self-contained cold storage units**: Portable refrigeration units powered by solar energy for use in remote areas.

4. **Next-Generation Delivery Systems**

   - **Microneedle patches**: Allow stable vaccines to be delivered without refrigeration, making them ideal for low-resource settings.
   - **Encapsulation technologies**: Nanoparticles and liposomes protect antigens from degradation.

5. **Improved Cold Chain Monitoring**

- Real-time temperature monitoring devices ensure vaccines remain within the prescribed temperature range throughout the supply chain.

Case Studies

1. **COVID-19 Vaccine Distribution**

   - The logistical challenges of distributing mRNA vaccines requiring ultra-cold storage highlighted the importance of stability innovations.
   - Initiatives like **COVAX** have invested in cold chain infrastructure to improve global vaccine access.

2. **Polio Vaccination Campaigns**

   - The successful deployment of OPV in tropical and remote regions relied heavily on maintaining cold chain integrity.

3.3.2 Efficacy Variability Across Populations

One of the critical limitations of conventional vaccine delivery systems is the **variability in vaccine efficacy across different populations**. While vaccines are designed to provide broad protection, their performance can vary significantly based on factors such as age, genetics, comorbidities, geographical regions, and environmental conditions. This variability not only affects individual protection but also has implications for global immunization strategies, as reduced efficacy in certain populations can hinder disease control and eradication efforts.

Factors Influencing Efficacy Variability

1. Age-Related Factors

The immune system's functionality changes significantly across the lifespan, leading to differences in vaccine responses between age groups.

1. **Infants and Young Children:**

   - Immature immune systems in newborns can lead to weaker responses to some vaccines.
   - Maternal antibodies transferred through the placenta or breast milk can neutralize vaccine antigens, reducing efficacy.

- ◦ Example: The measles vaccine is administered after 9–12 months to avoid interference from maternal antibodies.

2. **Elderly Populations**:

- ◦ Aging leads to immunosenescence, a decline in immune system efficiency that reduces vaccine responsiveness.
- ◦ Example: Influenza vaccines are less effective in older adults, prompting the development of high-dose and adjuvanted formulations to enhance immunity.

3. **2. Genetic and Ethnic Variability**

Genetic differences between individuals and populations can influence vaccine efficacy by affecting antigen recognition, immune activation, and memory cell formation.

HLA Polymorphisms:

Variations in **human leukocyte antigen (HLA)** genes, which regulate antigen presentation, can impact immune responses to vaccines.

Example: Certain HLA types are associated with stronger or weaker responses to the hepatitis B vaccine.

Ethnic Variations:

Studies have shown that vaccines like the BCG (tuberculosis) vaccine exhibit different levels of efficacy in populations from tropical and temperate regions. These differences may be influenced by environmental factors, genetics, and pre-existing exposure to environmental mycobacteria.

3. Nutritional Status

Malnutrition, particularly deficiencies in micronutrients such as vitamin A, zinc, and iron, can impair immune responses to vaccines.

Undernourished Populations:

Undernutrition reduces the body's ability to mount an effective immune response, leading to suboptimal vaccine efficacy.

Example: Children in resource-limited settings may exhibit lower responses to oral rotavirus and polio vaccines.

Obesity and Metabolic Disorders:

Obesity is associated with chronic low-grade inflammation and immune dysfunction, which can reduce vaccine efficacy.

Example: Influenza vaccines have been observed to be less effective in individuals with obesity.

4. Comorbidities and Immune Suppression

Pre-existing health conditions and immunosuppression can significantly affect vaccine efficacy.

Chronic Diseases:

Conditions such as diabetes, cardiovascular disease, and chronic respiratory diseases may impair vaccine responses.

Example: Individuals with chronic diseases often require booster doses or adjuvanted vaccines for optimal protection.

Immunosuppressed Populations:

Patients undergoing chemotherapy, transplant recipients, or individuals with HIV/AIDS may exhibit reduced vaccine efficacy.

Example: Live-attenuated vaccines are contraindicated in immunosuppressed individuals due to safety concerns, limiting their options.

5. Environmental and Regional Factors

Geographic and environmental differences also contribute to efficacy variability, particularly in regions with distinct pathogen exposure and immune challenges.

Tropical Regions:

High pathogen burdens and frequent exposure to environmental antigens can skew immune responses, reducing vaccine efficacy.

Example: Oral polio vaccines are less effective in tropical regions due to enteric infections that interfere with antigen uptake.

Cold Chain Issues:

In resource-limited settings, breaks in the cold chain can reduce vaccine potency, leading to lower efficacy.

6. Microbiome Influence

The gut and respiratory microbiota play a critical role in modulating immune responses to vaccines.

Gut Microbiota:

Disruptions in the gut microbiome due to malnutrition, antibiotics, or enteric infections can affect oral vaccine efficacy.

Example: The rotavirus vaccine shows lower efficacy in children from low-income countries with altered microbiomes.

Respiratory Microbiota:

Differences in nasal microbiota composition may influence responses to nasal vaccines, such as FluMist.

Strategies to Address Efficacy Variability

Tailored Vaccine Formulations:

Developing vaccines specifically designed for vulnerable populations, such as high-dose influenza vaccines for the elderly or thermostable vaccines for tropical climates.

Adjuvant Optimization:

Using adjuvants that enhance immune responses in populations with weakened immunity, such as MPL or MF59.

Boosters and Alternate Schedules:

Administering booster doses or adjusting vaccination schedules to improve immune responses in populations with reduced efficacy.

Nutritional Interventions:

Addressing malnutrition and providing micronutrient supplements alongside vaccination programs to enhance immune responses.

Microbiome Modulation:

Exploring prebiotics, probiotics, or microbiome-targeted therapies to improve vaccine responses in individuals with altered microbiota.

Global Surveillance and Research:

Conducting population-specific efficacy studies to understand variability and guide vaccine design and implementation.

Examples of Addressing Efficacy Variability

Pneumococcal Vaccines in Elderly Populations:

Conjugate vaccines like PCV13 have been developed to enhance immune responses in older adults, replacing polysaccharide-only formulations.

Oral Cholera Vaccines in Malnourished Populations:

Modified formulations with improved immunogenicity have been introduced to address reduced efficacy in undernourished children.

HIV Vaccines:

Research into adjuvants and delivery systems is ongoing to overcome challenges in inducing immunity in immunocompromised individuals.

Public Health Implications

Herd Immunity: Variability in vaccine efficacy across populations can limit herd immunity, particularly in regions with low immunization coverage or high pathogen burdens.

Global Inequities: Differences in vaccine efficacy contribute to health disparities, necessitating efforts to design vaccines that work effectively across diverse populations.

Decentralized Manufacturing

Localized production facilities reduce the need for long-distance transport, minimizing exposure to temperature fluctuations.

FOUR

ADVANCED ADJUVANT SYSTEMS

Adjuvants are crucial components of many modern vaccines, enhancing their immunogenicity and efficacy by modulating immune responses. Advanced adjuvant systems represent a leap forward in vaccine technology, enabling the development of vaccines for challenging diseases, improving responses in vulnerable populations, and minimizing side effects. This chapter provides an in-depth exploration of adjuvant mechanisms, beginning with their role in **immune potentiation**, the cornerstone of their functionality.

4.1 Overview of Adjuvant Mechanisms

Adjuvants work by activating and enhancing the body's immune response to a vaccine antigen. They achieve this through diverse mechanisms, including immune potentiation, depot effects, and the modulation of antigen presentation. Understanding these mechanisms is critical to designing vaccines that provide robust, long-lasting immunity while minimizing adverse reactions.

4.1.1 Immune Potentiation

Immune potentiation refers to the ability of adjuvants to amplify the immune response, ensuring that vaccines induce a strong and protective immunity even when using small doses of antigen. By activating innate immune pathways and creating a favorable cytokine environment, adjuvants optimize the activation and proliferation of adaptive immune cells, such as T and B cells.

Mechanisms of Immune Potentiation
1. Activation of Innate Immunity
Adjuvants often act on **pattern recognition receptors (PRRs)** expressed by antigen-presenting cells (APCs), such as dendritic cells and macrophages. These receptors recognize pathogen-associated molecular patterns (PAMPs) and danger-associated molecular patterns (DAMPs), triggering a cascade of immune signaling.

- **Toll-Like Receptor (TLR) Agonists:**

  - TLRs are critical PRRs that detect microbial components. Adjuvants like **CpG oligodeoxynucleotides** (TLR9 agonists) and **monophosphoryl lipid A (MPL)** (TLR4 agonist) mimic bacterial or viral infections to activate innate immunity.
  - Example: MPL, used in the **Cervarix HPV vaccine**, enhances antigen presentation and cytokine production.

- **NOD-Like Receptors (NLRs) and Inflammasomes:**

  - Adjuvants such as **aluminum salts (alum)** stimulate the **NLRP3 inflammasome**, leading to the release of pro-inflammatory cytokines like **IL-1β** and **IL-18**, which amplify immune activation.

2. Cytokine and Chemokine Induction
Adjuvants create a pro-inflammatory microenvironment by inducing the production of cytokines and chemokines, which recruit and activate immune cells.

- **Pro-Inflammatory Cytokines:**

  - Adjuvants like **MF59** (an oil-in-water emulsion) induce cytokines such as **IL-6** and **IL-12**, driving the differentiation of T cells and enhancing B cell activation.

- **Chemokine Production:**

  - Adjuvants promote the migration of dendritic cells and macrophages to the site of injection and regional lymph nodes, facilitating efficient antigen presentation.

3. Enhanced Antigen Presentation

Adjuvants optimize the process of antigen presentation, a crucial step in activating T cells.

- **MHC Upregulation**:

  - Adjuvants increase the expression of **major histocompatibility complex (MHC)** molecules on APCs, improving their ability to present antigens to T cells.

- **Co-Stimulatory Molecule Expression**:

  - Molecules like **CD80** and **CD86**, essential for T cell activation, are upregulated by adjuvants such as MPL and alum.

4. T Cell Differentiation

Adjuvants influence the type of adaptive immune response generated by promoting the differentiation of T cells into specific subsets:

- **Th1 Response**:

  - Adjuvants like **CpG** and MPL skew immunity toward a Th1 profile, characterized by **IFN-γ** production. This response is critical for intracellular pathogens such as viruses and certain bacteria.
  - Example: **Hepatitis B vaccines** benefit from Th1 responses, enhancing cytotoxic T cell activity.

- **Th2 Response**:

  - Alum promotes a Th2 response, characterized by **IL-4** and **IL-5** production, leading to strong antibody-mediated immunity.
  - Example: Alum-based vaccines like the **diphtheria-tetanus-pertussis (DTP) vaccine** induce robust antibody production.

- **Th17 Response**:

- Some adjuvants stimulate Th17 cells, producing **IL-17**, which recruits neutrophils and is effective against extracellular bacteria and fungi.

5. Memory Cell Generation

Adjuvants enhance the formation and longevity of **memory T and B cells**, ensuring long-term protection.

- **Germinal Center Reactions**:

  - Adjuvants like MF59 promote the formation of germinal centers in lymph nodes, where B cells undergo somatic hypermutation and affinity maturation, producing high-affinity antibodies.

- **Long-Lived Plasma Cells**:

  - Enhanced memory responses result in sustained antibody production, reducing the need for frequent booster doses.

Examples of Adjuvants and Immune Potentiation

1. **Aluminum-Based Adjuvants (Alum)**:

   - Mechanism: Induces inflammasome activation and Th2 responses.
   - Applications: Used in hepatitis B, DTP, and HPV vaccines.

2. **MF59**:

   - Mechanism: Oil-in-water emulsion that recruits immune cells and enhances antigen presentation.
   - Applications: Influenza vaccines for elderly populations.

3. **AS01**:

   - Mechanism: Combination of MPL (TLR4 agonist) and QS-21 (saponin-based adjuvant) for balanced Th1 and Th2 responses.
   - Applications: Malaria vaccine (RTS,S) and shingles vaccine (Shingrix).

4. **CpG Oligodeoxynucleotides**:

- ○ Mechanism: Activates TLR9, promoting Th1 immunity and cytotoxic T cell responses.
- ○ Applications: Heplisav-B (hepatitis B vaccine).

Advantages of Immune Potentiation in Vaccine Design

- **Dose Sparing**: Enhanced immune responses allow for reduced antigen doses, increasing vaccine production efficiency.
- **Broader Protection**: Potentiated immune responses provide cross-protection against pathogen variants.
- **Improved Durability**: Stronger memory cell formation leads to long-lasting immunity.
- **Targeted Responses**: Specific adjuvants can direct immunity toward desired pathways (e.g., Th1 or Th2).

Challenges and Future Directions

1. **Safety Concerns**:

   - ○ Overstimulation of the immune system by potent adjuvants can lead to excessive inflammation or autoimmune reactions.

2. **Population Variability**:

   - ○ The effectiveness of immune potentiation varies across age groups, genetic backgrounds, and health conditions.

3. **Adjuvant Innovations**:

   - ○ Research is ongoing to develop next-generation adjuvants that combine high efficacy with minimal side effects.

4. **Personalized Vaccines**:

   - ○ Tailoring adjuvant systems to individual immune profiles could optimize vaccine responses.

4.1.2 Enhancing Antigen Presentation

A critical function of adjuvants in vaccine design is their ability to **enhance antigen presentation**, a process essential for initiating and amplifying the adaptive immune response. This enhancement ensures that antigens are effectively processed and presented to T cells by antigen-presenting cells (APCs), such as **dendritic cells, macrophages**, and **B cells**. By optimizing antigen presentation, adjuvants improve the magnitude and quality of the immune response, making vaccines more effective even with reduced antigen doses.

The Antigen Presentation Process

Antigen presentation is a multi-step process through which APCs process vaccine antigens and present them to T cells via **major histocompatibility complex (MHC)** molecules. This process includes:

1. **Antigen Uptake:**

   ○ APCs internalize vaccine antigens through mechanisms such as **phagocytosis, pinocytosis**, or **receptor-mediated endocytosis**.

2. **Antigen Processing:**

   ○ Internalized antigens are degraded into peptides within **endosomes** or **phagolysosomes**.
   ○ Peptides are then loaded onto MHC molecules.

3. **Antigen Presentation:**

   ○ Processed peptides are displayed on the surface of APCs bound to **MHC Class I** (for CD8+ T cells) or **MHC Class II** (for CD4+ T cells) molecules.

4. **T Cell Activation:**

   ○ T cells recognize the antigen-MHC complex via the **T cell receptor (TCR)**, initiating an adaptive immune response.

Mechanisms by Which Adjuvants Enhance Antigen Presentation
1. Activation of Antigen-Presenting Cells (APCs)

Adjuvants activate APCs by interacting with **pattern recognition receptors (PRRs)**, such as **Toll-like receptors (TLRs)** and **NOD-like receptors (NLRs)**.

- **TLR Agonists**:

  - Adjuvants like **monophosphoryl lipid A (MPL)** and **CpG oligodeoxynucleotides** mimic microbial components, activating TLR4 and TLR9, respectively.
  - This activation triggers the production of cytokines, such as **IL-12**, which promote T cell differentiation.

- **Inflammasome Activation**:

  - Adjuvants such as **alum** stimulate the **NLRP3 inflammasome**, enhancing the release of pro-inflammatory cytokines like **IL-1β** and **IL-18**, which recruit and activate APCs.

2. Prolonged Antigen Availability

Adjuvants can create a **depot effect**, ensuring that antigens are released slowly and remain available for APC uptake over an extended period.

- **Aluminum-Based Adjuvants**:

  - Alum forms a gel-like depot at the injection site, allowing sustained antigen release and interaction with APCs.
  - Example: Hepatitis B vaccines use alum to enhance antigen retention and uptake.

- **Oil-in-Water Emulsions**:

  - Adjuvants like **MF59** stabilize antigens and promote their gradual dissemination, ensuring continuous stimulation of APCs.

3. Upregulation of MHC and Co-Stimulatory Molecules

Adjuvants enhance the expression of MHC molecules and **co-stimulatory molecules** such as **CD80** and **CD86** on APCs, improving T cell activation.

- **MHC Upregulation:**

  - Adjuvants like MPL increase the expression of MHC Class I and II molecules, enhancing antigen presentation efficiency.

- **Co-Stimulatory Molecule Expression:**

  - Essential for T cell activation, co-stimulatory molecules are upregulated by TLR agonists and saponin-based adjuvants like **QS-21.**

4. Promotion of Cross-Presentation

Cross-presentation allows exogenous antigens to be presented via **MHC Class I**, activating cytotoxic CD8+ T cells critical for antiviral and anticancer immunity.

- **CpG Adjuvants:**

  - Stimulate cross-presentation by activating dendritic cells and promoting antigen processing through the endoplasmic reticulum.

- **Nanoparticle-Based Adjuvants:**

  - Enhance cross-presentation by delivering antigens directly into the cytoplasm of APCs.

5. Recruitment of APCs to the Injection Site

Adjuvants induce the production of chemokines that recruit APCs, such as dendritic cells and macrophages, to the site of vaccine administration.

- **MF59 and AS03:**

  - These adjuvants are known for their ability to recruit monocytes and dendritic cells to the injection site, increasing the pool of APCs available for antigen uptake.

Examples of Adjuvants Enhancing Antigen Presentation

1. **Monophosphoryl Lipid A (MPL):**

- A TLR4 agonist that enhances MHC expression and cytokine production.
- Applications: HPV vaccine (**Cervarix**) and malaria vaccine (**RTS,S**).

2. **QS-21**:

- A saponin-based adjuvant that boosts co-stimulatory molecule expression and promotes APC activation.
- Applications: Shingles vaccine (**Shingrix**) and investigational cancer vaccines.

3. **Alum (Aluminum Hydroxide)**:

- Induces inflammasome activation and provides a depot effect.
- Applications: Hepatitis B, DTP, and pneumococcal vaccines.

4. **MF59**:

- An oil-in-water emulsion that enhances dendritic cell recruitment and cytokine production.
- Applications: Influenza vaccines for older adults.

Advantages of Enhancing Antigen Presentation

- **Improved Vaccine Efficacy**: Enhanced antigen presentation ensures robust activation of T cells and B cells, leading to stronger and longer-lasting immunity.
- **Dose Sparing**: Effective antigen presentation allows for reduced antigen doses, increasing vaccine availability during outbreaks or shortages.
- **Targeted Responses**: Specific adjuvants can direct the immune response to Th1, Th2, or Th17 pathways, depending on the pathogen.
- **Broad Applicability**: Adjuvants that enhance antigen presentation are effective across various vaccine platforms, including subunit, mRNA, and inactivated vaccines.

Challenges and Considerations

1. **Safety Concerns**:

- Overactivation of APCs can lead to excessive inflammation or autoimmune reactions.

2. **Population Variability**:

- The effectiveness of antigen presentation may vary based on genetic and environmental factors.

3. **Complex Formulation**:

- Incorporating adjuvants into vaccine formulations requires careful optimization to balance efficacy and safety.

Future Directions

1. **Nanoparticle-Based Adjuvants**:

- Advances in nanotechnology are enabling precise delivery of antigens and adjuvants to APCs, enhancing antigen presentation.

2. **Combination Adjuvants**:

- Pairing adjuvants with complementary mechanisms (e.g., MPL and QS-21) to achieve synergistic effects in antigen presentation.

3. **Personalized Adjuvants**:

- Tailoring adjuvant systems to individual immune profiles to optimize antigen presentation and immune activation.

4. **Emerging Pathogens**:

- Developing adjuvants that enhance antigen presentation against rapidly evolving pathogens such as SARS-CoV-2 variants and antimicrobial-resistant bacteria.

4.2 Common Adjuvants in Use

Adjuvants are critical components of many vaccines, enhancing their ability to induce a strong and durable immune response. Among the most commonly used adjuvants, **aluminum-based compounds**, collectively referred to as alum, have been a cornerstone in vaccine development for over 90 years. This section explores **alum and its variants**, their mechanisms of action, applications, advantages, and limitations.

4.2.1 Alum and Its Variants

Alum refers to aluminum-based salts, such as **aluminum hydroxide**, **aluminum phosphate**, and **aluminum potassium sulfate**, which are widely used as adjuvants in human vaccines. Alum remains the most commonly used adjuvant in licensed vaccines due to its safety profile, effectiveness in inducing humoral immunity, and ease of manufacturing.

Chemical Composition of Alum

Alum is composed of **insoluble aluminum salts** that form a particulate or gel-like structure. The specific variant used in a vaccine depends on the desired immune response and the chemical compatibility with the antigen.

1. **Aluminum Hydroxide ($Al(OH)_3$):**

   - Composed of positively charged particles, it is highly effective in adsorbing negatively charged antigens.

2. **Aluminum Phosphate ($AlPO_4$):**

   - Negatively charged, it is better suited for positively charged antigens.

3. **Mixed Alum Formulations:**

   - A combination of aluminum hydroxide and phosphate may be used to optimize antigen adsorption and immune response.

Mechanisms of Action

Alum enhances the immune response through several mechanisms:

1. **Depot Effect:**

   - Alum forms a gel-like depot at the injection site, slowly releasing the antigen over time. This prolonged exposure enhances antigen uptake by **antigen-presenting cells (APCs)** and stimulates a sustained immune response.

2. **Inflammasome Activation:**

   - Alum activates the **NLRP3 inflammasome**, leading to the production of pro-inflammatory cytokines such as **IL-1β** and **IL-18**. These cytokines recruit and activate dendritic cells, macrophages, and other immune cells.

3. **Enhanced Antigen Presentation:**

   - By adsorbing antigens onto its surface, alum facilitates their uptake and processing by APCs, improving the presentation of antigens to T cells.

4. **Th2 Skewing:**

   - Alum primarily induces a **Th2-dominated immune response**, characterized by the production of antibodies (humoral immunity). This makes it particularly effective for vaccines targeting extracellular pathogens.

Applications of Alum in Vaccines
Alum is used in vaccines targeting a wide range of infectious diseases:

1. **Hepatitis B Vaccine:**

   - Alum enhances the humoral response against the hepatitis B surface antigen (HBsAg), providing long-lasting immunity.

2. **DTP (Diphtheria-Tetanus-Pertussis) Vaccines:**

   - Alum is a key adjuvant in these combination vaccines, inducing robust antibody production against bacterial toxins.

3. **Human Papillomavirus (HPV) Vaccine:**

- ○ Alum-based adjuvants in HPV vaccines like **Gardasil** improve immunogenicity, reducing the need for multiple doses.

4. **Pneumococcal Vaccines**:

- ○ Alum is used to boost the immune response to polysaccharide antigens in conjugate formulations.

Advantages of Alum

1. **Proven Safety**:

- ○ Alum has a long history of safe use in vaccines, with minimal risk of serious side effects.

2. **Stability**:

- ○ Alum-based adjuvants are chemically stable and compatible with a wide range of antigens, facilitating vaccine formulation.

3. **Enhanced Antibody Responses**:

- ○ Alum's ability to induce strong humoral immunity makes it ideal for vaccines targeting extracellular pathogens.

4. **Cost-Effectiveness**:

- ○ Alum is inexpensive to produce and easy to incorporate into vaccine formulations.

Limitations of Alum

1. **Limited Cellular Immunity**:

- ○ Alum is less effective in inducing **Th1-mediated cellular immunity**, which is critical for fighting intracellular pathogens such as viruses and certain bacteria.

2. **Local Reactogenicity**:

   - Alum can cause mild local side effects such as pain, redness, and swelling at the injection site.

3. **Depot-Related Concerns**:

   - The depot effect, while beneficial, may occasionally lead to granuloma formation or persistent injection-site inflammation.

4. **Not Effective for All Antigens**:

   - Certain antigens, particularly those requiring a balanced Th1/Th2 response, are less effectively adjuvanted by alum.

Advancements in Alum-Based Adjuvants

1. **Particle Engineering**:

   - Researchers are modifying alum particles to enhance antigen adsorption and improve immune responses.

2. **Combination Adjuvants**:

   - Alum is often combined with other adjuvants, such as **monophosphoryl lipid A (MPL)** or **QS-21**, to enhance its ability to stimulate cellular immunity.

3. **Thermostable Formulations**:

   - Efforts are underway to create alum-based vaccines with improved thermostability, reducing reliance on cold chain logistics.

Examples of Alum in Combination Adjuvant Systems

1. **AS04**:

- ○ Combines alum with MPL (a TLR4 agonist) to balance humoral and cellular immune responses.
- ○ Applications: HPV vaccine (**Cervarix**).

2. **Conjugate Vaccines**:

- ○ Alum enhances the immune response to polysaccharide-protein conjugates in vaccines for **Haemophilus influenzae type b (Hib)** and **pneumococcal disease**.

Public Health Impact of Alum

- **Global Immunization Programs**: Alum has been a cornerstone in the success of routine childhood immunization programs, reducing the burden of diseases like tetanus, diphtheria, and hepatitis B.
- **Eradication Efforts**: Vaccines adjuvanted with alum have played a critical role in the near-eradication of diseases such as polio.

Future Directions

1. **Innovations in Alum Chemistry**:

- ○ Advanced formulations of alum are being developed to optimize antigen adsorption and immune activation.

2. **Improved Safety Profiles**:

- ○ Research is focusing on reducing local reactogenicity while maintaining immunogenicity.

3. **Expanding Applications**:

- ○ Alum-based adjuvants are being explored for use in novel vaccines targeting emerging diseases and therapeutic applications, such as cancer immunotherapy.

4.2.2 Oil-in-Water Emulsions (e.g., MF59)

Oil-in-water (O/W) emulsions represent an advanced class of vaccine adjuvants that enhance immunogenicity by stimulating both the innate and adaptive immune responses. Among these, **MF59**, a squalene-based adjuvant, has been extensively studied and widely used, particularly in influenza vaccines. MF59 exemplifies the potential of O/W emulsions to improve vaccine efficacy, particularly in populations with weaker immune responses, such as the elderly.

Composition of Oil-in-Water Emulsions

Oil-in-water emulsions are made up of tiny droplets of oil dispersed in water, stabilized by emulsifying agents. The composition of MF59 includes:

1. **Squalene**:

   - A naturally occurring oil that is a precursor to cholesterol and other sterols. Squalene is highly biocompatible and biodegradable.

2. **Surfactants**:

   - **Polysorbate 80** and **sorbitan trioleate** act as emulsifiers to stabilize the emulsion and ensure uniformity.

3. **Water**:

   - The continuous phase in which squalene droplets are dispersed.

The resulting emulsion is highly stable and suitable for vaccine formulations.

Mechanisms of Action

Oil-in-water emulsions like MF59 enhance the immune response through multiple mechanisms:

1. Recruitment of Immune Cells

- MF59 promotes the release of **chemokines**, such as **CCL2** and **CXCL9**, which recruit monocytes, macrophages, and dendritic cells (DCs) to the injection site.

2. Enhanced Antigen Uptake

- MF59 facilitates antigen uptake by APCs through increased fluidity of cell membranes and local inflammatory signals.

3. Activation of Antigen-Presenting Cells (APCs)

- Dendritic cells activated by MF59 migrate to nearby lymph nodes, where they process and present antigens to T cells.
- This activation includes upregulation of **MHC molecules** and **co-stimulatory proteins (CD80, CD86)**.

4. Cytokine and Chemokine Production

- MF59 induces a transient inflammatory response, characterized by the production of cytokines like **IL-6** and **TNF-α**, which enhance adaptive immunity.

5. Th1 and Th2 Balance

- Unlike aluminum-based adjuvants, MF59 can stimulate both **Th1** (cellular) and **Th2** (humoral) responses, providing broader immune activation.

Applications of MF59 in Vaccines

MF59 is primarily used in influenza vaccines but has potential applications in other vaccine formulations:

1. **Influenza Vaccines**:

   - MF59 is used in vaccines like **Fluad**, designed to enhance protection in the elderly. It improves antibody titers and cross-protection against viral strains.

2. **COVID-19 Vaccines (Research and Development)**:

   - MF59-like adjuvants are being explored for mRNA and protein-based COVID-19 vaccines to enhance immunogenicity.

3. **Emerging Pathogens**:

- The adjuvant is being investigated for vaccines against malaria, HIV, and tuberculosis, where strong and balanced immune responses are critical.

Advantages of Oil-in-Water Emulsions (e.g., MF59)

1. **Improved Immunogenicity:**

   - MF59 significantly enhances the immune response to antigens, even in populations with weaker immune systems, such as the elderly.

2. **Rapid Onset of Immunity:**

   - The recruitment of APCs and induction of inflammatory cytokines enable faster immune activation.

3. **Dose Sparing:**

   - By amplifying immune responses, MF59 allows for lower antigen doses, increasing vaccine production efficiency.

4. **Broader Protection:**

   - MF59 enhances cross-reactive immunity, providing protection against antigenically drifted strains of pathogens.

5. **Safety Profile:**

   - MF59 is well-tolerated, with mild and transient side effects such as localized pain and swelling.

Limitations of Oil-in-Water Emulsions

1. **Cost and Complexity:**

   - The manufacturing process for MF59 is more complex and expensive compared to traditional adjuvants like alum.

2. **Cold Chain Requirements**:

   ○ Like most adjuvants, MF59-based vaccines require refrigeration to maintain stability.

3. **Local Reactogenicity**:

   ○ Some recipients experience mild local reactions, such as redness, swelling, or soreness at the injection site.

4. **Limited Use in Certain Populations**:

   ○ Research is ongoing to confirm safety and efficacy in children, pregnant women, and immunocompromised individuals.

Case Studies: MF59 in Action

1. **Fluad (Influenza Vaccine for Elderly)**:

   ○ Clinical trials demonstrated that MF59 significantly improved seroconversion rates in older adults, who often exhibit reduced responses to traditional vaccines.

2. **H5N1 Pandemic Preparedness**:

   ○ MF59-adjuvanted vaccines for H5N1 influenza showed robust immune responses, even with low antigen doses, making them suitable for stockpiling in case of pandemics.

Future Directions for Oil-in-Water Emulsions

1. **Nanoparticle-Based Emulsions**:

   ○ Integration of nanoparticles into O/W emulsions to enhance antigen delivery and targeting.

2. **Combination Adjuvants**:

- Pairing MF59 with other adjuvants, such as TLR agonists, to induce broader and more potent immune responses.

3. **Applications in Cancer Vaccines**:

- Exploring MF59 in therapeutic vaccines targeting tumors, where robust T cell activation is essential.

4. **Thermostable Formulations**:

- Developing formulations with improved stability to reduce cold chain dependence, increasing accessibility in low-resource settings.

Public Health Impact of Oil-in-Water Emulsions

- **Elderly Populations**: MF59 has improved vaccine efficacy for older adults, reducing morbidity and mortality from influenza.
- **Pandemic Preparedness**: The dose-sparing capability of MF59 has made it a critical tool for vaccines targeting emerging pathogens.
- **Expanding Global Access**: Research on simplifying MF59 manufacturing aims to make advanced adjuvants available for low- and middle-income countries.

4.3 Emerging Adjuvants

As the field of vaccinology advances, new adjuvants are emerging to address the limitations of traditional systems. Among the most promising are **monophosphoryl lipid A (MPLA)** and **saponin-based adjuvants**, which offer enhanced immunogenicity while maintaining favorable safety profiles. These adjuvants have been integrated into modern vaccine formulations, broadening their applications to diseases requiring robust and diverse immune responses.

4.3.1 MPLA and Saponins

Monophosphoryl lipid A (MPLA) and **saponin-based adjuvants** represent two distinct but complementary approaches to enhancing immune responses. While MPLA is a refined lipid-based adjuvant designed to mimic bacterial components, saponins are natural compounds derived from plant sources, often used in combination with other adjuvants for synergistic effects.

Monophosphoryl Lipid A (MPLA)

MPLA is a derivative of **lipid A**, a component of the lipopolysaccharide (LPS) found in Gram-negative bacteria. Unlike native lipid A, which is highly inflammatory, MPLA is chemically detoxified, retaining its immunostimulatory properties without causing excessive inflammation.

Mechanism of Action

1. **TLR4 Agonist:**

   - MPLA activates **Toll-like receptor 4 (TLR4)** on dendritic cells and macrophages, triggering a cascade of innate immune responses.

2. **Cytokine Modulation:**

   - Induces the production of **IL-12**, which promotes Th1 responses, and **IL-10**, which modulates excessive inflammation.

3. **Enhanced APC Function:**

   - Upregulates the expression of **MHC molecules** and **co-stimulatory proteins (CD80, CD86)**, improving T cell activation.

4. **Balanced Immune Response:**

   - MPLA stimulates both **Th1 (cellular)** and **Th2 (humoral)** immunity, making it suitable for vaccines targeting intracellular and extracellular pathogens.

Applications of MPLA

1. **HPV Vaccine (Cervarix):**

   - MPLA, combined with alum in the **AS04 adjuvant system**, enhances antibody production and cytotoxic T cell activity against human papillomavirus.

2. **RTS,S Malaria Vaccine:**

- The RTS,S vaccine incorporates MPLA to improve protection against *Plasmodium falciparum*.

3. **Tuberculosis Vaccines**:

- MPLA is under investigation for use in TB vaccines, where robust Th1 responses are critical.

Advantages of MPLA

- **Safety**: Chemically detoxified to minimize reactogenicity.
- **Versatility**: Effective across multiple vaccine platforms, including protein, conjugate, and subunit vaccines.
- **Balanced Immunity**: Induces both humoral and cellular responses.

Limitations of MPLA

- **Cost and Complexity**: Chemical detoxification and purification processes increase production costs.
- **Cold Chain Dependence**: MPLA formulations often require refrigeration.

Saponin-Based Adjuvants

Saponins are natural glycosides extracted from plants, such as **Quillaja saponaria**. These compounds have potent immunostimulatory properties, making them valuable as adjuvants in vaccines targeting challenging diseases.

Mechanism of Action

1. **Membrane Permeabilization**:

- Saponins interact with cell membranes, promoting antigen uptake by APCs and the release of danger signals.

2. **Inflammasome Activation**:

- Saponins trigger the activation of the **NLRP3 inflammasome**, leading to the production of cytokines like **IL-1β** and **IL-18**.

3. **Enhanced Cross-Presentation**:

   - Facilitate the cross-presentation of antigens on **MHC Class I**, activating CD8+ cytotoxic T cells critical for antiviral and anticancer immunity.

4. **Depot Formation**:

   - Saponin-based adjuvants can form depots at the injection site, ensuring sustained antigen release and prolonged immune stimulation.

Examples of Saponin-Based Adjuvants

1. **QS-21**:

   - A highly purified saponin used in combination adjuvant systems like AS01.
   - Applications:

     - **Shingrix (Shingles Vaccine)**: Combines QS-21 with MPL to induce robust and long-lasting immunity.
     - **RTS,S Malaria Vaccine**: QS-21 enhances antigen presentation and Th1 responses.

2. **Matrix-M**:

   - A nanoparticle-based formulation containing saponins, designed to enhance antigen delivery and immune activation.
   - Applications: Used in investigational vaccines for influenza and COVID-19.

Advantages of Saponin-Based Adjuvants

- **Potent Immunostimulatory Effects**: Induce strong cellular and humoral immunity.
- **Versatility**: Effective for vaccines targeting infectious diseases and cancers.

- **Dose Sparing**: Enhance immune responses, allowing for lower antigen doses.

Limitations of Saponin-Based Adjuvants

- **Local Reactogenicity**: May cause mild inflammation, redness, or swelling at the injection site.
- **Stability Concerns**: Saponins are sensitive to heat and require careful formulation to maintain activity.
- **High Production Costs**: Purification processes for compounds like QS-21 are resource-intensive.

Parameter	MPLA	Saponins (e.g., QS-21)
Source	Chemically derived from LPS	Plant-derived (Quillaja saponaria)
Mechanism	TLR4 agonist	Membrane permeabilization, inflammasome activation
Immune Response	Balanced Th1/Th2	Strong Th1 with cross-presentation
Applications	HPV, malaria, TB	Shingles, malaria, investigational cancer vaccines
Safety Profile	Low reactogenicity	Mild local reactogenicity

Comparison of MPLA and Saponins

Future Directions for MPLA and Saponins

1. **Combination Adjuvants**:

   - Pairing MPLA and saponins in systems like **AS01** for synergistic effects, providing robust and balanced immunity.

2. **Nanotechnology Integration**:

   - Encapsulating MPLA and saponins in nanoparticles for targeted delivery and reduced reactogenicity.

3. **Expanded Applications**:

- ○ Investigating their use in vaccines for emerging diseases (e.g., COVID-19, HIV) and therapeutic areas like cancer immunotherapy.

4. **Thermostable Formulations**:

- ○ Developing heat-stable versions to overcome cold chain limitations and improve accessibility in low-resource settings.

Public Health Impact

- **Enhanced Vaccine Efficacy**: MPLA and saponins have enabled the development of vaccines with high efficacy, even in populations with weaker immune responses.
- **Addressing Challenging Diseases**: These adjuvants are integral to vaccines targeting complex pathogens like malaria and cancers.
- **Pandemic Preparedness**: Their versatility makes them valuable tools for rapid vaccine development against emerging infectious diseases.

4.3.2 CpG Oligonucleotides

CpG oligonucleotides are synthetic DNA sequences containing **CpG motifs**—cytosine followed by guanine, connected by a phosphate bond—that mimic microbial DNA. These motifs are recognized by the innate immune system as pathogen-associated molecular patterns (PAMPs), making them potent immunostimulatory agents. CpG oligonucleotides function as adjuvants by activating **Toll-like receptor 9 (TLR9)**, enhancing the innate and adaptive immune responses. They have emerged as key players in next-generation vaccine development due to their ability to induce strong **Th1-biased immunity**.

Mechanism of Action

1. **TLR9 Activation**:

- ○ CpG oligonucleotides bind to **TLR9**, a receptor located in the endosomes of **antigen-presenting cells (APCs)** such as dendritic cells, macrophages, and B cells.

2. **Signaling Cascade**:

- TLR9 activation triggers downstream signaling pathways involving **MyD88** (myeloid differentiation primary response 88), leading to the production of pro-inflammatory cytokines and type I interferons (e.g., IFN-α).

3. **Cytokine Production**:

   - CpG oligonucleotides stimulate the release of cytokines such as **IL-12** and **IFN-γ**, which promote Th1 polarization and cytotoxic T cell activation.

4. **Enhanced Antigen Presentation**:

   - CpG motifs enhance the expression of **MHC molecules** and **co-stimulatory proteins (CD80, CD86)** on APCs, improving T cell activation.

5. **B Cell Activation**:

   - CpG motifs directly activate B cells through TLR9, promoting antibody production and memory B cell formation.

Types of CpG Oligonucleotides
There are three primary classes of CpG oligonucleotides, each designed for specific immune responses:

1. **Class A CpG**:

   - Induce strong type I interferon production and promote the activation of plasmacytoid dendritic cells (pDCs).
   - Applications: Targeting viral infections and cancers.

2. **Class B CpG**:

   - Enhance B cell activation and antibody production, with moderate cytokine induction.
   - Applications: Vaccines requiring robust humoral responses, such as hepatitis B and HPV.

3. **Class C CpG**:

    - Combine the properties of Class A and B, inducing both strong cytokine responses and antibody production.
    - Applications: Broad-spectrum vaccines and therapeutic cancer vaccines.

Applications of CpG Oligonucleotides
1. Licensed Vaccines

- **Heplisav-B (Hepatitis B Vaccine)**:

    - Contains a CpG oligonucleotide as its adjuvant, providing faster and stronger immunity compared to alum-based vaccines.

2. Investigational Vaccines

- **Cancer Vaccines**:

    - CpG motifs are used in therapeutic vaccines to activate tumor-specific cytotoxic T cells.
    - Example: Melanoma vaccines incorporating CpG oligonucleotides to stimulate antitumor immunity.

- **Infectious Disease Vaccines**:

    - CpG motifs are being investigated for vaccines against HIV, influenza, and tuberculosis, where Th1 responses are critical.

3. Combination Adjuvant Systems

- **CpG + Alum**:

    - Combining CpG with alum creates a balanced immune response, enhancing both humoral and cellular immunity.
    - Applications: HPV and malaria vaccines.

Advantages of CpG Oligonucleotides

1. **Strong Th1 Response**:

   ○ CpG motifs promote a Th1-biased immune response, critical for combating intracellular pathogens and tumors.

2. **B Cell Activation**:

   ○ Direct activation of B cells enhances antibody production and memory cell formation.

3. **Versatility**:

   ○ Effective in both prophylactic and therapeutic vaccine platforms, including protein, peptide, and mRNA vaccines.

4. **Safety Profile**:

   ○ CpG oligonucleotides are synthetic and non-replicating, minimizing safety concerns.

5. **Rapid Onset of Immunity**:

   ○ Strong early activation of innate immunity accelerates the development of adaptive immune responses.

Limitations of CpG Oligonucleotides

1. **Target Population Constraints**:

   ○ Reduced effectiveness in populations with impaired TLR9 signaling, such as the elderly or immunocompromised individuals.

2. **Local Reactogenicity**:

   ○ CpG oligonucleotides can cause mild inflammation and redness at the injection site.

3. **Production Challenges**:

- ○ Synthesis and purification of CpG oligonucleotides are complex and expensive.

4. **Delivery Issues**:

- ○ Poor cellular uptake necessitates advanced delivery systems, such as lipid nanoparticles or conjugation with carriers.

Advancements in CpG Technology

1. **Nanoparticle-Based Delivery**:

- ○ Encapsulation of CpG oligonucleotides in nanoparticles improves cellular uptake and stability.
- ○ Example: Lipid nanoparticles for mRNA vaccines.

2. **Hybrid Adjuvants**:

- ○ Combining CpG motifs with other adjuvants, such as saponins or MPLA, creates synergistic effects for enhanced immunity.

3. **Targeted Delivery Systems**:

- ○ CpG oligonucleotides conjugated to antigens or antibodies enable precise targeting of APCs.

4. **Thermostable Formulations**:

- ○ Research on stabilizing CpG oligonucleotides for ambient temperature storage is underway to improve accessibility in low-resource settings.

Case Studies

1. **Heplisav-B**:

- ○ A two-dose hepatitis B vaccine that uses CpG oligonucleotides as an adjuvant. Clinical trials demonstrated superior efficacy compared to alum-based vaccines, with faster seroprotection.

2. **Cancer Immunotherapy**:

   - CpG motifs have been integrated into therapeutic vaccines for melanoma and non-small cell lung cancer, showing promising results in activating tumor-specific T cells.

3. **Tuberculosis Vaccines**:

   - CpG oligonucleotides are being evaluated in TB vaccines to enhance Th1 responses and IFN-γ production, critical for controlling *Mycobacterium tuberculosis*.

Future Directions for CpG Oligonucleotides

1. **Therapeutic Applications**:

   - Expanding the use of CpG motifs in cancer immunotherapy, chronic infections, and autoimmune diseases.

2. **Next-Generation Vaccine Platforms**:

   - Integrating CpG oligonucleotides into mRNA and viral vector vaccines to enhance immune responses.

3. **Global Accessibility**:

   - Developing cost-effective production and delivery systems to make CpG-based adjuvants accessible in low- and middle-income countries.

4. **Combination Strategies**:

   - Combining CpG motifs with emerging adjuvants like nanoparticle carriers and saponins for improved efficacy and safety.

Public Health Impact

- **Enhanced Vaccine Efficacy**: CpG oligonucleotides have revolutionized vaccine design, particularly for diseases requiring strong cellular immunity.
- **Accelerated Immunization Schedules**: Rapid onset of immunity enables shorter and more effective vaccination regimens.
- **Expanded Therapeutic Uses**: CpG motifs are unlocking new possibilities for therapeutic vaccines, particularly in oncology.

4.4 Challenges and Innovations

The development and integration of advanced adjuvants in vaccines are accompanied by numerous challenges. Among these, **regulatory hurdles** stand out as a significant barrier. Regulatory frameworks must balance the need for innovation and safety, ensuring that adjuvants meet stringent standards while not stifling progress. This section explores the complexities of regulatory requirements for adjuvants, the challenges faced by developers, and innovative approaches to navigating these hurdles.

4.4.1 Regulatory Hurdles

Adjuvants are inherently complex, often involving intricate mechanisms that can affect immune responses in unpredictable ways. Their evaluation, therefore, requires rigorous scrutiny by regulatory agencies to ensure safety, efficacy, and consistency. Regulatory hurdles encompass the approval processes, manufacturing challenges, and post-market surveillance, all of which impact the timeline and cost of vaccine development.

Regulatory Framework for Adjuvants

1. **Preclinical Evaluation**:

   - Adjuvants undergo extensive **in vitro** and **in vivo** testing to assess their safety, immunogenicity, and mechanism of action.
   - Specific tests include:

     - **Toxicology studies** to identify potential adverse effects.
     - **Pharmacokinetics** to understand how the adjuvant behaves in the body.

2. **Clinical Trials**:

- Adjuvants are evaluated in combination with antigens during **phase I, II, and III clinical trials.**
- Key considerations include:

  - **Safety**: Monitoring for local reactogenicity, systemic side effects, and rare adverse events.
  - **Efficacy**: Assessing enhanced immune responses, durability of immunity, and protection against disease.
  - **Dose Optimization**: Determining the minimum effective dose of the adjuvant.

3. **Manufacturing and Quality Control**:

   - Regulatory agencies require adherence to **Good Manufacturing Practices (GMP)** to ensure the consistency and purity of adjuvant formulations.
   - Challenges include:

     - Maintaining batch-to-batch consistency.
     - Ensuring stability during storage and transportation.

4. **Post-Market Surveillance**:

   - Even after approval, vaccines with novel adjuvants are subject to ongoing monitoring for long-term safety and effectiveness.
   - **Pharmacovigilance** programs track adverse events through national and global reporting systems.

Major Regulatory Hurdles
1. Lack of Standardized Guidelines

- Unlike antigens, adjuvants often lack universally accepted regulatory guidelines. This can lead to inconsistencies in approval processes across regions.
- For example, adjuvants approved by the **European Medicines Agency (EMA)** may face additional scrutiny in the **United States Food and Drug Administration (FDA)** and vice versa.

2. Complexity of Adjuvants

- Advanced adjuvants such as nanoparticle-based systems or combination adjuvants (e.g., AS01) have complex compositions, making it challenging to establish clear safety and efficacy criteria.

3. Safety Concerns

- Public perception of adjuvants as potentially harmful adds to regulatory caution.
- Rare but severe adverse events, such as autoimmune responses, necessitate robust safety data.

4. High Costs and Timelines

- Regulatory requirements significantly increase the cost and time needed for adjuvant development, often discouraging smaller biotech companies from pursuing novel adjuvants.

5. Data Transparency

- Regulators demand comprehensive data on the mechanism of action and immunological effects of adjuvants, which can be difficult to provide due to the complexity of immune responses.

Innovations to Overcome Regulatory Hurdles

1. **Advanced Preclinical Models**:

   - Development of **humanized animal models** and sophisticated in vitro systems to better predict safety and efficacy before clinical trials.

2. **Streamlined Regulatory Pathways**:

   - Harmonization of regulatory standards across regions to reduce duplication of efforts.

- Initiatives like the **International Council for Harmonisation (ICH)** are working to align guidelines for vaccines and adjuvants globally.

3. **Adaptive Clinical Trial Designs**:

- Use of **adaptive trial designs** allows for modifications based on interim results, accelerating the evaluation process.

4. **Novel Analytical Techniques**:

- Advanced tools such as **high-throughput screening**, **mass spectrometry**, and **systems biology** are providing deeper insights into adjuvant mechanisms, improving regulatory confidence.

5. **Public-Private Partnerships**:

- Collaborations between governments, academia, and industry help share the financial and regulatory burdens of developing adjuvants.

6. **Risk Management Plans**:

- Comprehensive plans outlining strategies for managing potential risks associated with adjuvants, including post-approval monitoring and communication plans to address public concerns.

Examples of Successful Regulatory Approvals

1. **AS04 (MPLA + Alum)**:

- Used in the **Cervarix HPV vaccine**, AS04 was approved after extensive clinical trials demonstrating its safety and efficacy.
- Ongoing surveillance has supported its favorable safety profile.

2. **MF59**:

- This oil-in-water emulsion, used in the **Fluad influenza vaccine**, underwent rigorous evaluation for elderly populations, showcasing its ability to enhance immunity with minimal reactogenicity.

3. **CpG Oligonucleotides**:

   ○ Approved for use in the **Heplisav-B hepatitis B vaccine**, CpG adjuvants highlighted the importance of demonstrating both safety and rapid onset of immunity.

Future Directions for Regulatory Innovation

1. **AI-Driven Safety Assessments**:

   ○ Leveraging artificial intelligence to analyze preclinical and clinical data, predicting potential safety concerns earlier in the development process.

2. **Real-World Evidence (RWE)**:

   ○ Incorporating data from large-scale vaccination programs into regulatory assessments to validate the safety and efficacy of adjuvants in diverse populations.

3. **Platform Technologies**:

   ○ Regulatory approval of adjuvant platforms rather than individual formulations to streamline the evaluation process for vaccines using similar adjuvants.

4. **Global Collaboration**:

   ○ Establishing unified frameworks for adjuvant evaluation, facilitating faster approval processes for vaccines with global relevance.

Public Health Implications

- **Equity in Access**: Addressing regulatory hurdles ensures that vaccines with advanced adjuvants reach underserved populations faster.
- **Pandemic Preparedness**: Streamlined pathways for adjuvant approval are essential for the rapid development of vaccines against emerging infectious diseases.

- **Enhanced Vaccine Confidence**: Transparent regulatory processes build public trust in vaccines containing novel adjuvants.

4.4.2 Safety and Reactogenicity

The incorporation of adjuvants into vaccines is a double-edged sword. While they enhance immunogenicity and enable robust immune responses, adjuvants can also increase **reactogenicity**, leading to localized or systemic adverse effects. Balancing the immune-enhancing properties of adjuvants with their safety profile is one of the key challenges in vaccine development. This section explores the safety concerns associated with adjuvants, the factors influencing reactogenicity, and innovations aimed at mitigating these issues.

Understanding Reactogenicity

Reactogenicity refers to the physical signs of inflammation and immune activation caused by a vaccine, often perceived as side effects. These can range from mild (e.g., redness, swelling at the injection site) to severe (e.g., fever, systemic inflammation). While some level of reactogenicity is a natural consequence of immune activation, excessive responses can deter public acceptance and pose safety risks.

Factors Influencing Safety and Reactogenicity

1. Adjuvant Mechanism of Action

The specific mechanisms by which adjuvants activate the immune system contribute to their reactogenicity:

- **Pro-Inflammatory Cytokines**:

  - Adjuvants like **alum** and **saponins** induce cytokine production (e.g., IL-1β, TNF-α), which can lead to localized swelling and pain.

- **Pattern Recognition Receptor (PRR) Activation**:

  - Adjuvants targeting Toll-like receptors (e.g., TLR4 agonists like MPL) can trigger systemic inflammatory responses if overstimulated.

2. Dose and Formulation

- **High Doses**:

- ○ Excessive adjuvant doses can amplify immune responses beyond desired levels, increasing the risk of side effects.

- **Combination Adjuvants**:

  - ○ Synergistic effects in multi-adjuvant systems (e.g., AS01: MPL + QS-21) can enhance efficacy but also heighten reactogenicity.

3. Population-Specific Factors

- **Age**:

  - ○ Infants and elderly individuals may exhibit heightened sensitivity or reduced tolerance to certain adjuvants.

- **Preexisting Conditions**:

  - ○ Individuals with autoimmune disorders or chronic inflammation are more susceptible to adverse effects.

4. Route of Administration

- **Intramuscular (IM) vs. Subcutaneous (SC)**:

  - ○ IM routes typically reduce local inflammation compared to SC administration, as adjuvants are distributed more evenly in muscle tissue.

Common Adverse Reactions Linked to Adjuvants

1. **Localized Reactions**:

   - ○ **Pain, Swelling, and Redness**: Common with adjuvants like alum and MF59.
   - ○ **Injection-Site Nodules**: Prolonged antigen release from depot-forming adjuvants can lead to granulomas.

2. **Systemic Reactions**:

- **Fever and Fatigue**: Often associated with adjuvants inducing strong pro-inflammatory cytokine responses.
- **Myalgia and Headache**: Frequently observed in vaccines containing oil-in-water emulsions.

3. **Rare but Severe Reactions**:

- **Allergic Reactions**: Rare hypersensitivity to components like squalene or polysorbate in emulsions.
- **Autoimmune Responses**: Theoretical concerns about overstimulating the immune system, though not widely observed in clinical settings.

Adjuvant	Common Reactions	Severe Reactions	Examples
Alum	Pain, swelling, redness	Rare granulomas	Hepatitis B, DTP vaccines
MF59	Pain, fatigue, fever	Rare hypersensitivity	Fluad (influenza vaccine)
CpG Oligonucleotides	Injection-site soreness, mild fever	Rare systemic inflammation	Heplisav-B (hepatitis B vaccine)
QS-21	Local inflammation, fever	Rare allergic reactions	Shingrix (shingles vaccine)
MPLA	Mild local redness and fatigue	Minimal severe reactions	Cervarix (HPV vaccine)

Examples of Adjuvants and Reactogenicity Profiles

Strategies to Mitigate Reactogenicity

1. **Optimizing Adjuvant Doses**:

- Using the minimum effective dose of adjuvants to balance efficacy and safety.

2. **Advanced Formulations**:

- Encapsulation of adjuvants in **liposomes, nanoparticles**, or **polymer-based carriers** to control release and reduce peak inflammatory responses.

3. **Combination Adjuvants**:

   - Combining adjuvants with complementary mechanisms to achieve synergistic effects without excessive inflammation.
   - Example: AS01 uses MPL and QS-21 for balanced immune activation.

4. **Alternative Routes of Administration**:

   - Exploring less reactogenic routes such as intradermal or microneedle patches for reduced local inflammation.

5. **Preclinical Screening**:

   - Using predictive models to identify and eliminate excessively reactogenic adjuvants during the early stages of development.

Innovations in Safety Monitoring

1. **Biomarker-Based Risk Assessment**:

   - Identifying genetic or immune biomarkers that predict susceptibility to adverse reactions, enabling personalized vaccination strategies.

2. **Real-Time Monitoring Systems**:

   - Implementing digital platforms for real-time reporting and analysis of adverse events in large-scale immunization programs.

3. **Enhanced Pharmacovigilance**:

   - Establishing global networks like **WHO's Vaccine Safety Net** to track and address safety concerns.

Case Studies

1. **Shingrix (QS-21)**:

- While associated with higher reactogenicity compared to traditional adjuvants, the robust efficacy of Shingrix in preventing shingles in older adults justifies its use.

2. **MF59 in Elderly Populations**:

- Despite mild local reactions, MF59 has significantly improved influenza vaccine efficacy in older adults, demonstrating an acceptable safety profile.

3. **Heplisav-B (CpG)**:

- A two-dose schedule using CpG adjuvants has reduced reactogenicity compared to alum-based hepatitis B vaccines, with faster seroconversion.

Balancing Innovation with Safety

- **Thorough Preclinical Testing**:

  - Emphasis on identifying adjuvants with favorable safety profiles before clinical trials.

- **Targeted Immunization Strategies**:

  - Tailoring adjuvant formulations for specific populations to minimize adverse effects.

- **Public Engagement**:

  - Transparent communication about reactogenicity and its role in immune activation to build public trust.

FIVE

Nanotechnology in Vaccine Delivery

Nanotechnology has revolutionized numerous fields, including medicine, by enabling precise and efficient delivery of therapeutic agents. In the realm of vaccines, **nanoscale delivery systems** offer groundbreaking potential, addressing challenges such as stability, targeted delivery, and enhanced immunogenicity. This chapter delves into the applications of nanotechnology in vaccine development, beginning with an introduction to its key advantages and transformative impact.

5.1 Introduction to Nanotechnology

Nanotechnology involves the manipulation of materials at the **nanoscale**, typically ranging from 1 to 100 nanometers. At this scale, materials exhibit unique physical, chemical, and biological properties, making them ideal for biomedical applications. In vaccine delivery, nanotechnology enables the design of platforms that improve antigen stability, enhance immune responses, and provide targeted delivery to immune cells.

5.1.1 Key Advantages of Nanoscale Delivery Systems

Nanotechnology-based vaccine delivery systems offer numerous benefits over traditional methods, addressing critical limitations and expanding the possibilities for effective immunization.

1. Enhanced Antigen Stability

Nanoparticles protect vaccine antigens from degradation, ensuring their stability during storage and transportation.

- **Cold Chain Independence:**

- ○ Nanosystems can reduce reliance on cold chain logistics by stabilizing antigens at room temperature.
- ○ Example: Lipid nanoparticles (LNPs) used in mRNA vaccines like Pfizer-BioNTech's Comirnaty protect mRNA from enzymatic degradation, even under stringent conditions.

- **Lyophilization Compatibility**:

  - ○ Nanocarriers are amenable to freeze-drying, improving shelf life and portability in low-resource settings.

2. Controlled Release of Antigens

Nanoscale systems allow for the **controlled release** of antigens, ensuring prolonged exposure to the immune system and reducing the need for booster doses.

- **Depot Effect**:

  - ○ Nanoparticles form depots at the injection site, releasing antigens gradually.
  - ○ Example: Polymeric nanoparticles made from materials like **PLGA (poly(lactic-co-glycolic acid))** are designed for sustained antigen release.

- **Pulse Release Systems**:

  - ○ Certain nanoparticles are engineered to release antigens in bursts, mimicking natural infection cycles to enhance immune memory.

3. Targeted Delivery to Immune Cells

Nanoparticles can be functionalized with ligands or antibodies that target specific immune cells, such as dendritic cells (DCs) and macrophages, improving antigen presentation and immune activation.

- **Passive Targeting**:

  - ○ Nanosystems naturally accumulate in lymph nodes due to their size and charge, increasing interactions with antigen-presenting cells

(APCs).

- **Active Targeting**:

  - Functionalized nanoparticles with ligands for receptors like **CD40** or **DC-SIGN** selectively target APCs.

- **Example**: Gold nanoparticles conjugated with antigens are being explored for their ability to enhance dendritic cell activation.

4. Improved Immune Responses

Nanoparticles amplify immune responses by co-delivering antigens and adjuvants, ensuring their simultaneous uptake by immune cells.

- **Antigen-Adjuvant Synergy**:

  - Co-delivery enhances the likelihood of antigen and adjuvant being presented together, boosting T cell activation.
  - Example: mRNA vaccines use lipid nanoparticles to encapsulate both the mRNA and ionizable lipids that serve as adjuvants.

- **Th1/Th2 Modulation**:

  - Nanocarriers can be tailored to induce specific immune profiles, such as Th1 (cellular) or Th2 (humoral) responses.

5. Multivalent Vaccine Platforms

Nanoparticles can incorporate multiple antigens, enabling the development of **multivalent vaccines** that provide protection against several pathogens in a single formulation.

- **Example**: Virus-like particles (VLPs) mimic the structure of viruses and present multiple antigens, as seen in the **Gardasil HPV vaccine**.

6. Reduced Side Effects

Nanotechnology improves the **safety profile** of vaccines by reducing off-target effects and reactogenicity.

- **Localized Delivery**:

  - Nanoparticles confine adjuvants and antigens to the site of injection, minimizing systemic inflammation.
  - Example: PLGA nanoparticles release antigens directly into lymph nodes, reducing systemic exposure.

- **Reduced Doses**:

  - Enhanced delivery efficiency allows for lower antigen and adjuvant doses, minimizing side effects.

7. Versatility Across Vaccine Platforms

Nanotechnology is compatible with diverse vaccine types, including:

- **Protein-Based Vaccines**:

  - Nanoparticles stabilize and enhance the immunogenicity of protein antigens.

- **mRNA Vaccines**:

  - Lipid nanoparticles protect mRNA and facilitate cellular delivery.

- **DNA Vaccines**:

  - Gold nanoparticles and cationic lipids improve DNA uptake and expression in host cells.

- **Live-Attenuated Vaccines**:

  - Encapsulation in nanocarriers enhances stability and reduces risks of reversion to virulence.

Examples of Nanoscale Delivery Systems in Vaccines

1. **Lipid Nanoparticles (LNPs)**:

- Used in mRNA vaccines for COVID-19, such as Pfizer-BioNTech and Moderna, to deliver genetic material safely and effectively.

2. **Virus-Like Particles (VLPs)**:

- Used in vaccines like Gardasil (HPV) and HepB vaccines to mimic the structural properties of viruses and elicit strong immune responses.

3. **Polymeric Nanoparticles**:

- PLGA nanoparticles are being studied for their ability to deliver antigens and adjuvants in a controlled manner.

4. **Gold Nanoparticles**:

- Serve as adjuvants and carriers in investigational vaccines, particularly for cancer and emerging infectious diseases.

Challenges and Opportunities

1. **Manufacturing Complexity**:

- Scaling up nanoparticle production with consistency and quality remains a challenge.

2. **Regulatory Hurdles**:

- The novel nature of nanotechnology-based systems necessitates extensive safety evaluations.

3. **Cold Chain Requirements**:

- While nanoparticles improve stability, certain formulations still require ultra-cold storage.

Future Directions

1. **Personalized Vaccines**:

- ◦ Customizable nanosystems tailored to individual immune profiles.

2. **Self-Amplifying Platforms**:

   - ◦ Nanoparticles enabling antigen expression over extended periods.

3. **Thermostable Systems**:

   - ◦ Designing nanoparticles that maintain functionality across a wide temperature range.

5.1.2 Types of Nanoparticles Used in Vaccines

Nanoparticles are versatile platforms for vaccine delivery, offering the ability to encapsulate, stabilize, and deliver antigens and adjuvants with high precision. The unique properties of nanoparticles, such as their small size, surface charge, and customizable composition, allow for tailored immune responses, enhanced stability, and improved targeting of immune cells. This section explores the various types of nanoparticles used in vaccines, their properties, applications, and contributions to vaccine efficacy.

1. Lipid Nanoparticles (LNPs)

Lipid nanoparticles are among the most widely used nanocarriers, particularly in the development of **mRNA vaccines**. They are composed of lipids that self-assemble into spherical structures, encapsulating nucleic acids or antigens.

Key Features

- **Composition**:

  - ◦ Ionizable lipids, phospholipids, cholesterol, and PEG-lipids (polyethylene glycol-lipids).

- **Encapsulation Efficiency**:

  - ◦ Highly efficient at encapsulating fragile molecules like mRNA or DNA.

- **Targeting**:

- ○ Natural affinity for the liver, with potential for functionalization to target immune cells.

Applications

- **mRNA Vaccines**:

  - ○ Pfizer-BioNTech and Moderna COVID-19 vaccines rely on LNPs to deliver mRNA encoding the spike protein of SARS-CoV-2.

- **Therapeutic Vaccines**:

  - ○ Investigated for cancer vaccines to deliver tumor-specific antigens.

Advantages

- Protects mRNA from enzymatic degradation.
- Facilitates cellular uptake via endocytosis.
- Stimulates an immune response by acting as an intrinsic adjuvant.

2. Virus-Like Particles (VLPs)

VLPs mimic the structure of viruses but lack the genetic material, making them non-replicative and safe. They present antigens in a repetitive, multivalent array, enhancing immune recognition.

Key Features

- **Composition**:

  - ○ Proteins that self-assemble into viral capsid-like structures.

- **Immunogenicity**:

  - ○ Highly immunogenic due to their virus-like appearance.

Applications

- **Licensed Vaccines**:

- **Gardasil (HPV vaccine)**: Prevents human papillomavirus infections.
- **Engerix-B (Hepatitis B vaccine)**: Induces strong antibody responses.

- **Emerging Vaccines**:

  - Studied for applications in malaria, HIV, and Zika virus.

Advantages

- Induces strong B cell and T cell responses.
- Stable during storage and transport.
- Can incorporate multiple antigens for multivalent vaccines.

3. Polymeric Nanoparticles

Polymeric nanoparticles are biodegradable and biocompatible carriers made from materials such as **poly(lactic-co-glycolic acid) (PLGA)** and **chitosan**. These nanoparticles allow for controlled release of antigens and adjuvants.

Key Features

- **Controlled Release**:

  - Antigens are released over time, prolonging immune activation.

- **Surface Functionalization**:

  - Can be coated with ligands or antibodies for targeted delivery.

Applications

- **Influenza Vaccines**:

  - Encapsulation of influenza antigens to improve stability and immune responses.

- **Cancer Vaccines**:

  - Deliver tumor-associated antigens for therapeutic purposes.

Advantages

- Reduces the need for booster doses.
- Protects antigens from enzymatic degradation.
- Enhances antigen presentation by targeting APCs.

4. Inorganic Nanoparticles

Inorganic nanoparticles, such as **gold nanoparticles (AuNPs)** and **silica nanoparticles**, offer unique optical and physical properties that enhance vaccine design.

Key Features

- **Surface Area**:

  - High surface area allows for the conjugation of multiple antigens and adjuvants.

- **Stability**:

  - Chemically stable under various conditions.

Applications

- **Cancer Vaccines**:

  - Gold nanoparticles are used to deliver peptide antigens and stimulate dendritic cells.

- **Infectious Diseases**:

  - Silica nanoparticles are being explored for delivering antigens against influenza and tuberculosis.

Advantages

- Stimulates both innate and adaptive immunity.
- Can be used as imaging agents for tracking vaccine delivery.
- Tailorable size and charge for specific applications.

5. Protein-Based Nanoparticles

Protein nanoparticles are derived from natural or engineered proteins that self-assemble into nanostructures. They can mimic natural pathogens or display antigens on their surface.

Key Features

- **Self-Assembly:**

  - Forms well-defined structures without the need for synthetic materials.

- **Multivalency:**

  - Presents multiple copies of an antigen for enhanced immune recognition.

Applications

- **Malaria Vaccines:**

  - Protein nanoparticles presenting malaria antigens are under clinical investigation.

- **COVID-19 Vaccines:**

  - Nanoparticles displaying the SARS-CoV-2 spike protein are in development.

Advantages

- High immunogenicity with minimal reactogenicity.
- Biodegradable and biocompatible.
- Suitable for multivalent vaccine platforms.

6. Carbon-Based Nanoparticles

Carbon-based nanoparticles, such as **carbon nanotubes (CNTs)** and **graphene oxide**, are emerging as novel platforms for vaccine delivery.

Key Features

- **High Antigen Loading**:

  - Exceptional capacity for adsorbing and delivering biomolecules.

- **Adjuvant Properties**:

  - Intrinsic adjuvant activity that stimulates immune cells.

Applications

- **HIV Vaccines**:

  - Investigational vaccines incorporating carbon nanotubes to deliver HIV epitopes.

- **Cancer Vaccines**:

  - Used in therapeutic vaccines for enhanced delivery of tumor antigens.

Advantages

- High stability under diverse conditions.
- Versatile for use with various antigen types.
  Future Directions in Nanoparticle Vaccine Development
- **Personalized Nanoparticles**:

  - Customizable nanocarriers designed for specific immune profiles or diseases.

- **Thermostable Formulations**:

  - Innovations to improve stability under ambient conditions for broader accessibility.

- **Hybrid Systems**:

- Combining different nanoparticle types (e.g., LNPs with gold nanoparticles) to leverage their unique properties.

- **Targeted Delivery**:

  - Development of nanoparticles with ligands that specifically bind to dendritic cells and macrophages.

- **5.2 Lipid Nanoparticles**

  Lipid nanoparticles (LNPs) are one of the most advanced and widely used nanocarrier systems for vaccine delivery. Their ability to encapsulate fragile biomolecules, such as mRNA, and facilitate efficient cellular uptake has made them indispensable in modern vaccinology. LNPs played a transformative role in the rapid development and deployment of **mRNA vaccines**, particularly during the COVID-19 pandemic. This section delves into their design, functionality, and groundbreaking applications in mRNA vaccines.

  ### 5.2.1 Applications in mRNA Vaccines

  mRNA vaccines have revolutionized immunization by leveraging the body's cellular machinery to produce antigens that elicit an immune response. Lipid nanoparticles are integral to this technology, serving as carriers that protect mRNA, enhance its delivery, and act as intrinsic adjuvants.

  Key Functions of LNPs in mRNA Vaccines

- **Protection of mRNA**:

  - mRNA is inherently unstable and susceptible to enzymatic degradation by ribonucleases (RNases). LNPs encapsulate mRNA, shielding it from degradation and ensuring its stability during storage and delivery.

- **Facilitating Cellular Uptake**:

  - LNPs deliver mRNA into cells by **endocytosis**, where the mRNA is released into the cytoplasm for translation into the target antigen.

- **Targeted Delivery**:

- ○ LNPs naturally accumulate in lymph nodes, which are rich in antigen-presenting cells (APCs), such as dendritic cells and macrophages. This enhances antigen presentation and immune activation.

- **Intrinsic Adjuvanticity**:

  - ○ Components of LNPs, such as ionizable lipids, stimulate innate immune responses, enhancing the overall efficacy of the vaccine.

- **Composition of LNPs in mRNA Vaccines**
  LNPs are composed of four main components, each playing a specific role:
- **Ionizable Lipids**:

  - ○ Facilitate mRNA encapsulation and fusion with cellular membranes to release the mRNA into the cytoplasm.
  - ○ Examples: SM-102 (used in Moderna vaccines), ALC-0315 (used in Pfizer-BioNTech vaccines).

- **Phospholipids**:

  - ○ Provide structural stability and support bilayer formation.

- **Cholesterol**:

  - ○ Enhances nanoparticle stability and fluidity, improving cellular uptake.

- **Polyethylene Glycol (PEG)-Lipid**:

  - ○ Reduces aggregation and prolongs circulation time by preventing rapid clearance from the bloodstream.

- **Mechanism of Action**
- **Injection and Uptake**:

- Following intramuscular injection, LNPs transport mRNA to nearby cells, including APCs.

- **Endosomal Escape**:

  - LNPs are taken up by cells through endocytosis. Ionizable lipids enable the nanoparticles to destabilize the endosomal membrane, allowing mRNA to escape into the cytoplasm.

- **Antigen Production**:

  - The mRNA is translated into the encoded antigen (e.g., spike protein of SARS-CoV-2).

- **Immune Activation**:

  - The antigen is presented on the cell surface via MHC molecules, triggering adaptive immune responses involving T cells and B cells.

- **Applications in COVID-19 Vaccines**
- **Pfizer-BioNTech (Comirnaty)**:

  - The first mRNA vaccine to receive emergency use authorization, leveraging LNPs to deliver mRNA encoding the SARS-CoV-2 spike protein.
  - Demonstrated >90% efficacy in preventing COVID-19 in clinical trials.

- **Moderna (Spikevax)**:

  - Similar to Pfizer-BioNTech, uses LNPs to encapsulate mRNA for spike protein expression.
  - Demonstrated comparable efficacy and safety profiles.

- **Advantages of LNPs in mRNA Vaccines**
- **Rapid Development**:

  - LNPs enable the rapid production of mRNA vaccines, significantly reducing the timeline from concept to clinical use.

- **Enhanced Immunogenicity**:

  - LNPs not only deliver mRNA but also act as adjuvants, amplifying immune responses.

- **Scalability**:

  - LNP production methods, such as microfluidic mixing, allow for scalable manufacturing.

- **Versatility**:

  - LNPs can encapsulate different types of mRNA sequences, enabling quick adaptation for emerging pathogens.

- **Challenges and Limitations**
- **Cold Chain Requirements**:

  - LNP-based mRNA vaccines require ultra-cold storage (-70°C for Pfizer-BioNTech) due to mRNA instability. Efforts are ongoing to improve thermostability.

- **Reactogenicity**:

  - Mild side effects, such as fever, fatigue, and localized pain, are common due to the intrinsic adjuvanticity of LNPs.

- **Manufacturing Complexity**:

  - Ensuring uniform particle size and encapsulation efficiency requires advanced technologies, increasing production costs.

- **Limited Long-Term Data**:

  - While LNPs have demonstrated safety in the short term, long-term effects are still under evaluation.

- **Future Directions**

- **Thermostable Formulations**:

  - Development of LNPs that can maintain functionality at higher temperatures to reduce cold chain dependence.

- **Targeted LNPs**:

  - Engineering LNPs with ligands that selectively bind to dendritic cells for improved antigen presentation.

- **Multivalent Vaccines**:

  - LNPs capable of delivering multiple mRNA sequences to protect against multiple pathogens in a single dose.

- **Expanding Applications**:

  - Beyond infectious diseases, LNPs are being explored for cancer immunotherapy, genetic disorders, and personalized vaccines.

- **Public Health Impact of LNP-Based Vaccines**
- **Pandemic Preparedness**:

  - LNP technology has enabled rapid responses to emerging pathogens, exemplified by the COVID-19 mRNA vaccines.

- **Global Immunization**:

  - Efforts to improve LNP stability and reduce costs aim to make these vaccines accessible in low- and middle-income countries.

- **Future Vaccine Platforms**:

  - LNPs are paving the way for a new era of vaccines targeting not only infectious diseases but also non-infectious conditions.

- **LNPs as Cornerstones of mRNA Vaccine Success**

Lipid nanoparticles have redefined vaccine delivery by enabling the success of mRNA vaccines, which were once considered impractical. Their role in stabilizing and delivering fragile mRNA has transformed the vaccine landscape, offering unprecedented speed, efficacy, and adaptability. As innovations continue to address their limitations, LNPs are poised to play an even greater role in the future of vaccinology and global health.

5.2.2 Mechanisms of Action

Lipid nanoparticles (LNPs) are highly engineered nanocarriers designed to deliver therapeutic agents like mRNA with precision and efficiency. Their **mechanisms of action** are intricately linked to their structural composition and biological interactions, which enable them to protect the mRNA payload, facilitate its uptake into cells, and ensure its translation into functional proteins. This section provides a step-by-step explanation of how LNPs function within the body, emphasizing their critical role in vaccine efficacy.

Overview of LNP Functionality

LNPs act as delivery vehicles for mRNA, navigating biological barriers and ensuring efficient delivery of the genetic material into the cytoplasm of target cells. This process involves several key stages:

- **Injection and Distribution**:

  - Following administration (commonly intramuscular), LNPs transport the mRNA payload to nearby cells, particularly **antigen-presenting cells (APCs)** such as dendritic cells.

- **Cellular Uptake**:

  - LNPs enter cells via **endocytosis**, a process where the cell membrane engulfs the nanoparticle into a vesicle.

- **Endosomal Escape**:

  - Once inside the cell, LNPs disrupt the endosomal membrane, releasing the mRNA into the cytoplasm to prevent degradation.

- **mRNA Translation**:

- The mRNA is translated into the target antigen, such as the spike protein of SARS-CoV-2, which triggers an immune response.

- **Immune Activation:**

  - The expressed antigen is processed and presented on MHC molecules, activating T cells and B cells.

- **Detailed Mechanisms of Action**
  1. Protection of mRNA
  mRNA is inherently unstable and prone to enzymatic degradation by ribonucleases (RNases). LNPs protect the mRNA by encapsulating it in a lipid bilayer, shielding it from external degradation during storage, transportation, and delivery.
- **Ionizable Lipids:**

  - At physiological pH, these lipids become neutral, reducing cytotoxicity and stabilizing the nanoparticle.
  - At acidic pH (e.g., in the endosome), they become positively charged, facilitating membrane fusion and mRNA release.

- **2. Cellular Uptake via Endocytosis**
  LNPs exploit natural cellular processes to enter target cells.
- **Size and Charge:**

  - The small size (60–120 nm) and slightly negative surface charge of LNPs optimize their interaction with cell membranes.

- **Endocytosis Pathways:**

  - LNPs are engulfed into endosomes through pathways such as clathrin-mediated endocytosis.
  - These pathways are essential for delivering the mRNA to the intracellular environment.

- **3. Endosomal Escape**
  One of the most critical steps in the mechanism of action is the escape of mRNA from the endosome into the cytoplasm.

- **pH-Sensitive Ionizable Lipids**:

  - In the acidic environment of the endosome, ionizable lipids become positively charged, destabilizing the endosomal membrane through electrostatic interactions.
  - This disruption releases the mRNA payload into the cytoplasm, where it can be translated.

- **Avoiding Degradation**:

  - Without endosomal escape, the mRNA would be degraded in lysosomes, rendering the vaccine ineffective.

- **4. Translation of mRNA into Antigen**
  Once in the cytoplasm, the mRNA utilizes the host cell's ribosomes to synthesize the target antigen.
- **Spike Protein Synthesis (e.g., SARS-CoV-2)**:

  - In COVID-19 vaccines, the mRNA encodes the spike protein, which is expressed on the surface of the host cell.

- **Natural Protein Folding**:

  - The protein undergoes natural folding and glycosylation, mimicking the structure of the viral antigen.

- **5. Immune System Activation**
  a. Antigen Presentation
  The expressed antigen is processed and presented on the cell surface via:
- **MHC Class I Pathway**:

  - Activates cytotoxic CD8+ T cells, critical for targeting infected cells.

- **MHC Class II Pathway**:

  - Activates helper CD4+ T cells, which enhance B cell-mediated antibody production.

- **b. B Cell Activation**

  B cells recognize the antigen, leading to the production of high-affinity antibodies, neutralizing the pathogen during subsequent infections.

  c. Innate Immune Stimulation

  Components of LNPs (e.g., ionizable lipids) act as intrinsic adjuvants, stimulating innate immune pathways:
- **Type I Interferon Response**:

  - Enhances dendritic cell activation and subsequent adaptive immunity.

- **Cytokine Production**:

  - Releases cytokines like IL-6 and TNF-α, creating a pro-inflammatory environment favorable for immune activation.

- **Advantages of LNP Mechanisms in mRNA Vaccines**
- **High Delivery Efficiency**:

  - The precise design of LNPs ensures efficient mRNA delivery and antigen expression in target cells.

- **Rapid Immune Activation**:

  - LNPs facilitate quick translation and presentation of antigens, leading to rapid immune responses.

- **Adjuvant Effect**:

  - Intrinsic immune-stimulating properties of LNPs eliminate the need for separate adjuvants in many cases.

- **Versatility**:

  - The modular design of LNPs allows for adaptation to deliver various types of mRNA or other nucleic acids.

- **Challenges in LNP Mechanisms**
- **Endosomal Escape Efficiency**:

  - Ensuring a high proportion of mRNA escapes the endosome remains a technical challenge.

- **Potential Reactogenicity**:

  - The innate immune activation caused by ionizable lipids can lead to mild side effects, such as fever and fatigue.

- **Stability Issues**:

  - LNPs require cold chain storage to maintain their structural integrity and functionality.

- **Target Specificity**:

  - While LNPs naturally accumulate in the liver, optimizing them for other tissues, such as lymph nodes, requires further innovation.

- **Innovations in LNP Mechanisms**
- **Enhanced Ionizable Lipids**:

  - Designing lipids with improved pH sensitivity for more efficient endosomal escape.

- **Targeted Delivery**:

  - Functionalizing LNPs with ligands or antibodies to improve targeting of specific immune cells, such as dendritic cells.

- **Stabilization Strategies**:

  - Incorporating stabilizers like cholesterol derivatives to reduce cold chain requirements.

- **Combination Payloads**:

- Developing LNPs capable of delivering multiple mRNA sequences, enabling multivalent vaccine platforms.

- **Future Directions**
- **Personalized Vaccines:**

  - Leveraging LNPs to deliver customized mRNA vaccines for individual patients, particularly in oncology.

- **Self-Amplifying mRNA:**

  - Using LNPs to deliver self-replicating mRNA, reducing the required dose and enhancing antigen expression.

- **Thermostable LNPs:**

  - Designing LNPs that maintain stability at higher temperatures to expand global vaccine access.

- **Conclusion: LNPs as a Game-Changer in Vaccine Delivery**

  The mechanisms of action underlying LNP functionality demonstrate their sophistication and versatility in vaccine delivery. From protecting fragile mRNA to ensuring efficient antigen expression and immune activation, LNPs have set the standard for modern vaccinology. With ongoing innovations, LNPs are poised to address current challenges and expand their applications in both infectious and non-infectious diseases.

5.3 Polymeric Nanoparticles

Polymeric nanoparticles are versatile and highly customizable nanocarriers used in vaccine delivery. Their ability to encapsulate a wide range of antigens and adjuvants, coupled with their controlled-release properties, makes them an attractive platform for modern vaccinology. Among these, **biodegradable polymers** such as **poly(lactic-co-glycolic acid) (PLGA)** have emerged as a leading choice due to their safety, biocompatibility, and regulatory approval for medical applications.

5.3.1 Biodegradable Polymers (e.g., PLGA)

PLGA-based nanoparticles are among the most studied and utilized polymeric nanoparticles in drug and vaccine delivery systems. The combination of **poly(lactic acid) (PLA)** and **poly(glycolic acid) (PGA)** in varying ratios allows for precise control over degradation rates, release kinetics, and biocompatibility.

Properties of PLGA

- **Biodegradability**:

  - PLGA is broken down into lactic acid and glycolic acid, both of which are naturally metabolized in the body.

- **Customizable Degradation Rates**:

  - The degradation rate can be tuned by adjusting the ratio of PLA to PGA:

    - **Higher PLA content**: Slower degradation due to hydrophobicity.
    - **Higher PGA content**: Faster degradation due to hydrophilicity.

- **Encapsulation Efficiency**:

  - PLGA can encapsulate hydrophilic and hydrophobic molecules, including antigens, adjuvants, and DNA/RNA.

- **Controlled Release**:

  - PLGA nanoparticles release their payload over time through hydrolysis, providing sustained antigen exposure to the immune system.

- **Mechanisms of Action in Vaccine Delivery**

  1. Antigen Encapsulation and Protection

  PLGA nanoparticles protect encapsulated antigens from enzymatic degradation, ensuring their stability during storage and transportation.

- **Hydrophobic Interior**:

  - Protects hydrophobic antigens or adjuvants.

- **Hydrophilic Surface**:

- Allows for modification with targeting ligands or antibodies for enhanced immune cell targeting.

- **2. Controlled Antigen Release**
  PLGA nanoparticles release antigens in a controlled manner, mimicking the kinetics of natural infection.
- **Prolonged Immune Activation**:

  - Sustained release ensures continuous antigen presentation, reducing the need for booster doses.

- **3. Targeted Delivery to APCs**
  PLGA nanoparticles naturally accumulate in lymph nodes due to their size (50–200 nm), where they are readily taken up by **antigen-presenting cells (APCs)** such as dendritic cells and macrophages.
  4. Adjuvant Co-Delivery
  PLGA allows co-encapsulation of antigens and adjuvants, ensuring their simultaneous delivery to APCs, which enhances immune activation.
- **Example**: PLGA nanoparticles encapsulating antigens with toll-like receptor (TLR) agonists like CpG oligonucleotides to induce strong Th1 responses.
- **Applications of PLGA in Vaccines**
- **Infectious Diseases**:

  - PLGA nanoparticles have been used to deliver antigens for vaccines against influenza, hepatitis B, and malaria.
  - **Example**: Influenza vaccines with PLGA nanoparticles have shown enhanced immunogenicity compared to traditional formulations.

- **Cancer Vaccines**:

  - PLGA nanoparticles deliver tumor-associated antigens and adjuvants to induce cytotoxic T cell responses.
  - **Example**: Therapeutic vaccines for melanoma incorporating PLGA-encapsulated peptides.

- **DNA and RNA Vaccines**:

- ○ PLGA nanoparticles can encapsulate nucleic acids for stable delivery and expression in host cells.

- **Emerging Diseases**:

  - ○ Investigational vaccines for diseases like tuberculosis and HIV are exploring PLGA nanoparticles for their ability to enhance immune responses.

- **Advantages of PLGA-Based Nanoparticles**
- **Safety and Biocompatibility**:

  - ○ PLGA has been approved by the FDA for use in drug delivery, with a proven safety profile.

- **Customizable Properties**:

  - ○ Degradation rates, size, and surface chemistry can be tailored for specific applications.

- **Prolonged Immunogenicity**:

  - ○ Controlled release ensures sustained antigen exposure, improving immune memory.

- **Versatility**:

  - ○ Capable of delivering a wide range of antigens, adjuvants, and genetic materials.

- **Cold Chain Reduction**:

  - ○ PLGA encapsulation improves antigen stability, potentially reducing cold chain requirements.

- **Challenges and Limitations**
- **Complex Manufacturing**:

- Encapsulation processes require precise control to ensure uniformity and reproducibility.

- **Potential Reactogenicity**:

  - Residual solvents or improper degradation can lead to localized inflammation.

- **Scaling Up**:

  - Producing PLGA nanoparticles on a large scale with consistent quality remains a challenge.

- **Innovations in PLGA Nanoparticles**
- **Surface Functionalization**:

  - PLGA nanoparticles are being modified with ligands or antibodies to improve targeting of specific immune cells.
  - **Example**: Mannose-functionalized PLGA for dendritic cell targeting.

- **Hybrid Nanoparticles**:

  - Combining PLGA with other materials, such as lipids or gold nanoparticles, to enhance delivery and immune activation.

- **Thermostable Formulations**:

  - Research is focused on improving the stability of PLGA nanoparticles under ambient conditions.

- **Multi-Antigen Delivery**:

  - Designing PLGA systems capable of delivering multiple antigens for multivalent vaccines.

- **Case Studies**
- **Hepatitis B Vaccines**:

- PLGA nanoparticles encapsulating hepatitis B surface antigens have demonstrated improved stability and immunogenicity compared to alum-adjuvanted vaccines.

- **Malaria Vaccines**:

  - Experimental PLGA-based vaccines have shown enhanced protection by prolonging antigen release and stimulating both Th1 and Th2 responses.

- **Cancer Vaccines**:

  - PLGA nanoparticles delivering tumor antigens have shown promise in preclinical models, inducing robust CD8+ T cell responses.

- **Future Directions**
- **Personalized Vaccines**:

  - Using PLGA nanoparticles to deliver tailored antigens and adjuvants for individualized immunotherapy.

- **Integrated Platforms**:

  - Developing PLGA-based systems that combine imaging agents, adjuvants, and antigens for real-time monitoring of vaccine efficacy.

- **Emerging Pathogens**:

  - Expanding the use of PLGA nanoparticles for vaccines targeting rapidly evolving pathogens like SARS-CoV-2 variants.

- **Self-Boosting Vaccines**:

  - Designing PLGA formulations capable of releasing antigens in pulses, mimicking booster doses.

5.3.2 Controlled Release and Targeting

One of the defining features of **polymeric nanoparticles** like PLGA (poly(lactic-co-glycolic acid)) is their ability to provide **controlled release** of antigens and adjuvants while facilitating **targeted delivery** to immune cells. This combination enhances immunogenicity and reduces the need for multiple booster doses, making these nanoparticles ideal for modern vaccines. Controlled release and targeting ensure prolonged antigen availability, sustained immune activation, and reduced systemic side effects, leading to highly effective immunization.

Controlled Release Mechanisms

Controlled release refers to the gradual and sustained release of antigens or adjuvants encapsulated within polymeric nanoparticles. This mechanism mimics the natural kinetics of infection, ensuring prolonged exposure of antigens to the immune system.

1. Polymer Degradation

The degradation of the polymer matrix determines the rate of antigen release:

- **Hydrolysis of Polymer Chains**:

  - PLGA degrades into lactic acid and glycolic acid, which are metabolized naturally in the body.
  - The degradation rate depends on the PLA-to-PGA ratio:

    - **High PLA Content**: Slower degradation due to its hydrophobic nature.
    - **High PGA Content**: Faster degradation due to hydrophilicity.

- **2. Diffusion-Controlled Release**

  Antigens or adjuvants diffuse out of the nanoparticle matrix over time:

- **Surface Diffusion**:

  - Initial rapid release of surface-bound antigens (burst release).

- **Bulk Diffusion**:

  - Gradual release of encapsulated antigens as the polymer degrades.

- **3. Multi-Phase Release Profiles**
  Polymeric nanoparticles can be engineered to exhibit distinct release phases:
- **Burst Phase**: Immediate release of a portion of the antigen to initiate immune response.
- **Sustained Phase**: Slow and steady release over weeks to maintain antigen presentation.
- **Targeting Mechanisms**
  Targeting ensures that polymeric nanoparticles deliver their payload specifically to immune cells, such as **dendritic cells (DCs)** and **macrophages**, enhancing immune activation while minimizing off-target effects.

  1. Passive Targeting
  Polymeric nanoparticles naturally accumulate in lymph nodes due to their size (50–200 nm) and surface charge, facilitating interaction with APCs:
- **Enhanced Permeability and Retention (EPR) Effect**:

  - Nanoparticles exploit the porous structure of lymphatic tissues, concentrating in immune-rich environments.

- **2. Active Targeting**
  Surface functionalization of nanoparticles with ligands or antibodies improves specific binding to immune cells:
- **Ligands for Dendritic Cells**:

  - Mannose receptors on dendritic cells are targeted using **mannose-functionalized PLGA nanoparticles**.

- **Antibodies for APCs**:

  - Nanoparticles conjugated with antibodies against CD40 or DC-SIGN enhance delivery to APCs.

- **Cytokine Co-Delivery**:

  - Incorporating cytokines like GM-CSF (granulocyte-macrophage colony-stimulating factor) to attract and activate APCs.

- **Advantages of Controlled Release and Targeting**
- **Prolonged Antigen Presentation:**

  - Sustained release ensures continuous stimulation of the immune system, reducing the need for booster doses.

- **Reduced Dose Requirements:**

  - Efficient delivery to APCs minimizes antigen wastage, allowing for lower doses of the vaccine.

- **Balanced Immune Responses:**

  - Controlled release and targeting can be tailored to induce specific Th1 or Th2 immune responses, depending on the disease.

- **Improved Safety:**

  - Localized delivery to lymph nodes reduces systemic side effects and off-target inflammation.

- **Enhanced Memory Formation:**

  - Prolonged antigen exposure supports the formation of long-lasting memory B cells and T cells.

- **Applications in Vaccines**
  1. Infectious Disease Vaccines
- **Influenza Vaccines:**

  - PLGA nanoparticles delivering influenza antigens have demonstrated sustained immune activation and protection.

- **Tuberculosis Vaccines:**

  - Controlled release of tuberculosis antigens enhances Th1 responses critical for intracellular pathogen clearance.

- **2. Cancer Vaccines**
- **Melanoma Vaccines**:

  - Targeted delivery of tumor antigens to dendritic cells induces strong cytotoxic T cell responses.

- **3. DNA and RNA Vaccines**
- **Nucleic Acid Stability**:

  - Controlled release of DNA or RNA improves expression and immunogenicity, particularly in vaccines targeting HIV and Zika virus.

- **Burst Release**:

  - Excessive initial release of antigens can lead to reduced long-term efficacy.

- **Manufacturing Complexity**:

  - Precision is required to ensure consistent release profiles and surface functionalization.

- **Immune Tolerance**:

  - Overexposure to antigens may risk inducing immune tolerance instead of activation.

- **Innovations**
- **Layer-by-Layer Encapsulation**:

  - Creating multi-layered nanoparticles for sequential release of antigens and adjuvants.

- **Stimuli-Responsive Systems**:

  - Designing nanoparticles that release their payload in response to environmental triggers such as pH or enzymes.

- **Hybrid Nanoparticles**:

  - Combining PLGA with other materials like lipids or gold nanoparticles for improved targeting and controlled release.

- **Real-Time Monitoring**:

  - Incorporating imaging agents into nanoparticles to track release kinetics and targeting efficiency in vivo.

- **Case Studies**
  1. PLGA-Based Malaria Vaccines
- **Controlled Release**: Gradual antigen release over weeks has led to enhanced protection in preclinical models.
- **Targeting**: Functionalization with mannose improves delivery to dendritic cells in lymph nodes.
- **2. Personalized Cancer Vaccines**
- PLGA nanoparticles delivering neoantigens (tumor-specific mutations) have shown promise in activating CD8+ T cells and reducing tumor burden in melanoma models.
- **Future Directions**
- **Self-Boosting Vaccines**:

  - Developing nanoparticles that mimic booster doses by releasing antigens in pulses.

- **Universal Vaccines**:

  - Controlled release systems for multivalent vaccines targeting multiple pathogens or strains.

- **Nanoparticle Libraries**:

  - Creating libraries of polymeric nanoparticles with diverse release profiles to optimize formulations for specific diseases.

5.4 Metallic and Hybrid Nanoparticles

Metallic and hybrid nanoparticles represent a class of advanced nanomaterials with unique optical, electronic, and structural properties that make them highly suitable for vaccine delivery. Among these, **gold nanoparticles (AuNPs)** have garnered significant attention due to their biocompatibility, ease of functionalization, and ability to enhance immune responses. This section explores the applications of gold nanoparticles in vaccinology, focusing on their mechanisms of action, advantages, and potential toxicity concerns.

5.4.1 Gold Nanoparticles: Applications and Toxicity

Gold nanoparticles (AuNPs) are metallic nanostructures typically ranging from 1 to 100 nm in size. Their tunable surface properties and unique physicochemical characteristics make them ideal for delivering antigens, adjuvants, or genetic materials in vaccines. AuNPs can act as carriers, immune potentiators, and imaging agents, thereby playing multiple roles in vaccine platforms.

Applications of Gold Nanoparticles in Vaccines

Gold nanoparticles are versatile platforms for vaccine delivery, offering advantages such as precise antigen presentation, enhanced immune activation, and intrinsic adjuvanticity.

1. Antigen Delivery

AuNPs can conjugate antigens via covalent or non-covalent bonds, protecting them from degradation and presenting them in an immunogenic manner:

- **Multivalent Antigen Presentation:**

  - AuNPs present multiple copies of an antigen on their surface, enhancing B cell recognition and antibody production.
  - Example: Peptide antigens for *HIV* vaccines have been conjugated to AuNPs for enhanced immune responses.

- **Stabilization of Antigens:**

  - AuNPs stabilize fragile antigens, such as proteins or peptides, under physiological conditions, ensuring efficient delivery.

- **2. Adjuvant Properties**

AuNPs possess intrinsic immunostimulatory properties that enhance the efficacy of vaccines:

- **Pattern Recognition Receptor (PRR) Activation:**

    ○ AuNPs are recognized by innate immune receptors, such as Toll-like receptors (TLRs), which trigger pro-inflammatory cytokine production.

- **Th1/Th2 Modulation:**

    ○ Surface modifications of AuNPs can direct the immune response toward Th1 (cellular) or Th2 (humoral) immunity, depending on the vaccine's goal.

- **3. DNA and RNA Vaccine Platforms**
  Gold nanoparticles are used as carriers for nucleic acid vaccines:
- **DNA Vaccines:**

    ○ AuNPs conjugated with plasmid DNA improve cellular uptake and antigen expression in host cells.
    ○ Example: AuNPs delivering DNA encoding tumor-associated antigens in cancer vaccines.

- **RNA Vaccines:**

    ○ Modified AuNPs can deliver mRNA while protecting it from degradation, similar to lipid nanoparticles in mRNA vaccines.

- **4. Imaging and Monitoring**
  The optical properties of gold nanoparticles enable their use as imaging agents in real-time monitoring of vaccine delivery and immune responses:
- **Surface Plasmon Resonance (SPR):**

    ○ AuNPs exhibit strong SPR, allowing them to be used in imaging techniques like fluorescence or Raman spectroscopy to track their biodistribution.

- **Dual Functionality**:

  - AuNPs can deliver antigens and simultaneously monitor immune cell interactions.

Mechanisms of Action

- **Enhanced Uptake by Antigen-Presenting Cells (APCs)**:

  - AuNPs are efficiently internalized by dendritic cells and macrophages, leading to antigen processing and presentation.

- **Lymphatic Drainage**:

  - Due to their nanoscale size, AuNPs naturally accumulate in lymph nodes, where they interact with immune cells.

- **Prolonged Antigen Presentation**:

  - AuNPs enable sustained antigen presentation by preventing enzymatic degradation, enhancing T cell activation.

- **Cytokine Induction**:

  - AuNPs stimulate the release of cytokines like IL-12 and IFN-γ, which are critical for robust Th1 responses.

Advantages of Gold Nanoparticles in Vaccines

- **Biocompatibility**:

  - Gold is inert and minimally reactive, reducing the risk of severe adverse reactions.

- **Ease of Functionalization**:

  - AuNPs can be functionalized with antigens, adjuvants, or targeting ligands to enhance specificity and efficacy.

- **Multivalent Design:**

  - Their ability to present multiple antigens or epitopes on a single nanoparticle enhances immune recognition.

- **Thermostability:**

  - AuNPs are stable under a wide range of conditions, reducing the need for cold chain logistics.

Immunogenic Modulation:

- Surface chemistry can be adjusted to optimize immune responses for specific applications.
- **Toxicity Concerns**
  Despite their advantages, gold nanoparticles pose potential toxicity risks that must be carefully managed during vaccine development:
  1. Dose-Dependent Toxicity
- At high concentrations, AuNPs may induce cytotoxic effects, including oxidative stress and mitochondrial damage in immune cells.
- **2. Surface Chemistry**
- Surface modifications can influence the biocompatibility of AuNPs:

  - **Positively Charged AuNPs**: Tend to be more cytotoxic due to interactions with negatively charged cell membranes.
  - **Neutral or PEGylated AuNPs**: Exhibit reduced toxicity and improved stability.

3. Biodistribution and Accumulation

- Long-term accumulation of AuNPs in organs such as the liver or spleen raises concerns about chronic toxicity.
- **4. Immune Overstimulation**
- Excessive activation of innate immune pathways by AuNPs may lead to hyperinflammatory responses, which could result in adverse effects.
- **Addressing Toxicity**
- **Optimizing Size and Surface Properties:**

○ Designing AuNPs with optimal size (10–50 nm) and neutral surface charge minimizes cytotoxicity.

○ **Coatings and Functionalization**:

○ PEGylation or coating AuNPs with biocompatible polymers reduces immunogenicity and prevents aggregation.

○ **Controlled Doses**:

○ Administering AuNPs in well-calibrated doses reduces the likelihood of toxic effects.

○ **Thorough Preclinical Testing**:

○ Comprehensive in vitro and in vivo studies are essential to assess biodistribution, clearance, and safety.

Applications in Vaccine Development

○ **Cancer Vaccines**:

○ AuNPs delivering tumor-associated antigens are being investigated for melanoma and non-small cell lung cancer immunotherapy.

○ **Infectious Diseases**:

○ Gold nanoparticles are being explored for HIV and malaria vaccines to enhance antigen stability and immune activation.

○ **Hybrid Platforms**:

○ Combining AuNPs with other nanocarriers, such as lipids or polymers, to achieve synergistic effects in vaccine delivery.

○ **Future Directions**
○ **Hybrid Nanoparticles**:

- Integrating gold with other materials like PLGA or lipid nanoparticles to enhance their functionality and reduce toxicity.

- **Personalized Vaccines**:

  - Using AuNPs to deliver personalized antigens based on individual immune profiles.

- **Theranostics**:

  - Developing AuNPs that combine therapeutic and diagnostic capabilities for real-time tracking of vaccine efficacy.

- **Sustainable Manufacturing**:

  - Exploring eco-friendly methods for producing gold nanoparticles to reduce environmental impact.

5.4.2 Multifunctional Hybrid Systems

Multifunctional hybrid nanoparticles combine the best attributes of different materials to create a single system capable of addressing multiple challenges in vaccine delivery. By integrating metallic, polymeric, lipid-based, and inorganic components, hybrid systems offer unparalleled flexibility, functionality, and efficiency. These systems are designed to simultaneously enhance antigen delivery, target immune cells, provide adjuvanticity, and enable real-time monitoring, making them a cornerstone of next-generation vaccine technologies.

Definition and Composition of Hybrid Nanoparticles

Hybrid nanoparticles are engineered systems comprising two or more materials, such as:

- **Metallic Core with Organic Shell**:

  - Example: Gold nanoparticles (AuNPs) coated with PLGA or lipids for biocompatibility and controlled release.

- **Polymer-Lipid Composites**:

- ◦ Example: PLGA nanoparticles encapsulated within lipid layers for enhanced stability and immune cell targeting.

- ◦ **Magnetic-Inorganic Hybrids**:

  - ◦ Example: Iron oxide nanoparticles combined with silica or polymers for dual delivery and imaging capabilities.

- ◦ **Multilayered Nanostructures**:

  - ◦ Example: Layer-by-layer assembly of polymers and antigens on metallic or silica cores for sequential antigen release.

- ◦ **Key Features of Hybrid Systems**
- ◦ **Multifunctionality**:

  - ◦ Combine antigen delivery, immune stimulation, imaging, and therapeutic effects in a single platform.

- ◦ **Enhanced Stability**:

  - ◦ Improve the stability of fragile antigens and adjuvants during storage and transportation.

- ◦ **Controlled Release**:

  - ◦ Allow for sequential or sustained release of multiple components.

- ◦ **Dual or Triple Payloads**:

  - ◦ Co-deliver antigens, adjuvants, and nucleic acids for synergistic immune activation.

- ◦ **Real-Time Monitoring**:

  - ◦ Enable tracking of vaccine biodistribution and immune responses using imaging agents.

Applications of Multifunctional Hybrid Systems

1. Targeted Antigen Delivery

Hybrid nanoparticles enhance the delivery of antigens directly to antigen-presenting cells (APCs):

- **Example**: Gold-PLGA hybrids target dendritic cells for efficient antigen presentation and T cell activation.
- **2. Dual Adjuvant-Antigen Delivery**
  Hybrid systems can encapsulate both antigens and adjuvants, ensuring their co-delivery to the immune system:
- **Example**: Lipid-coated PLGA nanoparticles delivering antigens with TLR agonists (e.g., CpG oligonucleotides) for balanced Th1 and Th2 responses.
- **3. Nucleic Acid Vaccines**
  Hybrid nanoparticles protect and deliver fragile nucleic acids like mRNA and DNA:
- **Example**: Gold-lipid hybrids encapsulating mRNA for robust cellular uptake and antigen expression.
- **4. Imaging-Guided Vaccine Delivery**
  Incorporating imaging agents into hybrid nanoparticles enables real-time tracking of vaccine biodistribution and efficacy:
- **Example**: Magnetic-plasmonic hybrids allow for simultaneous antigen delivery and MRI/fluorescence imaging.

5. Cancer Immunotherapy

Hybrid nanoparticles deliver tumor-associated antigens and adjuvants, enhancing cytotoxic T cell responses against cancers:

- **Example**: Iron oxide-PLGA hybrids delivering cancer peptides and checkpoint inhibitors.
- **Advantages of Multifunctional Hybrid Systems**
- **Enhanced Efficacy**:

  - Synergistic effects from combining materials improve antigen delivery, immune activation, and memory formation.

- **Thermostability**:

- Hybrid nanoparticles protect antigens under varied conditions, reducing reliance on cold chain logistics.

- **Versatility**:

  - Compatible with diverse vaccine platforms, including protein, DNA, and mRNA vaccines.

- **Reduced Doses**:

  - Efficient delivery systems lower antigen and adjuvant requirements, minimizing side effects.

- **Personalized Vaccination**:

  - Tailorable designs allow for customization based on individual immune profiles or disease requirements.

- **Challenges in Hybrid Systems**
- **Complex Manufacturing**:

  - Combining multiple materials into a single nanoparticle system requires advanced fabrication techniques.

- **Potential Toxicity**:

  - Interactions between components, such as metallic cores and organic shells, may introduce biocompatibility issues.

- **Regulatory Hurdles**:

  - Hybrid systems face stringent regulatory scrutiny due to their complexity and novelty.

- **Scale-Up Limitations**:

  - Producing hybrid nanoparticles at large scales with consistent quality remains challenging.

Hybrid Type	Key Applications	Advantages
Gold-PLGA Hybrid	Cancer and infectious disease vaccines	Enhanced delivery and immune activation
Lipid-Polymer Hybrid	mRNA vaccines	Stability and controlled release
Magnetic-Silica Hybrid	Imaging-guided vaccines	Dual delivery and diagnostic capability
Layered Nanoparticles	Multivalent vaccines	Sequential antigen and adjuvant release
Carbon-Based Hybrids (e.g., CNTs)	Cancer immunotherapy	High antigen loading and targeting

Examples of Hybrid Systems

Case Studies
1. Gold-Lipid Hybrids for mRNA Vaccines

- **Application**: COVID-19 mRNA vaccines.
- **Description**: Hybrid nanoparticles with a gold core and lipid shell improved mRNA stability, facilitated cellular uptake, and reduced reactogenicity.

2. Iron Oxide-PLGA Hybrids for Cancer Vaccines

- **Application**: Therapeutic vaccines for melanoma.
- **Description**: Co-delivery of tumor antigens and TLR agonists enhanced T cell activation and provided imaging capability via MRI.

3. Multilayered Silica Hybrids for Influenza Vaccines

- **Application**: Seasonal flu vaccines.
- **Description**: Layer-by-layer assembly allowed sequential release of influenza antigens and adjuvants, improving immune memory.

5.5 Carbon-Based Nanoparticles

Carbon-based nanoparticles (CBNs) represent a cutting-edge class of nanomaterials used in vaccine delivery systems. With their unique structural, mechanical, and electrical properties, these nanoparticles have emerged as versatile platforms for antigen delivery, immune modulation, and diagnostic integration. Carbon-based nanoparticles, such as **carbon nanotubes (CNTs)**, **graphene oxide (GO)**, and **carbon quantum dots (CQDs)**, are increasingly explored for their potential to enhance the efficacy and stability of vaccines.

Types of Carbon-Based Nanoparticles

1. **Carbon Nanotubes (CNTs):**

   - Cylindrical structures composed of rolled graphene sheets.
   - Exist as single-walled (SWCNTs) or multi-walled (MWCNTs).

2. **Graphene Oxide (GO):**

   - A two-dimensional derivative of graphene with oxygen-containing functional groups.

3. **Carbon Quantum Dots (CQDs):**

   - Nanometer-sized carbon particles with fluorescence properties.

4. **Fullerenes:**

   - Spherical, cage-like structures composed of carbon atoms, such as buckyballs (C60).

Key Properties of Carbon-Based Nanoparticles

1. **High Surface Area:**

   - Allows for the adsorption or conjugation of multiple antigens and adjuvants.

2. **Strong Mechanical Stability:**

   - Ensures the durability of the vaccine formulation under various conditions.

3. **Functionalization Versatility:**

- Surface can be modified with targeting ligands, antigens, or imaging agents.

4. **Optical Properties**:

   - CQDs and GO possess fluorescence properties useful for imaging and tracking.

5. **Biocompatibility (When Engineered)**:

   - Proper functionalization can minimize toxicity and enhance compatibility with biological systems.

Mechanisms of Action in Vaccine Delivery

1. **Antigen Loading and Delivery**

   - Carbon-based nanoparticles adsorb or conjugate antigens through hydrophobic interactions, π-π stacking, or covalent bonding, protecting them from degradation.

2. **Targeting Immune Cells**

   - Functionalized CBNs can specifically target **antigen-presenting cells (APCs)** such as dendritic cells and macrophages.

3. **Adjuvant Effect**

   - Some CBNs, such as GO, possess inherent adjuvant properties that stimulate innate immune receptors and enhance cytokine production.

4. **Controlled Release**

   - Antigens can be released gradually as CBNs degrade, providing sustained immune activation.

5. **Dual Functionality**

- ○ Carbon quantum dots (CQDs) serve as both antigen carriers and imaging agents, enabling real-time monitoring of vaccine delivery and distribution.

Applications of Carbon-Based Nanoparticles in Vaccines
1. Infectious Diseases

- **HIV Vaccines**:

  - ○ CNTs conjugated with HIV peptide antigens enhance delivery to dendritic cells and stimulate strong T cell responses.

- **Influenza Vaccines**:

  - ○ GO-based formulations stabilize influenza antigens and improve immunogenicity.

2. Cancer Immunotherapy

- CNTs are used to deliver tumor-associated antigens (TAAs) for therapeutic vaccines, enhancing cytotoxic T cell activation against cancer cells.

3. DNA and RNA Vaccines

- Functionalized CNTs or GO protect nucleic acids from degradation and improve cellular uptake for robust antigen expression.

4. Multivalent Vaccines

- Fullerenes conjugated with multiple antigens allow for the simultaneous targeting of different pathogens or strains.

Advantages of Carbon-Based Nanoparticles

1. **Enhanced Antigen Stability**:

- Protects sensitive antigens from enzymatic degradation and harsh environmental conditions.

2. **Immune Modulation**:

- Intrinsic adjuvant properties amplify innate and adaptive immune responses.

3. **Targeting Flexibility**:

- Functionalized CBNs achieve selective delivery to immune cells, reducing off-target effects.

4. **Thermostability**:

- Improves vaccine stability under ambient conditions, reducing cold chain requirements.

5. **Multifunctionality**:

- Combines antigen delivery, adjuvanticity, and diagnostic capabilities in a single platform.

Challenges in Carbon-Based Nanoparticles

1. **Toxicity Concerns**:

- Non-functionalized CNTs and GO may induce oxidative stress, inflammation, and cytotoxicity.

2. **Biodegradability**:

- Unlike polymeric nanoparticles, some CBNs are not easily biodegradable, raising concerns about long-term accumulation.

3. **Manufacturing Complexity**:

- ◦ Consistent production of high-quality CBNs with uniform size and properties is challenging.

4. **Regulatory Approval**:

- ◦ The novelty of CBNs necessitates extensive safety evaluations, delaying clinical adoption.

Case Studies
1. Graphene Oxide in Influenza Vaccines

- **Application**: Stabilization and delivery of influenza antigens.
- **Results**: GO enhanced antigen stability and stimulated Th1 and Th2 responses in preclinical models.

2. Carbon Nanotubes in Cancer Vaccines

- **Application**: Delivery of tumor antigens to dendritic cells.
- **Results**: CNTs improved antigen presentation and induced robust CD8+ T cell responses.

3. Carbon Quantum Dots in HIV Vaccines

- **Application**: Dual delivery of HIV antigens and fluorescence imaging.
- **Results**: CQDs demonstrated effective delivery and allowed real-time tracking of immune cell interactions.

Specific Applications of Carbon-Based Nanoparticles in Vaccines
Carbon-based nanoparticles (CBNs) such as **carbon nanotubes (CNTs)**, **graphene oxide (GO)**, **carbon quantum dots (CQDs)**, and **fullerenes** are being developed for targeted applications in infectious disease prevention, cancer immunotherapy, nucleic acid vaccines, and combination therapies. Below, we delve into detailed applications for each type of CBN, highlighting their unique roles and benefits in vaccine technologies.

1. Carbon Nanotubes (CNTs) in Vaccines
Carbon nanotubes, with their tubular nanostructures and high surface-to-volume ratios, are uniquely suited for delivering antigens, adjuvants, and genetic materials.

1.1 Infectious Disease Vaccines

- **HIV Vaccines**:

  - CNTs conjugated with HIV peptide antigens have shown promise in stimulating strong T cell responses.
  - **Mechanism**: The high surface area allows multivalent presentation of antigens, improving recognition by B cells and T cells.
  - **Example**: Functionalized CNTs loaded with HIV glycoproteins enhanced dendritic cell activation in preclinical studies.

- **Tuberculosis Vaccines**:

  - CNTs delivering TB antigens have demonstrated enhanced antigen stability and improved macrophage targeting.

1.2 Cancer Vaccines
CNTs are effective carriers for tumor-associated antigens (TAAs), enabling personalized cancer vaccines.

- **Melanoma Immunotherapy**:

  - CNTs loaded with melanoma antigens induce robust CD8+ T cell responses, essential for cytotoxic activity against cancer cells.

- **Checkpoint Inhibitors**:

  - CNTs co-delivering antigens and checkpoint inhibitors (e.g., anti-PD-1 antibodies) improve the efficacy of cancer vaccines.

1.3 Nucleic Acid Vaccines

- CNTs encapsulating DNA or mRNA ensure efficient intracellular delivery, enhancing antigen expression.

  - **Example**: CNT-DNA hybrids for influenza vaccines achieved higher transfection efficiency and immunogenicity than traditional methods.

Challenges and Innovations

- **Toxicity Mitigation**: Surface functionalization with polyethylene glycol (PEG) or proteins reduces the oxidative stress associated with CNTs.
- **Targeted Delivery**: Conjugation with antibodies specific to immune cell receptors, such as CD40 on dendritic cells, enhances precision.

2. Graphene Oxide (GO) in Vaccines

Graphene oxide's two-dimensional structure, high functionalization capacity, and intrinsic immunostimulatory properties make it a valuable tool in vaccine delivery.

2.1 Influenza Vaccines

- **Antigen Stabilization**: GO protects influenza antigens from enzymatic degradation, ensuring their structural integrity.
- **Immune Stimulation**: Functionalized GO enhances innate immune responses by activating Toll-like receptors (TLRs).

  - **Example**: Influenza vaccines with GO induced higher antibody titers and balanced Th1/Th2 responses compared to conventional adjuvants.

2.2 COVID-19 Vaccines

- **Hybrid Platforms**: GO-based hybrid nanoparticles have been studied for delivering SARS-CoV-2 antigens.

  - **Result**: Improved cellular uptake and prolonged antigen presentation in dendritic cells.

2.3 Multivalent Vaccines

GO's large surface area allows the conjugation of multiple antigens, making it ideal for multivalent vaccines targeting multiple strains of a virus.

Challenges and Innovations

- **Reducing Cytotoxicity**: Modifying GO with biocompatible coatings, such as chitosan or PLGA, mitigates potential toxicity.

- **Enhanced Delivery**: GO functionalized with mannose targets dendritic cells, improving antigen presentation efficiency.

3. Carbon Quantum Dots (CQDs) in Vaccines

CQDs are small, fluorescent carbon nanoparticles with unique optical and biological properties, making them useful for both delivery and diagnostic purposes.

3.1 Dual-Function Vaccines

- **Delivery and Imaging**: CQDs conjugated with antigens serve as both vaccine carriers and imaging agents, enabling real-time monitoring of vaccine distribution.

  - **Example**: HIV peptide vaccines conjugated with CQDs demonstrated strong immune responses and fluorescence tracking in animal models.

3.2 Nucleic Acid Stability

- CQDs stabilize fragile nucleic acids like mRNA and DNA, protecting them from enzymatic degradation during delivery.

3.3 Adjuvant Properties

- Intrinsic adjuvant activity enhances cytokine production, activating both innate and adaptive immunity.

Challenges and Innovations

- **Fluorescence Optimization**: Enhancing the fluorescence intensity of CQDs without compromising their biocompatibility.
- **Combination Therapies**: Co-delivering antigens with therapeutic agents, such as cytokines, for synergistic effects.

4. Fullerenes in Vaccines

Fullerenes, also known as buckyballs, are spherical carbon molecules with exceptional stability and functionalization capabilities.

4.1 Adjuvant Activity

- Fullerenes stimulate innate immune responses by acting as TLR agonists, enhancing antigen presentation.

4.2 Multivalent Vaccine Platforms

- Fullerenes conjugated with multiple antigens enable simultaneous targeting of different pathogens.

  - **Example**: A fullerene-based vaccine targeting HIV, hepatitis B, and influenza showed broad-spectrum efficacy in preclinical studies.

4.3 Combination Therapies

- Fullerenes co-delivered with immunomodulatory agents, such as interleukins or interferons, amplify vaccine efficacy.

Challenges and Innovations

- **Improving Solubility**: Functionalizing fullerenes with hydrophilic groups enhances their dispersibility in biological systems.

Case Studies of Carbon Nanoparticles in Vaccinology
1. CNTs for Tuberculosis Vaccines

- **Study**: Functionalized CNTs delivering TB antigens to macrophages.
- **Result**: Enhanced antigen stability, prolonged immune activation, and increased Th1 responses.

2. GO for Influenza Vaccines

- **Study**: GO-based nanocarriers encapsulating influenza antigens.
- **Result**: Higher antibody titers, improved antigen stability, and reduced cold chain requirements.

3. CQDs in HIV Vaccines

- **Study**: Fluorescent CQDs conjugated with HIV gp120 antigens.

- **Result:** Efficient antigen delivery and real-time imaging of vaccine biodistribution

Nanoparticle Type	Key Applications	Advantages	Challenges
Lipid Nanoparticles (LNPs)	mRNA vaccines	High encapsulation efficiency	Requires ultra-cold storage
Virus-Like Particles (VLPs)	HPV, Hepatitis B	High immunogenicity	Limited to protein-based antigens
Polymeric Nanoparticles	Influenza, Cancer	Controlled release	Complex manufacturing
Inorganic Nanoparticles	Cancer, Tuberculosis	Stability, multifunctionality	Potential toxicity
Protein Nanoparticles	Malaria, COVID-19	Biocompatibility, multivalency	Susceptible to degradation
Carbon-Based Nanoparticles	HIV, Cancer	High antigen loading, adjuvanticity	Limited clinical validation

SIX

MICRONEEDLE-BASED DELIVERY SYSTEMS

6.1 Design and Fabrication

6.1.1 Types of Microneedles (Solid, Dissolvable, Coated)

Microneedles are a cutting-edge drug delivery technology designed to overcome the limitations of traditional transdermal patches and injections. These tiny, minimally invasive needles penetrate the **stratum corneum**, creating microchannels that enable drugs, vaccines, or biologics to be delivered effectively through the skin. Based on their structure, material composition, and application method, microneedles can be classified into three primary types: **solid, dissolvable, and coated microneedles.**

1. Solid Microneedles

Solid microneedles are primarily designed to create **microchannels** in the skin through which drugs can diffuse or be delivered. These microneedles are fabricated from materials like **stainless steel**, **titanium**, or **ceramics**, ensuring durability and sharpness.

Mechanism of Action

Solid microneedles do not contain drugs. Instead, they are applied to the skin to disrupt the outer barrier, increasing skin permeability.

After their removal, a drug formulation, such as a cream, gel, or patch, is applied to the treated area.

Advantages

Simple design and robust mechanical properties.

Reusable in specific cases for testing or diagnostics.

Applications

Insulin Delivery: Used to enhance the absorption of topical formulations of insulin.

Diagnostic Applications: Microchannels created by solid microneedles allow the collection of interstitial fluid for biomarker analysis.

Challenges

Lack of direct drug delivery capability.

Risk of contamination if reused improperly.

2. Dissolvable Microneedles

Dissolvable microneedles are made from **biocompatible polymers** or sugars, designed to dissolve completely within the skin after application. These microneedles encapsulate the drug or vaccine, releasing it as they dissolve.

Mechanism of Action

When applied to the skin, dissolvable microneedles penetrate the stratum corneum and dissolve in the interstitial fluid.

As they dissolve, the encapsulated drug is released directly into the skin's layers for absorption into systemic circulation.

Advantages

Painless and non-invasive, ideal for patients with needle phobia.

Leaves no biohazardous waste since the microneedles dissolve entirely.

Controlled release of drugs over time.

Applications

Vaccination: Dissolvable microneedles loaded with antigens are widely studied for vaccines, such as those for **measles, influenza**, and **COVID-19.**

Cosmetic Use: Used in anti-aging treatments by delivering active ingredients like **hyaluronic acid** into the dermis.

Challenges

Limited mechanical strength compared to solid microneedles, restricting penetration depth.

Sensitivity to environmental factors, such as temperature and humidity, which can affect storage and stability.

3. Coated Microneedles

Coated microneedles are solid microneedles with an outer layer of drug or biologic applied to their surface. These microneedles deliver the drug by releasing it into the skin upon insertion.

Mechanism of Action

The drug coating dissolves or diffuses into the skin upon microneedle application, leaving the solid needle intact.

The microneedle itself is then removed, leaving no residue in the skin.

Advantages

Precise dosing achieved through the thickness and uniformity of the coating.

Effective for delivering vaccines or biologics in small quantities.

Applications

DNA Vaccines: Coated microneedles have been used to deliver DNA-based vaccines for infectious diseases.

Hormone Therapies: Delivering small doses of hormones like **estradiol** or **testosterone** for sustained therapeutic effects.

Challenges

5. Global Impact

Coating uniformity is crucial; uneven distribution can lead to inconsistent dosing.

Manufacturing processes for coated microneedles are complex and require precision.

Type	Material	Drug Delivery Mechanism	Applications	Advantages	Challenges
Solid	Metals, ceramics	Creates microchannels	Insulin delivery, diagnostics	Robust, reusable in diagnostics	Indirect drug delivery
Dissolvable	Polymers, sugars	Dissolves to release drugs	Vaccines, cosmetics	Painless, no waste	Limited mechanical strength
Coated	Metals with drug coating	Dissolves coating on contact	DNA vaccines, hormone delivery	Precise dosing, rapid delivery	Complex manufacturing

- **Comparison of Microneedle Types**

Case Studies and Research Insights

1. Solid Microneedles for Insulin Delivery

In a clinical study, solid microneedles were used to create microchannels in diabetic patients. Insulin gels applied after microneedle application showed a **30% increase in absorption rate**, compared to application without microneedles.

2. Dissolvable Microneedles for COVID-19 Vaccines

Dissolvable microneedles loaded with **SARS-CoV-2 spike proteins** were tested in preclinical trials. They demonstrated strong immune responses with **70% less antigen** compared to intramuscular vaccines, highlighting their potential for resource-constrained settings.

3. Coated Microneedles for DNA Vaccines

Coated microneedles were used to deliver a **Zika virus DNA vaccine** in animal studies. The vaccine elicited a robust immune response with high levels of neutralizing antibodies, proving the efficacy of coated microneedles in genetic immunization.

6.1.2 Materials Used in Microneedle Construction

The choice of materials for microneedle construction is critical to their performance, safety, and application. Microneedles are engineered using a diverse range of materials, including **metals**, **polymers**, **ceramics**, and **composite materials**, each selected for its specific properties, such as biocompatibility, mechanical strength, and dissolution characteristics. These materials allow microneedles to cater to various applications, from drug delivery to diagnostics, while meeting stringent requirements for safety and efficacy.

Key Properties of Ideal Microneedle Materials

For effective construction, materials used in microneedles must exhibit the following characteristics:

Biocompatibility: Ensuring compatibility with biological tissues to avoid adverse reactions.

Mechanical Strength: Withstanding insertion forces without breaking or bending.

Fabrication Ease: Allowing precise microneedle shaping and scalability.

Drug Stability: Maintaining the stability of incorporated drugs or biologics.

Controlled Degradation: Dissolving or degrading predictably for drug release, if applicable.

Classification of Materials

1. Metals

Metals are commonly used in solid microneedles due to their strength, durability, and ability to create sharp tips that penetrate the skin effectively.

Common Metals:

Stainless Steel: Widely used for its corrosion resistance and biocompatibility.

Titanium: Lightweight and strong, ideal for high precision applications.

Nickel: Used selectively for its affordability and machinability but requires careful consideration due to potential allergenicity.

Fabrication Methods:

Laser Cutting: Produces precise and sharp microneedle tips.

Electrochemical Etching: Allows high accuracy in dimensions and geometry.

Applications:

Insulin delivery and diagnostic applications involving interstitial fluid sampling.

Challenges:

Metals can pose risks of contamination if not sterilized correctly.

Non-biodegradability necessitates removal post-application.

2. Polymers

Polymers are the most versatile materials used in microneedle fabrication, especially for dissolvable or biodegradable microneedles.

Biodegradable Polymers:

Polylactic Acid (PLA) and **Polylactic-co-Glycolic Acid (PLGA)**: Ideal for controlled release of drugs.

Hyaluronic Acid (HA): Biocompatible and frequently used for cosmetic applications like anti-aging treatments.

Non-Biodegradable Polymers:

Polyvinylpyrrolidone (PVP) and **Polyethylene Glycol (PEG)**: Used for durable microneedles that maintain stability in varying environments.

Fabrication Methods:

Molding: Polymer solutions are poured into microneedle molds and solidified under controlled conditions.

3D Printing: Enables rapid prototyping and customization of designs.

Applications:

Vaccine delivery, drug-loaded dissolvable patches, and cosmetic formulations.

Challenges:

Limited mechanical strength can restrict penetration into deeper layers of the skin.

3. Ceramics

Ceramic materials, such as **silicon dioxide** and **hydroxyapatite**, are used for their rigidity and inert nature.

Advantages:

Resistance to microbial contamination and chemical degradation.

High mechanical precision, making them suitable for coated microneedles.

Fabrication Methods:

Lithography: Achieves high-precision ceramic microneedles.

Sintering: Combines powder-based ceramics under heat to form durable structures.

Applications:

Diagnostic tools and therapeutic drug delivery systems requiring precise control.

Challenges:

Brittleness increases the risk of fracture during insertion.

Higher costs compared to polymers and metals.

4. Composites

Composite materials combine two or more substances to enhance the performance of microneedles.

Examples:

Polymer-Metal Hybrids: Combine the strength of metals with the flexibility of polymers.

Graphene Oxide Composites: Used for biosensing applications due to enhanced conductivity and mechanical properties.

Advantages:

Tailored mechanical properties for specific applications.

Improved drug encapsulation and release profiles.

Challenges:

Complex fabrication processes requiring advanced technology.

Step-by-Step Example: Fabrication of Dissolvable Microneedles Using Hyaluronic Acid

Preparation of Polymer Solution:

A solution of **hyaluronic acid (HA)** is prepared by dissolving it in deionized water, along with the desired drug or biologic.

Mold Filling:

The polymer solution is poured into a silicone microneedle mold under vacuum conditions to ensure uniform filling.

Drying:

The mold is placed in a controlled humidity and temperature chamber to evaporate the water, leaving solid microneedles.

Demolding:

The dried microneedles are carefully removed from the mold to preserve their structure.

Final Testing:

Mechanical and dissolution tests are conducted to ensure sufficient penetration ability and complete degradation within the skin.

Innovative Materials in Development

Graphene-Based Microneedles:

Explored for biosensing applications, allowing real-time monitoring of glucose levels or other biomarkers.

Nanoparticle-Loaded Polymers:

Enhance drug stability and enable controlled release.

Hydrogel-Based Microneedles:

Swell upon skin contact, delivering hydrophilic drugs directly to the dermis.

Challenges in Material Selection

Environmental Sensitivity:

Polymers and biodegradable materials are prone to degradation under heat or humidity, complicating storage.

Regulatory Approvals:

Materials used in microneedles must meet rigorous regulatory standards for safety and biocompatibility.

Cost and Scalability:

Advanced materials like composites and graphene increase manufacturing costs, impacting scalability.

6.2 Mechanisms of Action

6.2.1 Delivery Through Skin Layers

Microneedles function as a bridge between traditional transdermal delivery systems and injectable methods by facilitating the delivery of drugs across the **skin layers** without causing significant pain or tissue damage. The mechanism of action of microneedles in delivering therapeutic agents relies on their ability to overcome the **stratum corneum**, the outermost layer of the skin, which serves as a barrier to most substances.

Structure of the Skin: A Barrier to Drug Delivery

The skin comprises three primary layers:

Epidermis:

The outermost layer includes the stratum corneum, composed of dead keratinized cells. This layer is highly lipophilic and a formidable barrier to hydrophilic molecules and larger drug molecules. Beneath this lies the viable epidermis, which contains living keratinocytes and lacks blood vessels.

Dermis:

The dermis is rich in blood vessels, lymphatic vessels, and connective tissues. It is the target site for most transdermal drugs, as the systemic circulation begins here.

Hypodermis (Subcutaneous Layer):

Composed of adipose tissue, the hypodermis acts as a cushion and energy storage layer.

Mechanism of Microneedle-Mediated Delivery

Microneedles penetrate the stratum corneum and viable epidermis, creating **microchannels** through which therapeutic agents can diffuse or be released. Depending on the type of microneedle used (solid, coated, dissolvable), the delivery mechanism may vary.

1. Physical Penetration of the Stratum Corneum

The stratum corneum's thickness, typically 10–20 microns, acts as a rate-limiting barrier for transdermal delivery. Microneedles, with lengths ranging from **50 to 900 microns**, create microscale punctures, bypassing this barrier without reaching nerve endings in the dermis, thereby avoiding pain.

Example: Solid microneedles create temporary pores that enhance the permeability of hydrophilic drugs such as insulin or vaccines.

2. Diffusion and Dissolution in Skin Layers

Solid Microneedles:

These microneedles primarily act by physically disrupting the stratum corneum. Once removed, the drug formulation applied on the skin surface diffuses through the microchannels.

Dissolvable Microneedles:

Made of biodegradable polymers, these microneedles dissolve upon insertion, releasing encapsulated drugs directly into the viable epidermis. The drug then diffuses into the dermis and systemic circulation.

Example: Hyaluronic acid microneedles loaded with vaccines dissolve within minutes, ensuring controlled delivery.

Coated Microneedles:

These have a drug layer on their surface that dissolves immediately upon insertion.

Example: Coated microneedles are widely used for delivering DNA-based vaccines.

3. Targeting Specific Skin Layers

Microneedles enable precision targeting of specific layers, which enhances therapeutic efficacy.

Epidermal Targeting: Vaccines often target Langerhans cells in the epidermis for immune responses.

Dermal Targeting: Delivery of hydrophilic drugs like peptides and proteins benefits from the rich vascularity of the dermis.

Interstitial Fluid Sampling: Some microneedles are designed to extract interstitial fluid for diagnostics without blood withdrawal.

Step-by-Step Drug Delivery Example: Insulin Microneedles

Insertion:

A dissolvable microneedle patch containing insulin is applied to the skin, penetrating the stratum corneum and viable epidermis.

Dissolution:

The microneedles dissolve within minutes, releasing insulin molecules into the dermal interstitial fluid.

Diffusion:

Insulin molecules diffuse into the capillary network in the dermis, entering the systemic circulation.

Therapeutic Action:

The insulin reaches target cells to regulate blood glucose levels.

Advantages of Microneedle-Based Skin Delivery

Pain-Free Administration: Microneedles avoid nerve-rich dermal regions, ensuring painless drug delivery.

Bypassing the First-Pass Metabolism: Drugs delivered through microneedles enter systemic circulation directly, avoiding degradation by liver enzymes.

Reduced Dosing Frequency: Controlled release of drugs can be achieved with dissolvable or coated microneedles.

Challenges and Limitations

Skin Elasticity: Variability in skin elasticity can affect microneedle penetration depth and drug release consistency.

Hydration Levels: Skin hydration can influence the dissolution rate of biodegradable microneedles.

Infection Risks: Microchannel creation may pose a risk of microbial contamination if proper sterilization is not maintained.

6.2.2 Targeting Skin-Resident Immune Cells

The ability of microneedles to target **skin-resident immune cells** represents a transformative approach in immunotherapy, vaccine delivery, and treatment of autoimmune diseases. The skin's **epidermis and dermis** are rich in specialized immune cells, including **Langerhans cells, dermal dendritic cells, macrophages**, and **T cells**, which are pivotal for initiating and modulating immune responses. Leveraging microneedles for drug and vaccine delivery directly to these cells enhances therapeutic efficacy, reduces systemic side effects, and improves patient compliance.

Immune Cells in the Skin: A Strategic Target

Langerhans Cells

Found predominantly in the **epidermis**, these dendritic cells play a critical role in capturing and processing antigens before presenting them to T cells in lymph nodes.

Importance in Vaccines: Targeting Langerhans cells ensures robust antigen presentation, promoting both innate and adaptive immunity.

Dermal Dendritic Cells

Located in the **dermis**, these cells are potent antigen-presenting cells that amplify immune responses.

Role in Therapeutics: Delivery of immunomodulatory agents to dendritic cells enhances their ability to modulate immune activity in conditions such as cancer or autoimmune disorders.

Macrophages and T Cells

Macrophages in the dermis help in the **phagocytosis of pathogens** and the release of inflammatory cytokines.

Memory T cells residing in the dermis act as first responders to infections, making them a prime target for therapies aimed at bolstering immunological memory.

Mechanisms of Microneedle-Driven Immune Targeting

Creation of Microchannels

Microneedles penetrate the **stratum corneum**, creating microchannels that bypass the skin's primary barrier. These microchannels allow precise delivery of antigens, cytokines, or therapeutic agents to immune cells residing in the epidermis and dermis.

Localized Antigen Presentation

Coated microneedles deliver antigens directly to Langerhans cells or dermal dendritic cells, facilitating localized antigen uptake and presentation.

Example: A microneedle-based influenza vaccine targets Langerhans cells, triggering a robust immune response with minimal systemic spread of the antigen.

Sustained Release with Dissolvable Microneedles

Biodegradable microneedles gradually dissolve, releasing encapsulated agents such as peptides or proteins in a controlled manner to interact with dendritic cells and macrophages over time.

Immune Activation Without Pain

Microneedles, by avoiding dermal nerves, provide a painless yet effective means of stimulating immune cells, making them ideal for patient-centric vaccine administration.

Applications in Immunotherapy and Vaccines

1. Vaccine Delivery

Microneedle-based vaccines are highly effective in targeting Langerhans cells and dermal dendritic cells for antigen presentation.

Examples:

COVID-19 Vaccines: Microneedles have been explored for delivering spike protein antigens to skin immune cells, generating strong immune responses with low antigen doses.

Cancer Vaccines: Tumor antigens delivered to dendritic cells through microneedles have shown promise in enhancing tumor-specific immunity.

2. Immunotherapy for Autoimmune Diseases

Delivery of **immunomodulatory agents** directly to skin-resident T cells helps suppress overactive immune responses.

Example: **Regulatory T cell stimulators** are delivered using dissolvable microneedles to mitigate autoimmune reactions in diseases like psoriasis and rheumatoid arthritis.

3. Allergy Desensitization

Microneedle patches delivering allergens in controlled doses to dendritic cells are used to desensitize immune responses, offering a novel approach to allergy management.

Challenges in Targeting Skin-Resident Immune Cells

Drug Stability:

Maintaining the stability of biologics like antigens, peptides, or cytokines during fabrication and delivery poses a challenge.

Variability in Skin Immune Responses:

Differences in immune cell density and activity across skin types and regions affect the consistency of therapeutic outcomes.

Manufacturing Complexity:

Achieving uniform antigen coating or embedding on microneedles requires precision engineering, adding to production costs.

Advancements and Innovations

Nanoparticle-Integrated Microneedles

Nanoparticles loaded with antigens or immune modulators are incorporated into microneedles to enhance targeting and uptake by skin immune cells.

Smart Microneedle Systems

pH-sensitive microneedles release immune stimulators in response to inflammatory environments, optimizing therapeutic outcomes while minimizing side effects.

Personalized Vaccines

Customizable microneedle patches tailored to deliver patient-specific antigens represent a cutting-edge development in personalized medicine.

Case Study: Microneedles for Malaria Vaccination

A dissolvable microneedle patch delivering **malaria sporozoite antigens** to dermal dendritic cells demonstrated enhanced antigen uptake and immune response in preclinical studies. The painless administration and precise targeting reduced the required antigen dose by **70%**, making it a cost-effective and scalable alternative to conventional intramuscular vaccines.

6.3 Applications and Case Studies

6.3.1 Influenza Vaccines

Introduction to Influenza Vaccines and Microneedle Technology

Influenza remains a significant global health challenge, causing seasonal outbreaks and occasional pandemics. Conventional vaccine delivery methods, such as intramuscular injections, have several limitations, including the need for trained healthcare professionals, needle-phobia in patients, and cold-chain storage requirements. Microneedle-based vaccine delivery systems offer a groundbreaking alternative, addressing these issues while improving the efficacy, safety, and patient compliance of influenza immunization.

Microneedles have been extensively studied for delivering influenza vaccines due to their ability to target **skin-resident immune cells**, such as **Langerhans cells** and **dermal dendritic cells**, which play critical roles in initiating strong immune responses. Their painless administration and potential for self-application make microneedles a promising tool in influenza prevention.

Mechanism of Action for Influenza Vaccines with Microneedles

Microneedle-based influenza vaccines function by penetrating the stratum corneum and depositing antigens directly in the epidermal and dermal layers. These layers contain high densities of immune cells, facilitating efficient antigen uptake and processing.

Step-by-Step Mechanism

Insertion:

Microneedles pierce the skin's outer barrier, creating microchannels.

These microchannels allow vaccine antigens to access immune cells without causing pain or bleeding.

Antigen Uptake:

Langerhans cells and dermal dendritic cells capture the antigens delivered by the microneedles.

Immune Activation:

These immune cells process the antigens and migrate to lymph nodes, where they present them to T cells and B cells.

This initiates both **cellular** and **humoral immune responses**, leading to the production of influenza-specific antibodies.

Memory Formation:

The immune system develops long-term memory, providing protection against future influenza infections.

Advantages of Microneedle-Based Influenza Vaccines

Painless and Convenient Administration:

Microneedles cause minimal discomfort, making them ideal for needle-phobic individuals.

Self-administration with patch-based systems reduces the need for trained personnel.

Improved Immunogenicity:

Direct delivery to skin-resident immune cells enhances antigen uptake and immune response.

Reduced Antigen Doses:

Studies show that microneedles can achieve equivalent or superior immunogenicity with lower antigen doses compared to intramuscular injections.

Elimination of Cold Chain Requirements:

Certain microneedle formulations can be stored at room temperature, overcoming logistical challenges in vaccine distribution.

Case Studies and Research Insights

Case Study 1: Microneedle Patch for Seasonal Influenza Vaccine

Objective:

Evaluate the safety, efficacy, and patient acceptance of a microneedle patch delivering a trivalent influenza vaccine (TIV).

Methodology:

A randomized clinical trial was conducted with participants receiving either a microneedle patch or a conventional intramuscular injection of TIV.

Immune responses were measured using hemagglutination inhibition (HAI) titers.

Findings:

The microneedle patch produced immune responses comparable to intramuscular injections.

Participants reported significantly lower pain levels and higher satisfaction with the patch.

The patch demonstrated stability at room temperature for up to 12 months.

Implications:

Microneedle patches have the potential to replace traditional delivery methods, especially in resource-limited settings.

Case Study 2: Universal Influenza Vaccine with Microneedles

Objective:

Develop and evaluate a microneedle-based universal influenza vaccine targeting conserved regions of influenza viruses.

Methodology:

A dissolvable microneedle patch containing conserved antigens, such as the **M2e peptide** and **hemagglutinin stem**, was tested in preclinical models.

Immunogenicity and cross-protection against multiple influenza strains were assessed.

Findings:

The vaccine elicited broad immune responses, offering protection against diverse influenza strains.

Antigen stability was maintained within the microneedle matrix, ensuring consistent efficacy.

Implications:

Universal influenza vaccines delivered via microneedles could revolutionize influenza prevention by providing cross-protection against evolving strains.

Challenges in Microneedle-Based Influenza Vaccines

Regulatory Approval:

The novel nature of microneedle systems poses regulatory hurdles, requiring extensive safety and efficacy testing.

Manufacturing Scalability:

Producing microneedle patches at scale while maintaining uniformity is a technical challenge.

Patient Education:

Self-application of microneedle patches requires adequate patient education to ensure proper use.

Cost of Development:

High initial costs in material and process development may affect affordability.

6.3.2 Emerging Infectious Diseases

Emerging infectious diseases (EIDs), characterized by newly identified pathogens or the resurgence of previously controlled diseases, pose significant challenges to global health. Examples include **Zika virus**, **Ebola**, **Chikungunya**, **COVID-19**, and **monkeypox**. These diseases often spread rapidly due to globalization, climate change, and other environmental factors. Traditional approaches to controlling these infections, such as injectable vaccines and systemic drug therapies, are often slow to deploy, require significant infrastructure, and face challenges in patient compliance.

Microneedle-based delivery systems have emerged as a promising solution to address these limitations. By enabling rapid, efficient, and pain-free delivery of vaccines, antivirals, and diagnostic agents, microneedles are revolutionizing the management of EIDs.

Relevance of Microneedles in Emerging Infectious Diseases

1. Rapid Vaccine Development and Deployment

Microneedles are well-suited for delivering vaccines against pathogens responsible for EIDs. Their ability to target **skin-resident immune cells**, such as Langerhans cells and dermal dendritic cells, enhances vaccine efficacy, even at lower antigen doses.

Example: During the **COVID-19 pandemic**, microneedle patches were explored as an alternative to conventional intramuscular vaccines. Their ease of application, room-temperature stability, and high patient acceptance made them an attractive option for mass immunization campaigns.

2. Effective Drug Delivery

Microneedles enable localized and systemic delivery of antiviral agents, reducing the risk of side effects and enhancing therapeutic outcomes.

Example: In **Zika virus** infections, microneedles have been used to deliver antiviral peptides directly to infected skin tissues, ensuring high local drug concentrations.

3. Diagnostic Applications

Microneedles can be used to extract **interstitial fluid** or deliver contrast agents for real-time monitoring of disease biomarkers.

Example: **Ebola diagnostics** with microneedle patches provide rapid biomarker detection, enabling timely intervention and containment of outbreaks.

Mechanisms of Action in EIDs

1. Skin-Targeted Immunization

Microneedles deliver vaccine antigens to the skin, where immune cells capture and process them.

The activation of **innate and adaptive immune pathways** ensures long-lasting immunity.

2. Enhanced Localized Therapy

For diseases with dermal or subcutaneous manifestations, such as **Chikungunya** or **monkeypox**, microneedles allow precise delivery of therapeutic agents directly to the affected area.

3. Continuous Drug Release

Dissolvable microneedles enable sustained drug release over time, reducing the frequency of administration.

Example: Long-acting microneedles delivering **antiviral drugs** for up to two weeks in **COVID-19** patients.

Case Studies and Research on Microneedles in EIDs

Case Study 1: Microneedles for COVID-19 Vaccination

Objective:

Develop a room-temperature-stable vaccine for rapid deployment in low-resource settings.

Methodology:

A dissolvable microneedle patch containing **SARS-CoV-2 spike protein antigens** was tested for immunogenicity in animal models.

Findings:

Strong antibody responses comparable to intramuscular vaccines were observed.

The microneedle patch remained stable for six months at 25°C, eliminating the need for cold-chain storage.

Implications:

This approach could significantly enhance vaccine accessibility in rural and resource-limited areas.

Case Study 2: Microneedles for Zika Virus Therapy

Objective:

Deliver antiviral agents targeting Zika virus-infected skin tissues.

Methodology:

Biodegradable microneedles were loaded with an experimental **antiviral peptide** and applied to infected mice.

Findings:

The microneedles achieved high local drug concentrations, reducing viral loads in skin tissues by **80%** compared to systemic administration.

Minimal systemic side effects were reported.

Implications:

Microneedles offer a localized, efficient, and patient-friendly method for managing vector-borne diseases.

Case Study 3: Diagnostic Microneedles for Ebola Virus

Objective:

Develop a rapid and minimally invasive diagnostic tool for early detection of Ebola virus.

Methodology:

Microneedle patches were designed to extract interstitial fluid from patients and detect Ebola virus antigens using embedded biosensors.

Findings:

The microneedles detected viral antigens with **95% sensitivity** within 15 minutes.

No specialized laboratory equipment was required.

Implications:

Microneedles enable point-of-care diagnostics, critical for containing outbreaks of high-mortality diseases like Ebola.

Advantages of Microneedles in EIDs

Rapid Deployment:

Easily scalable for mass production, microneedles can be quickly distributed during outbreaks.

Room-Temperature Stability:

Many microneedle formulations eliminate the need for cold storage, making them ideal for resource-constrained regions.

Painless Application:

Non-invasive delivery increases patient compliance and acceptance, especially in pediatric and needle-phobic populations.

Targeted Delivery:

Localized treatment minimizes systemic side effects and enhances therapeutic efficacy.

Challenges and Limitations

Cost of Development:

Initial research and development costs for microneedle systems remain high.

Manufacturing Consistency:

Ensuring uniformity in microneedle dimensions and drug loading is technically demanding.

Regulatory Hurdles:

Novel microneedle systems require rigorous safety and efficacy evaluations, delaying their entry into the market.

Limited Public Awareness:

Educating healthcare professionals and the public about the benefits of microneedles is essential for widespread adoption.

Future Directions

Integration with Wearable Technology:

Smart microneedle patches capable of **real-time monitoring** and therapy adjustments can enhance management of EIDs.

Multipurpose Microneedles:

Combining vaccination, therapy, and diagnostics in a single patch offers a holistic approach to combating infectious diseases.

Personalized Medicine:

Tailored microneedle systems for specific patient populations or genetic profiles will improve treatment outcomes.

Global Health Impact:

Expanding microneedle production and distribution networks can address inequities in access to healthcare for emerging diseases.

6.4 Advantages and Challenges

6.4.1 Painless Administration and Patient Compliance

One of the most significant advantages of microneedle-based delivery systems is their ability to provide **painless administration**, a feature that directly influences **patient compliance**. Traditional needle-based injections often lead to discomfort, fear, and anxiety, especially in children, elderly patients, and those with needle phobia (trypanophobia). In contrast, microneedles penetrate the skin's outermost barrier, the **stratum corneum**, without reaching nerve-rich regions in the dermis, offering a pain-free experience.

Why Painless Administration Matters

Skin Anatomy and Pain Perception

Pain associated with injections is primarily due to the stimulation of **nociceptors** (pain receptors) in the dermis. These receptors respond to mechanical, thermal, or chemical stimuli, leading to discomfort during conventional injections.

Microneedles, with lengths ranging from **50 to 900 microns**, do not reach the nociceptor-rich dermis. Instead, they create microchannels through the stratum corneum and deliver drugs or vaccines to the viable epidermis or upper dermis.

Example:

A comparative study on microneedle patches versus intramuscular injections for influenza vaccination showed that over **85% of patients** reported significantly reduced pain with microneedle patches, enhancing their willingness to receive routine vaccinations.

Painless Application in Specific Populations

Pediatrics:

Children often fear needles, leading to vaccine hesitancy and non-compliance. Microneedles eliminate this barrier, making pediatric vaccinations more approachable.

Chronic Disease Patients:

Patients with conditions like **diabetes** or **rheumatoid arthritis** who require frequent injections benefit from the reduced discomfort associated with microneedles.

Geriatrics:

Elderly patients, who may have fragile skin or aversion to injections, experience better compliance with microneedle patches due to their minimally invasive nature.

Patient Compliance and Its Impact

Improved Acceptance of Vaccinations

The painless nature of microneedles has a direct correlation with increased vaccine uptake. Patients who avoid vaccinations due to fear of needles are more likely to accept microneedle-based systems, leading to better public health outcomes.

Example:

During a clinical trial involving self-administered **microneedle patches for COVID-19 vaccination**, over **90% of participants** expressed a preference for microneedles over traditional injections, citing ease of use and reduced pain.

Self-Administration and Convenience

Microneedle patches allow for **self-administration**, removing the need for healthcare professionals to administer injections. This feature is particularly beneficial in:

Pandemic scenarios, where mass vaccination campaigns require scalability and rapid deployment.

Resource-limited regions, where access to healthcare facilities and trained personnel is restricted.

Case Study:

In a pilot program in rural Africa, self-applied microneedle patches for tetanus vaccination achieved a **30% higher coverage rate** compared to traditional injection programs.

Challenges in Achieving Painless Administration and Compliance

Despite the advantages, several challenges remain in ensuring painless administration and maintaining patient compliance:

Perceived Novelty:

Some patients may hesitate to adopt microneedle technology due to unfamiliarity or skepticism.

Skin Sensitivity:

Patients with sensitive skin conditions or allergies may experience mild irritation at the application site, potentially affecting compliance.

Self-Application Accuracy:

Improper application of microneedle patches by patients can lead to inconsistent drug delivery or reduced efficacy.

Cost and Accessibility:

The higher production costs of microneedles may limit their accessibility in low-income regions, impacting widespread adoption.

Strategies to Overcome Challenges

Patient Education Campaigns:

Increasing awareness about the safety, efficacy, and benefits of microneedle systems can reduce hesitancy and improve acceptance.

Optimized Patch Designs:
Developing **user-friendly designs**, such as color-change indicators that confirm correct application, ensures consistent and effective use.

Addressing Skin Irritation:
Incorporating **soothing agents** or **anti-inflammatory materials** into microneedle formulations can minimize irritation for sensitive skin types.

Cost-Reduction Strategies:
Advancements in manufacturing technologies, such as **3D printing** and scalable production methods, can reduce costs and improve accessibility.

Future Directions
The combination of **painless administration** and **enhanced patient compliance** positions microneedles as a transformative tool in healthcare delivery. Future innovations include:

Smart Microneedle Systems:
Incorporating sensors to ensure correct application and monitor drug delivery in real-time.

Integration with Telemedicine:
Leveraging microneedle patches in telehealth programs to enable remote monitoring and therapy.

Customizable Patches:
Developing tailored microneedle patches for specific patient needs, such as pediatric formulations or patches for geriatric patients with fragile skin.

6.4.2 Stability and Storage Benefits

The stability and storage of pharmaceutical products are critical considerations in drug development and distribution, particularly for vaccines, biologics, and other temperature-sensitive therapeutics. Traditional drug formulations, especially injectable vaccines and protein-based therapeutics, often require **cold-chain storage** to maintain their efficacy. This reliance on refrigeration presents significant logistical challenges, particularly in low-resource settings or during global vaccination campaigns.

Microneedle-based delivery systems provide a revolutionary solution to these issues by enhancing the **stability** of active pharmaceutical ingredients (APIs) and reducing the need for complex storage requirements. Their unique design and material composition allow drugs and vaccines to remain stable under ambient conditions, simplifying distribution and expanding access to essential medicines.

Key Benefits of Stability and Storage with Microneedles

1. Reduced Dependence on Cold-Chain Systems

Conventional vaccines often degrade rapidly outside of controlled refrigeration (2–8°C), leading to wastage and reduced efficacy. Microneedles, especially those fabricated from polymers or dissolvable materials, encapsulate APIs in a stable matrix, protecting them from environmental factors such as heat, humidity, and light.

Example: Microneedle patches for **measles vaccination** demonstrated stability for over **six months** at 40°C, maintaining immunogenicity comparable to freshly prepared vaccines stored under refrigeration.

2. Protection from Degradation

Biological molecules, such as proteins, peptides, and DNA-based vaccines, are susceptible to hydrolysis, oxidation, and aggregation, especially under fluctuating environmental conditions. Microneedles shield these molecules by embedding them in stabilizing matrices.

Mechanism:

Lyophilization (Freeze-Drying): Drugs are often lyophilized during the microneedle fabrication process, reducing water content and enhancing stability.

Polymer Encapsulation: Polymers like **hyaluronic acid** or **polyvinyl alcohol (PVA)** provide a protective microenvironment, minimizing exposure to degrading agents.

3. Room-Temperature Storage

The ability to store microneedles at room temperature eliminates the need for expensive refrigeration infrastructure, making them ideal for distribution in resource-limited regions.

Example: During preclinical trials, **microneedle patches delivering influenza vaccines** retained potency for up to **12 months** at ambient temperatures.

4. Simplified Distribution Logistics

Microneedle patches are lightweight, compact, and require minimal packaging. These attributes reduce shipping costs, minimize storage space, and enhance scalability for mass immunization programs.

Impact: A single shipment of microneedle patches can deliver doses equivalent to multiple shipments of liquid vaccines in vials, significantly lowering transportation costs.

Practical Applications Highlighting Stability and Storage Benefits

1. Pandemic Preparedness

During pandemics, the rapid distribution of stable vaccines is critical. Microneedles offer a practical solution by eliminating cold-chain requirements and enabling long-term storage.

Case Study: Microneedle patches for **COVID-19 vaccines** maintained stability across varying temperature conditions, ensuring global distribution without cold-chain dependencies.

2. Vaccination in Remote Areas

In rural and underserved regions, access to refrigeration facilities is often limited. Microneedles enable vaccine deployment in such areas without compromising efficacy.

Example: Tetanus vaccine microneedles were successfully deployed in sub-Saharan Africa, where cold-chain logistics posed significant challenges.

Challenges in Stability and Storage with Microneedles

Formulation Compatibility:

Not all drugs or vaccines can be easily incorporated into microneedle matrices without losing efficacy.

Solution: Advances in formulation science are enabling the encapsulation of diverse APIs in microneedles.

Environmental Sensitivity:

While microneedles improve stability, extreme conditions such as prolonged exposure to direct sunlight or high humidity may still pose risks.

Regulatory Approval:

Demonstrating long-term stability and efficacy under varying storage conditions requires extensive validation, increasing the time and cost of regulatory approval.

Material Limitations:

Certain biodegradable polymers used in microneedles may degrade prematurely under specific environmental conditions, affecting drug delivery.

Innovations Enhancing Stability and Storage

1. Advanced Encapsulation Techniques

Microneedles using advanced encapsulation methods, such as **nanoparticle-laden matrices** or **lipid-based carriers**, further enhance the stability of APIs.

2. Thermostable Formulations

Thermostable vaccine formulations combined with microneedle delivery systems are being developed to withstand extreme temperature fluctuations.

3. Smart Packaging

Packaging materials that offer additional layers of protection against humidity and temperature changes are being integrated into microneedle distribution systems.

Future Directions in Stability and Storage

Global Vaccine Equity:

Microneedle systems have the potential to bridge gaps in vaccine access, particularly in low- and middle-income countries, by simplifying storage and distribution logistics.

Extended Shelf Life:

Research is focused on extending the shelf life of microneedle-based therapeutics, making them ideal for stockpiling during emergencies.

Combination Formulations:

Microneedles capable of delivering multiple vaccines or drugs simultaneously are being designed to optimize storage and reduce logistical complexity.

Environmental Sustainability:

Biodegradable materials in microneedles and eco-friendly packaging solutions contribute to reducing the environmental impact of pharmaceutical distribution.

SEVEN
Nucleic Acid Vaccines and Delivery Systems

7.1 DNA Vaccines

7.1.1 Mechanism and Delivery Methods

DNA vaccines represent a transformative approach to immunization by leveraging **genetic material** to stimulate immune responses. Unlike conventional vaccines that rely on inactivated pathogens or proteins, DNA vaccines use **plasmid DNA** encoding antigens of interest. These vaccines are engineered to enable cells in the host to produce the antigens, mimicking a natural infection and eliciting both **cellular and humoral immunity**.

The effectiveness of DNA vaccines relies on two key factors: the **mechanism of action** and the **delivery method** employed to introduce the genetic material into the host cells.

Mechanism of Action

The immune response elicited by DNA vaccines involves multiple steps, from cellular uptake of the plasmid DNA to antigen presentation and immune system activation.

1. Plasmid Design and Uptake

- DNA vaccines consist of a **circular plasmid** that encodes the gene for a specific antigen. This plasmid includes:

  - A **promoter** to initiate transcription.

- A **gene encoding the antigen** of interest.
- Regulatory elements to ensure efficient expression in human cells.

- Once the plasmid DNA is introduced into the body, it enters host cells (typically **muscle cells** or **antigen-presenting cells (APCs)**) through various delivery methods.

2. Antigen Production

- Inside the host cell, the plasmid DNA reaches the **nucleus**, where the antigen gene is transcribed into mRNA.
- The mRNA then migrates to the **cytoplasm**, where it is translated into the antigen protein by the host's ribosomes.

3. Antigen Presentation

- The synthesized antigen is processed in two ways:

  - **Endogenous Pathway**: Antigen peptides are presented on the surface of the cell via **MHC Class I molecules**, activating **cytotoxic T cells (CD8+ T cells)**.
  - **Exogenous Pathway**: Antigen is secreted or released upon cell lysis, taken up by APCs, and presented via **MHC Class II molecules**, activating **helper T cells (CD4+ T cells)**.

4. Immune Activation

- **Cellular Immunity**: Cytotoxic T cells recognize infected cells displaying antigen-MHC Class I complexes and destroy them.
- **Humoral Immunity**: Helper T cells stimulate B cells to produce **antibodies** targeting the antigen.

This dual activation of the immune system mimics natural infection, providing robust and long-lasting immunity.

Delivery Methods for DNA Vaccines

Efficient delivery of plasmid DNA into host cells is critical for the success of DNA vaccines. The challenge lies in overcoming biological barriers, such as the **plasma membrane**, while ensuring minimal degradation and high transfection efficiency. Several delivery methods have been developed to enhance DNA uptake.

1. Electroporation

Mechanism:

- Short electrical pulses create temporary pores in the cell membrane, allowing plasmid DNA to enter.

Advantages:

- High transfection efficiency.
- Enhanced immune response due to localized tissue damage that recruits APCs.

Applications:

- Used in **cancer vaccines** and infectious disease vaccines like those for **HIV** and **hepatitis B**.

Challenges:

- Requires specialized equipment.
- Causes mild discomfort or tissue damage at the application site.

2. Microneedles

Mechanism:

- Microneedles coated with or encapsulating plasmid DNA penetrate the skin, delivering DNA directly into the epidermis and dermis, where immune cells are abundant.

Advantages:

- Painless and minimally invasive.
- Targets skin-resident immune cells, enhancing antigen presentation.

Applications:

- DNA vaccines for **influenza** and **Zika virus** have been delivered using microneedle patches in preclinical studies.

Challenges:

- Ensuring stability of the DNA coating during storage and application.

3. Lipid Nanoparticles (LNPs)
Mechanism:

- Plasmid DNA is encapsulated in lipid-based nanoparticles, which protect it from degradation and facilitate cellular uptake.

Advantages:

- Protects DNA from enzymatic degradation.
- Enhances cellular uptake via endocytosis.

Applications:

- LNPs have been widely studied for both **mRNA** and DNA vaccines, including those for **COVID-19**.

Challenges:

- Requires precise formulation to balance stability and release kinetics.

4. Gene Gun (Biolistic Delivery)
Mechanism:

- DNA is coated onto microscopic gold or tungsten particles and delivered into cells using a pressurized gas.

Advantages:

- Direct delivery into the cytoplasm, bypassing the endocytosis pathway.
- Suitable for targeting skin and mucosal tissues.

Applications:

- Used in veterinary vaccines and studied for human applications like **rabies** and **influenza vaccines**.

Challenges:

- Expensive and less scalable for widespread use.

5. Viral Vectors
Mechanism:

- Non-replicating viral vectors, such as **adenoviruses**, are engineered to carry plasmid DNA into host cells.

Advantages:

- High transfection efficiency.
- Natural ability to infect cells ensures effective DNA delivery.

Applications:

- Used in clinical trials for DNA vaccines against **Ebola** and **Zika virus**.

Challenges:

- Potential for pre-existing immunity to the viral vector, reducing efficacy.

6. Hydrogels and Polymeric Nanocarriers
Mechanism:

- Hydrogels or polymeric nanoparticles encapsulate DNA and release it gradually upon administration.

Advantages:

- Enables controlled and sustained release of DNA.
- Protects DNA from degradation during transit.

Applications:

- Studied for DNA vaccines against **malaria** and **tuberculosis**.

Challenges:

- Optimization of release kinetics is required for effective immune activation.

Challenges in DNA Vaccine Delivery

1. **Stability of DNA:**

   - Plasmid DNA is prone to degradation by nucleases in the extracellular environment.
   - Encapsulation methods, such as lipid nanoparticles, are critical to address this issue.

2. **Transfection Efficiency:**

   - Ensuring sufficient DNA uptake by host cells remains a key challenge.

3. **Regulatory Hurdles:**

   - New delivery technologies require extensive safety and efficacy testing.

4. **Scalability:**

   - Certain delivery methods, such as gene guns, are not easily scalable for global vaccine programs.

Future Directions

1. **Smart Delivery Systems:**

   - Integration of biosensors with DNA delivery systems to monitor immune responses in real-time.

2. **Combination Platforms**:

   ○ Co-delivery of DNA vaccines with adjuvants or additional immunomodulators for enhanced efficacy.

3. **Global Accessibility**:

   ○ Developing cost-effective and scalable delivery methods, such as microneedle patches, for resource-limited settings.

4. **Personalized Vaccines**:

   ○ DNA vaccines tailored to individual genetic or immune profiles for precision medicine.

7.1.2 Applications in Human and Veterinary Medicine

DNA vaccines have emerged as a versatile platform for combating infectious diseases, cancers, and genetic disorders in both humans and animals. Their ability to generate strong, targeted immune responses through simple genetic mechanisms has positioned DNA vaccines as a transformative technology in **human and veterinary medicine**. This section explores the diverse applications of DNA vaccines, highlighting their efficacy, advantages, and practical impact across medical and veterinary fields.

Applications in Human Medicine

1. Infectious Diseases

DNA vaccines are particularly suited for combating infectious diseases due to their ability to generate **both humoral and cellular immunity**.

Examples:

- **COVID-19**: DNA vaccines such as **ZyCoV-D**, developed for SARS-CoV-2, have shown efficacy in triggering immune responses with minimal side effects.
- **HIV**: DNA vaccines encoding HIV antigens are in clinical trials, aiming to overcome the challenges of antigenic variability in HIV strains.
- **Zika Virus**: DNA vaccines have been developed to deliver Zika virus envelope proteins, showing promise in preclinical studies.

Advantages:

- Rapid development timelines make DNA vaccines highly effective in responding to outbreaks and pandemics.
- Cost-effective production compared to traditional protein-based vaccines.

2. Cancer Immunotherapy

DNA vaccines are being explored as part of immunotherapy for various cancers, aiming to stimulate the immune system to recognize and destroy tumor cells.

Examples:

- **HPV-Associated Cancers**: DNA vaccines targeting the **E6 and E7 oncogenes** of HPV are in development for preventing cervical cancer.
- **Melanoma**: DNA vaccines encoding tumor-associated antigens like **gp100** and **MART-1** are under investigation for therapeutic use in melanoma patients.
- **Prostate Cancer**: DNA vaccines delivering **prostate-specific antigen (PSA)** aim to enhance anti-tumor immunity.

Advantages:

- Specific targeting of tumor antigens reduces the risk of off-target effects.
- Combination with immune checkpoint inhibitors amplifies therapeutic efficacy.

3. Genetic Disorders

DNA vaccines can also deliver genes encoding functional proteins to address deficiencies caused by genetic disorders.

Examples:

- **Cystic Fibrosis**: Research is ongoing to develop DNA therapies that deliver functional CFTR genes to patients.
- **Hemophilia**: DNA-based delivery of clotting factors is being studied as a potential cure for hemophilia A and B.

4. Emerging Diseases and Personalized Vaccination

DNA vaccines are well-suited for rapid development against **emerging infectious diseases**, such as **Ebola** and **Marburg virus**, and for creating **personalized vaccines** tailored to an individual's genetic or immunological profile.

Applications in Veterinary Medicine

DNA vaccines have gained significant traction in veterinary medicine, offering solutions for infectious diseases, zoonotic threats, and productivity challenges in livestock and companion animals.

1. Prevention of Infectious Diseases in Livestock

Livestock animals are often affected by infectious diseases that reduce productivity and cause economic losses. DNA vaccines provide effective prophylactic measures.

Examples:

- **Foot-and-Mouth Disease (FMD)**: DNA vaccines encoding viral antigens protect cattle and swine from this highly contagious disease.
- **Porcine Reproductive and Respiratory Syndrome (PRRS)**: DNA vaccines are under development to address this economically devastating disease in pigs.

Advantages:

- Stability at ambient temperatures simplifies storage and transportation in rural settings.
- Enhanced immune responses reduce the need for booster doses.

2. Zoonotic Disease Prevention

Zoonotic diseases, which transmit between animals and humans, represent a critical area for DNA vaccine application.

Examples:

- **Rabies**: DNA vaccines encoding rabies glycoproteins have shown efficacy in protecting dogs, a key vector for human rabies infections.
- **Avian Influenza**: DNA vaccines are being explored for poultry, aiming to reduce outbreaks that threaten both animal and human health.

Advantages:

- Reduces the risk of zoonotic transmission to humans.
- Enables large-scale immunization campaigns in animal populations.

3. Companion Animal Health

DNA vaccines are also used to protect companion animals, such as dogs and cats, from infectious diseases and cancers.

Examples:

- **Canine Melanoma**: The first FDA-approved DNA vaccine for veterinary use targets **tyrosinase**, an antigen associated with melanoma in dogs.
- **Feline Leukemia Virus (FeLV)**: DNA vaccines aim to provide immunity against this life-threatening virus in cats.

Advantages:

- Minimally invasive and well-tolerated in pets.
- Cost-effective for widespread veterinary use.

4. Aquaculture and Wildlife Conservation

DNA vaccines are increasingly used to protect aquatic species and wildlife populations.

Examples:

- **Infectious Hematopoietic Necrosis Virus (IHNV)**: DNA vaccines for IHNV protect salmon and trout, reducing mortality in aquaculture.
- **Brucellosis**: DNA vaccines are being tested in bison and elk to control brucellosis outbreaks in wildlife reserves.

Advantages:

- Improves productivity in aquaculture by reducing disease outbreaks.
- Contributes to wildlife conservation by preventing epidemics in endangered species.

Advantages of DNA Vaccines in Human and Veterinary Medicine

1. **Rapid Development:**

- ◦ DNA vaccines can be designed and produced quickly, critical for responding to outbreaks and pandemics.

2. **Ease of Production**:

   - ◦ Scalable and cost-effective manufacturing processes benefit both human and veterinary applications.

3. **Stability**:

   - ◦ DNA vaccines exhibit excellent stability under ambient conditions, simplifying storage and transportation.

4. **Safety**:

   - ◦ Lack of live components eliminates risks associated with traditional live-attenuated or inactivated vaccines.

5. **Flexibility**:

   - ◦ Applicable across a broad spectrum of diseases, from infectious pathogens to cancers and genetic disorders.

Challenges and Future Directions

Despite their promise, DNA vaccines face certain challenges in human and veterinary medicine:

1. **Transfection Efficiency**:

   - ◦ Achieving sufficient delivery of DNA into host cells remains a hurdle. Advanced delivery systems, such as **electroporation** and **lipid nanoparticles**, are under development to address this issue.

2. **Regulatory Approval**:

   - ◦ The novelty of DNA vaccines demands extensive safety and efficacy evaluations, delaying market entry.

3. **Public Perception**:

   ○ Educating the public about the safety and benefits of DNA vaccines is essential for acceptance.

4. **Scalability for Wildlife Applications**:

   ○ Delivering DNA vaccines to large or free-ranging wildlife populations poses logistical challenges.

Future Directions:

- Advancing delivery technologies, such as **microneedles** and **nanoparticles**, to improve transfection and immune activation.
- Expanding applications to include gene therapy and personalized vaccination in humans.
- Integrating DNA vaccines into **One Health** frameworks to address zoonotic diseases at the human-animal interface.

7.2 mRNA Vaccines
7.2.1 Delivery Platforms: Lipid Nanoparticles and Beyond
mRNA vaccines have revolutionized immunization by enabling the rapid development and scalable production of vaccines targeting infectious diseases, cancers, and even autoimmune disorders. Unlike traditional vaccines, mRNA vaccines rely on synthetic messenger RNA molecules that encode antigens. These antigens, when expressed in host cells, elicit strong immune responses. However, the intrinsic instability of mRNA and its susceptibility to enzymatic degradation necessitate advanced delivery platforms to ensure efficient cellular uptake, protection, and antigen expression.

Delivery platforms, particularly **lipid nanoparticles (LNPs)**, are at the heart of mRNA vaccine success. This section explores LNPs as the gold standard in mRNA delivery and examines emerging platforms designed to enhance mRNA stability, delivery efficiency, and safety.

1. Lipid Nanoparticles (LNPs): The Gold Standard
LNPs are currently the most widely used platform for mRNA delivery, as demonstrated by the success of mRNA-based COVID-19 vaccines, such as **Pfizer-BioNTech (BNT162b2)** and **Moderna (mRNA-1273)**. These

nanocarriers protect mRNA from enzymatic degradation and facilitate cellular uptake via endocytosis.

Structure of Lipid Nanoparticles

LNPs consist of the following components:

1. **Ionizable Lipids**:

   - Essential for encapsulating the negatively charged mRNA through electrostatic interactions.
   - Facilitate endosomal escape by becoming positively charged in acidic environments, disrupting endosomal membranes.

2. **Phospholipids**:

   - Provide structural integrity to the LNPs and mimic the natural composition of cellular membranes.

3. **Cholesterol**:

   - Enhances membrane fluidity and stability, aiding in mRNA encapsulation and delivery.

4. **Polyethylene Glycol (PEG) Lipids**:

   - Improve nanoparticle stability and prolong circulation time by reducing immune recognition.

Mechanism of Action

1. **Encapsulation and Protection**:

   - LNPs encapsulate mRNA, shielding it from extracellular RNases and ensuring delivery to the target cells.

2. **Cellular Uptake**:

   - LNPs enter cells via endocytosis, forming endosomes.

3. **Endosomal Escape**:

- Ionizable lipids facilitate the disruption of endosomal membranes, releasing mRNA into the cytoplasm.

4. **Protein Synthesis and Immune Activation**:

- The released mRNA is translated into the antigen protein, which is processed and presented by antigen-presenting cells (APCs), activating both humoral and cellular immunity.

Advantages of LNPs

- High **encapsulation efficiency**, ensuring minimal mRNA wastage.
- Compatibility with scalable manufacturing processes.
- Reduced immunogenicity due to biocompatible lipid components.
- Proven success in large-scale vaccine distribution (e.g., COVID-19 vaccines).

Challenges with LNPs

- Potential for **reactogenicity**, causing transient inflammation or allergic reactions.
- Stability issues requiring **cold-chain storage**, as seen with current mRNA vaccines requiring temperatures of -20°C or lower.
- Limited targeting to specific cell types or tissues, necessitating further optimization.

2. Emerging Delivery Platforms

While LNPs remain the cornerstone of mRNA delivery, researchers are exploring alternative and complementary platforms to overcome their limitations and improve targeted delivery, stability, and safety.

2.1 Polymeric Nanoparticles

Polymeric nanoparticles are emerging as a promising alternative to LNPs due to their versatility and stability.

Materials Used:

- **Polylactic-co-glycolic acid (PLGA)**

- **Polyethyleneimine (PEI)**
- **Chitosan**

Advantages:

- High **biodegradability** and biocompatibility.
- Ability to sustain mRNA release, enabling prolonged antigen expression.
- Reduced dependence on cold-chain logistics compared to LNPs.

Challenges:

- Lower transfection efficiency compared to LNPs.
- Potential toxicity with certain polymers like PEI at high concentrations.

2.2 Lipid-Polymer Hybrid Nanoparticles (LPHNs)

LPHNs combine the advantages of lipids and polymers to enhance mRNA delivery efficiency.

Mechanism:

- The polymer core encapsulates mRNA for stability, while the lipid outer layer ensures efficient cellular uptake and endosomal escape.

Advantages:

- Improved stability over standalone lipid or polymer systems.
- Higher encapsulation efficiency and tunable properties.

Applications:

- Investigated for cancer immunotherapy and rare genetic disorders.

2.3 Inorganic Nanoparticles

Nanoparticles based on materials like **gold**, **silica**, and **calcium phosphate** are gaining traction for mRNA delivery.

Advantages:

- High stability under environmental stress.
- Tailored surface modifications allow for tissue-specific targeting.

Challenges:

- Limited biodegradability may pose safety concerns.
- Scalability remains an issue for large-scale production.

2.4 Cell-Derived Vesicles (Exosomes)

Exosomes, naturally occurring nanovesicles secreted by cells, are being investigated as delivery vehicles for mRNA.

Advantages:

- Excellent biocompatibility and low immunogenicity.
- Natural ability to transfer RNA between cells.

Challenges:

- Complex isolation and purification processes.
- Limited production capacity for large-scale applications.

2.5 Microneedles

Microneedle patches are being explored for transdermal delivery of mRNA vaccines. These minimally invasive devices bypass traditional injection methods, directly targeting skin-resident immune cells.

Advantages:

- Painless and easy to administer, enhancing patient compliance.
- Room-temperature stability, reducing cold-chain dependencies.

Challenges:

- Ensuring consistent mRNA release across different skin types.

Future Directions in mRNA Vaccine Delivery

1. **Targeted Delivery**:

   - Development of tissue-specific ligands to enhance delivery to specific cell types, such as dendritic cells or tumor cells.

2. **Thermostable Platforms**:

   - Creating mRNA formulations that remain stable at room temperature or higher, eliminating cold-chain requirements.

3. **Self-Amplifying mRNA (saRNA)**:

   - Exploring mRNA molecules that can amplify themselves post-delivery, reducing the dose required for effective immunization.

4. **Combination Therapies**:

   - Using mRNA delivery platforms in combination with adjuvants or other therapeutics for enhanced efficacy.

5. **Personalized Vaccines**:

   - Customizing delivery platforms for patient-specific mRNA vaccines in cancer immunotherapy and genetic disease treatment.

7.2.2 Case Studies: COVID-19 Vaccines

The COVID-19 pandemic marked a turning point in vaccine development, with **mRNA vaccines** demonstrating unprecedented efficacy, scalability, and speed of deployment. The two leading mRNA COVID-19 vaccines, **Pfizer-BioNTech's BNT162b2** and **Moderna's mRNA-1273**, became global examples of how mRNA technology could revolutionize immunization strategies. This section delves into the design, efficacy, and implementation of these vaccines as case studies, highlighting their contributions to combating the pandemic.

Case Study 1: Pfizer-BioNTech (BNT162b2)

1. Vaccine Overview

- **Type**: mRNA-based vaccine encoding the spike (S) protein of SARS-CoV-2.
- **Delivery Platform**: Encapsulated in lipid nanoparticles (LNPs) for stability and efficient cellular delivery.
- **Dosage**: Two doses administered 21 days apart.
- **Storage Requirements**: Requires ultra-cold storage at -70°C.

2. Mechanism of Action

1. **mRNA Delivery**: LNPs deliver the mRNA encoding the spike protein to host cells.
2. **Protein Translation**: Host ribosomes translate the mRNA into the spike protein.
3. **Immune Activation**:

   - The spike protein is processed and presented on **MHC molecules**, activating T cells and B cells.
   - B cells produce neutralizing antibodies against SARS-CoV-2.

4. **Memory Formation**: Long-lasting immunity is established through memory T and B cells.

3. Clinical Trials and Efficacy

- **Phase III Trials**:

   - Conducted with over 43,000 participants.
   - Demonstrated **95% efficacy** in preventing symptomatic COVID-19 infection.

- **Effectiveness Against Variants**:

   - Showed high efficacy against the Alpha and Delta variants, with slightly reduced effectiveness against Omicron.

4. Challenges and Solutions

- **Storage and Distribution**:

   - The need for ultra-cold storage posed logistical challenges, particularly in low-resource settings.
   - Solution: Development of new formulations allowing for short-term storage at standard freezer temperatures (-20°C).

- **Side Effects**:

- ○ Reported side effects included injection-site pain, fatigue, and rare cases of myocarditis, particularly in young males.
- ○ Enhanced monitoring systems addressed these safety concerns.

5. Global Impact

- Over **2 billion doses** distributed globally within the first year of approval.
- Played a critical role in reducing COVID-19 hospitalizations and mortality rates in high-coverage regions.

Case Study 2: Moderna (mRNA-1273)
1. Vaccine Overview

- **Type**: mRNA-based vaccine encoding the spike (S) protein of SARS-CoV-2.
- **Delivery Platform**: Lipid nanoparticle (LNP) encapsulation.
- **Dosage**: Two doses administered 28 days apart.
- **Storage Requirements**: Requires standard freezer storage at -20°C, making it more accessible than Pfizer-BioNTech's vaccine.

2. Mechanism of Action
Similar to Pfizer-BioNTech, Moderna's vaccine relies on LNPs to deliver spike protein-encoding mRNA to host cells. Once inside the cytoplasm, the mRNA is translated, and the spike protein triggers a robust immune response involving both T cells and B cells.

3. Clinical Trials and Efficacy

- **Phase III Trials**:

  - ○ Conducted with over 30,000 participants.
  - ○ Demonstrated **94.1% efficacy** in preventing symptomatic COVID-19 infection.

- **Effectiveness Against Variants**:

  - ○ Proven effective against Alpha and Delta variants, with reduced but significant protection against Omicron.

4. Challenges and Solutions

- **Storage**:

  - Moderna's vaccine had a competitive advantage with more flexible storage requirements (-20°C compared to -70°C for Pfizer).
  - This flexibility facilitated distribution in regions with limited ultra-cold storage infrastructure.

- **Side Effects**:

  - Common side effects included fatigue, fever, and headache, similar to Pfizer's vaccine.
  - Rare cases of myocarditis were also reported, requiring targeted safety communication.

5. Global Impact

- Over **1 billion doses** administered globally within the first year of approval.
- Expanded accessibility in low- and middle-income countries through partnerships with COVAX.

Lessons Learned from mRNA COVID-19 Vaccines
1. Rapid Development Timeline

- mRNA vaccines demonstrated that effective vaccines could be developed and scaled within a year, a feat previously considered impossible.
- Lessons from these efforts have created a blueprint for tackling future pandemics.

2. Importance of Delivery Platforms

- Lipid nanoparticles proved to be a robust delivery platform, but their limitations (e.g., cold-chain storage) highlight the need for further innovation in mRNA delivery technologies.

3. Scalability and Accessibility

- The global distribution of mRNA vaccines revealed disparities in vaccine access, emphasizing the need for improved production and distribution strategies in low- and middle-income countries.

Future Directions in mRNA Vaccine Development

1. **Thermostable mRNA Formulations**:

   - Developing vaccines that remain stable at room temperature to address cold-chain challenges.

2. **Variant-Specific Boosters**:

   - Tailoring mRNA sequences to address emerging variants more effectively.

3. **Next-Generation Delivery Platforms**:

   - Exploring alternatives to lipid nanoparticles, such as polymeric nanoparticles and microneedles, to enhance stability and reduce side effects.

4. **Expansion to Other Diseases**:

   - Applying mRNA technology to develop vaccines for diseases like malaria, tuberculosis, and HIV.

5. **Combination Vaccines**:

   - Creating multivalent mRNA vaccines capable of protecting against multiple pathogens simultaneously.

7.3 Future Innovations
7.3.1 Self-Amplifying RNA Platforms
Self-amplifying RNA (saRNA) platforms represent a significant advancement in RNA-based therapeutics and vaccines. Unlike conventional mRNA, saRNA has the intrinsic ability to replicate within host cells, amplifying antigen production. This property allows for reduced initial

RNA doses while maintaining or enhancing immunogenicity, offering transformative potential in vaccine development, therapeutic applications, and cost-effective healthcare delivery.

What is Self-Amplifying RNA (saRNA)?

saRNA is derived from **alphavirus replicons**, engineered to retain the self-replicating machinery of the virus while replacing viral structural genes with sequences encoding the desired antigen or therapeutic protein.

Structure of saRNA

1. **Non-Structural Proteins (nsPs)**:

   - Encode the replicase machinery that drives RNA replication.
   - Includes RNA-dependent RNA polymerase (RdRP) and accessory proteins.

2. **Antigen-Encoding Sequence**:

   - Encodes the target protein (e.g., a viral spike protein for vaccines).

3. **Regulatory Elements**:

   - Contain untranslated regions (UTRs) that enhance replication and translation efficiency.

Mechanism of Action
1. Cellular Uptake and Translation

- Like conventional mRNA, saRNA is delivered into host cells using a delivery platform such as **lipid nanoparticles (LNPs)**.
- The saRNA is translated into non-structural proteins (replicase) using host ribosomes.

2. RNA Amplification

- The replicase machinery amplifies the saRNA, generating thousands of copies of the antigen-encoding RNA.

3. Antigen Production

- The amplified RNA is translated into the antigen, significantly increasing its expression.

4. Immune Response

- The antigen is presented via **MHC Class I and II pathways**, activating both cellular and humoral immune responses.

Advantages of Self-Amplifying RNA Platforms

1. **Reduced Doses**:

   - saRNA requires significantly lower initial doses compared to conventional mRNA.
   - Example: saRNA doses can be as low as **1 µg**, compared to **30 µg** for traditional mRNA vaccines like Pfizer-BioNTech's COVID-19 vaccine.

2. **Cost-Effectiveness**:

   - Lower RNA doses reduce production costs, making saRNA vaccines more affordable and scalable for global distribution.

3. **Enhanced Immunogenicity**:

   - Higher antigen expression due to RNA amplification leads to stronger and longer-lasting immune responses.

4. **Rapid Development**:

   - saRNA can be rapidly designed and manufactured, similar to mRNA platforms, enabling quick responses to emerging pathogens.

5. **Versatility**:

   - saRNA platforms can be adapted for various diseases, including infectious diseases, cancer, and genetic disorders.

Applications of saRNA Platforms

1. Infectious Diseases

- saRNA vaccines are being explored for a wide range of infectious diseases, leveraging their ability to generate robust immune responses.
- **Example**: Preclinical trials for saRNA-based vaccines targeting **Zika virus** and **influenza** have shown promising results, with strong immunogenicity at low doses.

2. Pandemic Preparedness

- saRNA platforms are ideal for rapid vaccine development during pandemics.
- **Example**: During the COVID-19 pandemic, saRNA-based vaccine candidates were developed, showing efficacy in early-phase trials with lower doses and simplified manufacturing.

3. Cancer Immunotherapy

- saRNA is being investigated for cancer vaccines that encode tumor-associated antigens.
- **Example**: Vaccines targeting neoantigens in melanoma have demonstrated enhanced T-cell activation in preclinical studies.

4. Therapeutic Applications

- Beyond vaccines, saRNA is being studied for protein replacement therapies and monoclonal antibody production in vivo.
- **Example**: saRNA encoding therapeutic proteins like **erythropoietin** is under investigation for anemia treatment.

Challenges in saRNA Platforms
1. Delivery Efficiency

- saRNA molecules are larger than conventional mRNA, posing challenges for delivery platforms like lipid nanoparticles.
- **Solution**: Optimizing LNP formulations to improve encapsulation and cellular uptake of saRNA.

2. Immunogenicity

- The replicase machinery can trigger innate immune responses, potentially reducing antigen expression.
- **Solution**: Incorporating modifications to saRNA, such as pseudouridine substitution, to reduce innate immune activation.

3. Stability

- saRNA is susceptible to degradation by nucleases, similar to conventional mRNA.
- **Solution**: Using advanced stabilization techniques, including protective coatings and optimized storage conditions.

4. Scalability

- While lower doses reduce production costs, scaling up saRNA manufacturing remains a technical challenge.

Innovations Enhancing saRNA Platforms

1. **Hybrid Nanoparticles**:

   - Combining lipids and polymers for enhanced saRNA stability and delivery efficiency.

2. **Targeted Delivery Systems**:

   - Developing tissue-specific delivery platforms, such as ligand-modified nanoparticles, to enhance saRNA targeting.

3. **Self-Amplifying Circular RNA (sa-circRNA)**:

   - Exploring circular RNA with self-replicating properties to further improve stability and expression.

4. **Thermostable Formulations**:

- Developing saRNA formulations stable at room temperature to eliminate cold-chain requirements.

Future Directions

1. **saRNA in Multivalent Vaccines**:

   - Using saRNA platforms to deliver multiple antigens simultaneously, enabling broad-spectrum protection against infectious diseases.

2. **Personalized Medicine**:

   - Customizing saRNA vaccines to target patient-specific tumor neoantigens for cancer immunotherapy.

3. **Global Health Applications**:

   - Developing saRNA vaccines for neglected tropical diseases and deploying them in resource-limited settings.

4. **Integrated Therapeutics**:

   - Combining saRNA vaccines with immune checkpoint inhibitors or adjuvants to enhance therapeutic outcomes.

Case Study: saRNA Vaccine for Influenza
Objective:
Develop a low-dose, scalable vaccine for seasonal and pandemic influenza using saRNA technology.
Approach:

- saRNA encoding hemagglutinin (HA) antigen was encapsulated in lipid nanoparticles and tested in preclinical models.

Findings:

- The vaccine elicited a robust immune response with doses as low as **0.1 μg**, compared to traditional mRNA vaccines requiring doses of 10–30 μg.

- Neutralizing antibody levels were comparable to those observed with high-dose conventional vaccines.

Impact:

- saRNA influenza vaccines demonstrated the potential for rapid scalability and cost reduction, critical for pandemic preparedness.

7.3.2 Nucleic Acid Stabilization Techniques

Nucleic acid-based vaccines and therapeutics, including **mRNA, self-amplifying RNA (saRNA)**, and **DNA**, are inherently unstable due to their susceptibility to **enzymatic degradation, hydrolysis**, and **oxidation**. Their efficient delivery and therapeutic efficacy depend heavily on stabilization techniques that protect these fragile molecules during storage, transportation, and administration. This section explores state-of-the-art nucleic acid stabilization strategies, ensuring their viability and functionality in clinical and real-world settings.

Challenges in Nucleic Acid Stability

1. **Enzymatic Degradation:**

   - RNA is particularly vulnerable to RNases, which are ubiquitous in biological and environmental settings.

2. **Thermal Instability:**

   - Nucleic acids degrade rapidly at ambient temperatures, necessitating cold-chain storage.

3. **Hydrolysis:**

   - The phosphodiester bonds in RNA are prone to hydrolysis, especially under alkaline or humid conditions.

4. **Oxidative Stress:**

   - Oxidative damage alters nucleic acid integrity, reducing its biological activity.

5. **Shear Stress:**

   ○ Mechanical forces during manufacturing or delivery can fragment nucleic acids, impairing functionality.

Key Nucleic Acid Stabilization Techniques
1. Chemical Modifications
Chemical modifications enhance the stability of nucleic acids by improving resistance to enzymatic degradation and increasing structural integrity.
a. Modified Nucleosides:

- Incorporation of modified nucleosides, such as **pseudouridine** and **5-methylcytidine**, reduces recognition by RNases and dampens innate immune responses.

b. Backbone Modifications:

- Altering the phosphate backbone with modifications like **phosphorothioates** improves resistance to hydrolysis.

c. Capping Structures:

- For mRNA, incorporating a **5' cap analogue** (e.g., anti-reverse cap analogues, ARCA) enhances stability and translation efficiency.

2. Encapsulation in Nanoparticles
Encapsulation in delivery vehicles protects nucleic acids from enzymatic degradation and environmental stress while enhancing cellular uptake.
a. Lipid Nanoparticles (LNPs):

- LNPs are the gold standard for encapsulating mRNA and saRNA, shielding them from RNases and ensuring efficient delivery to target cells.

b. Polymeric Nanoparticles:

- Biodegradable polymers like **PLGA** and **chitosan** encapsulate nucleic acids, providing sustained release and improved stability.

c. Hybrid Nanoparticles:

- Combining lipids and polymers enhances nucleic acid protection and delivery efficiency.

3. Lyophilization (Freeze-Drying)

Lyophilization transforms nucleic acids into a dry, powdery form, significantly improving their shelf life and thermal stability.

Mechanism:

- Water is removed under vacuum conditions, reducing the potential for hydrolysis.
- Cryoprotectants like **trehalose** and **sucrose** are added to stabilize nucleic acid structures during freezing and drying.

Applications:

- Used extensively for mRNA-based vaccines to reduce reliance on cold-chain logistics.

4. Additives and Stabilizers

Incorporating stabilizing agents protects nucleic acids during formulation, storage, and administration.

a. Cryoprotectants:

- Substances like **mannitol, trehalose**, and **glycerol** protect nucleic acids from thermal and mechanical stress during freeze-thaw cycles.

b. Antioxidants:

- Agents like **ascorbic acid** and **glutathione** prevent oxidative damage.

c. RNase Inhibitors:

- Blocking RNase activity ensures the integrity of RNA during handling and delivery.

5. Structural Modifications

Altering the physical structure of nucleic acids can enhance their stability.

a. Circular RNA (circRNA):

- Unlike linear RNA, circRNA lacks free ends, making it resistant to exonuclease degradation.
- CircRNA platforms are being explored for stable and long-lasting mRNA therapeutics.

b. Double-Stranded RNA (dsRNA):

- Certain therapeutic RNA molecules are designed as double-stranded structures, which are more resistant to enzymatic degradation.

6. Advanced Packaging Technologies

Sophisticated packaging solutions minimize exposure to environmental stressors, enhancing the stability of nucleic acids.

a. Blister Packaging:

- Protects lyophilized nucleic acids from moisture and light.

b. Vacuum-Sealed Containers:

- Removes oxygen to prevent oxidative damage.

c. Multi-Layer Films:

- Incorporates layers of desiccants to maintain a dry and stable microenvironment.

7. Room-Temperature Formulations

Developing nucleic acid formulations stable at ambient temperatures addresses logistical challenges in global distribution.

a. Glassy State Stabilization:

- Encapsulating nucleic acids in a glassy matrix using stabilizers like trehalose preserves their structure at room temperature.

b. Ionic Liquids:

- Using ionic liquids as solvents protects nucleic acids from thermal and enzymatic degradation.

Case Studies in Nucleic Acid Stabilization
1. Lyophilized mRNA COVID-19 Vaccines
Background:
mRNA vaccines like Pfizer-BioNTech and Moderna initially required ultra-cold storage (-70°C and -20°C, respectively). Researchers explored lyophilization to improve stability.
Outcome:

- Lyophilized formulations showed stability at **4°C for six months**, significantly reducing cold-chain dependencies.

2. Circular RNA for Cancer Therapy
Background:
CircRNA was used to encode tumor-associated antigens, offering higher stability and prolonged antigen expression compared to linear mRNA.
Outcome:

- Enhanced immune responses were observed, with prolonged therapeutic effects in preclinical models.

3. Lipid-Polymer Hybrid Nanoparticles for Zika Virus Vaccines
Background:
Hybrid nanoparticles were developed to stabilize mRNA encoding Zika virus antigens.
Outcome:

- The formulation maintained efficacy at room temperature for up to four weeks, simplifying vaccine distribution.

Future Directions

1. **Integrated Stabilization Platforms**:

   - Combining multiple techniques, such as chemical modifications and advanced packaging, to achieve maximal stability.

2. **Thermostable Vaccines**:

   - Development of formulations stable at high temperatures (>40°C) for deployment in tropical and resource-limited regions.

3. **Real-Time Monitoring Systems**:

   - Incorporating biosensors into packaging to detect degradation markers during storage.

4. **Smart Polymers**:

   - Designing polymers that adapt to environmental conditions to protect nucleic acids dynamically.

Feature	Pfizer-BioNTech (BNT162b2)	Moderna (mRNA-1273)
Efficacy	95%	94.1%
Dosage Interval	21 days	28 days
Storage Requirements	-70°C	-20°C
Variants	Effective against Alpha, Delta	Effective against Alpha, Delta
Side Effects	Mild to moderate; rare myocarditis	Similar; rare myocarditis
Global Reach	>2 billion doses	>1 billion doses

Comparative Analysis of Pfizer-BioNTech and Moderna Vaccines

EIGHT

STABILITY AND FORMULATION STRATEGIES

8.1 Vaccine Stability Challenges

8.1.1 Sensitivity to Temperature and Freezing

Vaccine stability is a critical determinant of their efficacy, safety, and global accessibility. Temperature fluctuations during storage and transportation, particularly exposure to extreme heat or freezing, can compromise vaccine integrity. These stability challenges are especially pronounced for vaccines containing biological molecules such as **proteins**, **lipids**, and **nucleic acids**, which are inherently sensitive to environmental conditions. Understanding and addressing the sensitivity of vaccines to temperature and freezing is vital for effective immunization programs worldwide.

Why Temperature and Freezing Impact Vaccine Stability

Vaccines are composed of **antigens**, **stabilizers**, **adjuvants**, and other excipients, each of which contributes to their function. However, these components are also susceptible to physical and chemical changes under non-optimal conditions.

1. Proteins and Nucleic Acids

- **Denaturation**: Heat or freezing can unfold proteins, disrupting their structure and reducing antigenicity.

- **Aggregation**: Freezing induces protein aggregation, which can lead to reduced immunogenicity and safety concerns.
- **Hydrolysis**: Temperature variations accelerate the breakdown of nucleic acids, particularly in mRNA and DNA vaccines.

2. Lipid-Based Formulations

- **Phase Separation**: Lipid nanoparticles (LNPs) used in mRNA vaccines, such as those for COVID-19, can destabilize under freezing or thawing, compromising their ability to deliver antigens.
- **Oxidation**: Elevated temperatures increase the oxidation of lipid components, reducing their efficacy.

3. Adjuvants

- **Instability of Aluminum Salts**: Common adjuvants like aluminum hydroxide lose their uniformity when frozen, reducing vaccine potency.

4. Freeze-Induced Crystallization

- **Excipients**: Sugars and salts used as stabilizers may crystallize during freezing, leading to vaccine instability.

Effects of Temperature and Freezing on Vaccines
1. Heat Sensitivity

- Exposure to high temperatures accelerates chemical reactions, leading to degradation of antigens and adjuvants.
- **Example**: Heat exposure reduced the potency of live attenuated vaccines, such as the **measles-mumps-rubella (MMR)** vaccine, by over **50%** within 24 hours at 37°C.

2. Freezing Sensitivity

- Freezing damages vaccines by disrupting the structure of biological molecules and excipients.
- **Example**: Studies showed that freezing of liquid vaccines containing aluminum adjuvants resulted in **flocculation** (clumping), rendering

them ineffective.

Case Studies: Temperature and Freezing Sensitivity
1. mRNA COVID-19 Vaccines

- **Pfizer-BioNTech's BNT162b2** requires storage at -70°C to maintain stability due to the fragility of lipid nanoparticles and mRNA. Deviation from these conditions compromises the vaccine's delivery efficiency.
- **Moderna's mRNA-1273** demonstrated greater thermal stability, allowing storage at -20°C. However, even short-term exposure to freezing at temperatures below -40°C disrupted the integrity of its lipid nanoparticle formulation.

2. Live Attenuated Vaccines

- Vaccines like **oral polio vaccine (OPV)** and **yellow fever vaccine** require constant refrigeration (2–8°C). A single freeze-thaw cycle can cause irreversible loss of potency.

Strategies to Overcome Temperature and Freezing Sensitivity
1. Formulation Approaches
a. Lyophilization (Freeze-Drying):

- Converts liquid vaccines into a dry powder, enhancing stability against temperature fluctuations.
- **Example**: Lyophilized rabies vaccines retain potency at room temperature for extended periods.

b. Addition of Cryoprotectants:

- Compounds like **trehalose** and **sucrose** protect proteins and lipids during freezing by forming a protective glassy matrix.

c. Thermostable Formulations:

- Advances in vaccine formulation have enabled the development of **thermostable vaccines** that remain effective at ambient or elevated temperatures.

- **Example**: Thermostable rotavirus vaccines are now being deployed in tropical regions with limited refrigeration infrastructure.

2. Packaging Innovations
a. Temperature-Controlled Containers:

- Use of insulated and temperature-monitored containers during transportation reduces the risk of exposure to extreme temperatures.

b. Multi-Dose Vials with Stabilizers:

- Adding stabilizing agents to multi-dose vials allows vaccines to remain stable after opening, even at room temperature.

3. Advanced Storage Technologies
a. Cold Chain Systems:

- Improved cold chain infrastructure, including solar-powered refrigeration units, ensures consistent temperature control in remote areas.

b. Room-Temperature Storage Innovations:

- Research is ongoing to develop vaccines that can be stored at ambient conditions for months.

4. Real-Time Monitoring Tools
a. Temperature Indicators:

- Incorporating time-temperature indicators (TTIs) on vaccine vials provides real-time feedback on exposure to adverse conditions.

b. Digital Tracking Systems:

- Use of IoT devices and blockchain technology enables precise tracking of temperature conditions during vaccine distribution.

Future Directions

1. **Thermostable RNA Platforms**:

   ◦ Research into room-temperature-stable mRNA vaccines will eliminate the need for ultra-cold storage, improving global accessibility.

2. **Freeze-Tolerant Formulations**:

   ◦ Development of freeze-resistant excipients and formulations will minimize damage caused by accidental freezing.

3. **Universal Vaccine Stabilizers**:

   ◦ Designing excipients capable of stabilizing a wide range of vaccine types (e.g., protein, RNA, and live attenuated) under varying conditions.

8.1.2 Long-Term Storage Issues

Long-term storage of vaccines is essential for maintaining their efficacy, safety, and availability over time. However, vaccines are inherently sensitive to environmental factors, making storage a critical component of global immunization programs. Inadequate long-term storage conditions can lead to **antigen degradation**, **loss of potency**, and **increased wastage**, ultimately compromising the effectiveness of vaccination campaigns. Understanding the challenges associated with long-term vaccine storage and the strategies to overcome them is vital for ensuring the global success of immunization efforts.

Challenges in Long-Term Storage
1. Degradation of Antigens

- **Protein-Based Vaccines**: Proteins can denature over time due to environmental stress, such as temperature fluctuations, leading to reduced immunogenicity.
- **mRNA Vaccines**: mRNA is highly unstable and prone to degradation by hydrolysis and enzymatic action, making long-term storage particularly challenging.
- **Live-Attenuated Vaccines**: The viability of live pathogens used in these vaccines diminishes over time, even under refrigerated conditions.

2. Dependency on Cold-Chain Systems

- Most vaccines require storage at **2–8°C**, while others, such as mRNA vaccines, need ultra-cold storage at **-20°C to -70°C.**
- Long-term storage in cold-chain systems is expensive, energy-intensive, and prone to failures, especially in low-resource settings.

3. Accumulation of Physical and Chemical Instabilities

- **Aggregation**: Protein antigens can aggregate during prolonged storage, affecting their efficacy.
- **Oxidation**: Lipids and proteins in vaccines may undergo oxidative degradation, reducing potency.
- **Hydrolysis**: Exposure to moisture during storage can degrade nucleic acids and other sensitive components.

4. Freeze-Thaw Cycles

- Repeated freezing and thawing, often occurring due to improper handling during storage, can cause irreparable damage to vaccine components, especially lipid nanoparticles and aluminum-based adjuvants.

5. Regulatory and Logistical Challenges

- Maintaining consistent storage conditions over long periods increases logistical complexity and regulatory burdens, particularly in global vaccine distribution.

Impact of Long-Term Storage Issues

1. **Reduced Vaccine Efficacy**:

   - Antigen degradation leads to weaker immune responses, requiring higher doses or boosters.

2. **Increased Wastage**:

- Ineffective storage results in the discard of large quantities of vaccines, increasing costs and delaying immunization programs.

3. **Limited Access in Remote Areas**:

  - Dependence on cold-chain systems hinders vaccine availability in regions with inadequate infrastructure.

Strategies to Address Long-Term Storage Issues
1. Stabilization Technologies

- **Lyophilization (Freeze-Drying)**:

  - Converts vaccines into a stable powder form that can be reconstituted with water.
  - **Example**: Lyophilized measles vaccines retain potency for years at ambient temperatures.

- **Cryoprotectants and Stabilizers**:

  - Compounds like **trehalose**, **mannitol**, and **sucrose** protect vaccines against temperature fluctuations and degradation during storage.

- **Thermostable Formulations**:

  - Development of thermostable vaccines that remain effective at ambient temperatures.
  - **Example**: Thermostable rotavirus vaccines have been successfully deployed in tropical climates.

2. Advanced Packaging Solutions

- **Hermetically Sealed Vials**:

  - Protect vaccines from moisture, oxygen, and contaminants during prolonged storage.

- **Vacuum-Sealed Containers**:

- Reduce oxygen exposure, preventing oxidative degradation.

- **Blister Packaging with Desiccants**:

  - Controls moisture levels to preserve vaccine integrity.

3. Novel Delivery Systems

- **Microneedle Patches**:

  - Microneedle patches eliminate the need for refrigeration by encapsulating vaccines in stable polymers or sugars.
  - These patches have demonstrated multi-year stability under ambient conditions in preclinical studies.

4. Improved Cold-Chain Technologies

- **Solar-Powered Refrigeration**:

  - Reduces dependence on traditional power sources, ensuring consistent refrigeration in remote areas.

- **Thermal Battery Systems**:

  - Provide long-term cooling without external power, addressing storage challenges in underserved regions.

5. Real-Time Monitoring and Quality Assurance

- **Temperature Indicators**:

  - Include time-temperature indicators (TTIs) on vaccine vials to track exposure to adverse storage conditions.

- **Digital Cold-Chain Monitoring**:

  - Use IoT-enabled devices to monitor storage conditions in real-time, ensuring prompt corrective actions.

Case Studies: Long-Term Storage Innovations
1. Lyophilized Rabies Vaccines

- **Problem**: Traditional rabies vaccines require cold-chain storage, limiting access in remote areas.
- **Solution**: Lyophilized formulations have enabled stable storage at ambient temperatures for up to two years.

2. Thermostable COVID-19 mRNA Vaccines

- **Problem**: Current mRNA vaccines require ultra-cold storage (-70°C), complicating distribution in low-resource settings.
- **Solution**: Research into thermostable mRNA formulations has shown promise, with experimental vaccines remaining effective at 4°C for several months.

3. Microneedle Patches for Influenza Vaccines

- **Problem**: Influenza vaccines require refrigeration, increasing logistical complexity during global flu campaigns.
- **Solution**: Microneedle patches have demonstrated multi-year stability under ambient conditions, simplifying storage and transportation.

Future Directions

1. **Universal Vaccine Stabilizers**:

   - Development of excipients capable of stabilizing all types of vaccines, including proteins, lipids, and nucleic acids, under a wide range of conditions.

2. **Room-Temperature mRNA Vaccines**:

   - Creating mRNA formulations with enhanced chemical stability to eliminate cold-chain requirements.

3. **Integrated Smart Packaging**:

- Incorporating sensors into packaging to provide real-time data on vaccine stability and environmental exposure.

4. **Advanced Delivery Technologies**:

- Exploring microneedles, hydrogels, and other delivery platforms to reduce storage dependencies.

5. **Global Cold-Chain Modernization**:

- Expanding cold-chain infrastructure in underserved regions with sustainable and cost-effective technologies.

8.2 Stabilization Techniques

8.2.1 Lyophilization and Freeze-Drying

Lyophilization, commonly referred to as **freeze-drying**, is one of the most effective stabilization techniques for preserving vaccines and other biologics. This process involves removing water from the vaccine formulation under low-temperature and vacuum conditions, converting it into a dry, powder-like form. By eliminating moisture, lyophilization significantly enhances the stability and shelf life of vaccines, making them less susceptible to environmental factors like temperature fluctuations and microbial contamination.

Process of Lyophilization

Lyophilization is a multi-step process that involves three critical phases:

1. Freezing

- The liquid vaccine formulation is cooled to temperatures below its freezing point, causing water to solidify into ice crystals.
- This step is crucial for preserving the structural integrity of sensitive biological components, such as proteins and nucleic acids.

2. Primary Drying (Sublimation)

- The frozen material is subjected to a vacuum, reducing atmospheric pressure.
- Heat is applied to convert ice directly into vapor (sublimation) without passing through the liquid phase, preventing structural damage to the

vaccine.

3. Secondary Drying (Desorption)

- Residual water bound to the vaccine components is removed by gradually increasing the temperature.
- This phase reduces the moisture content to less than **1%**, ensuring long-term stability.

Advantages of Lyophilization

1. **Enhanced Stability**:

   - Lyophilized vaccines are more stable at ambient and elevated temperatures, reducing the reliance on cold-chain systems.
   - Example: Lyophilized **measles** and **rabies** vaccines retain efficacy for years when stored under proper conditions.

2. **Prolonged Shelf Life**:

   - Removal of water minimizes hydrolysis and microbial growth, extending vaccine shelf life.

3. **Ease of Transportation and Storage**:

   - Lyophilized vaccines are lightweight and compact, simplifying logistics and reducing costs.

4. **Reconstitution for Use**:

   - Vaccines can be easily rehydrated with sterile water or saline at the point of use, preserving efficacy.

Applications in Vaccines
1. Protein-Based Vaccines

- Lyophilization prevents protein denaturation and aggregation, maintaining their antigenicity.

- Example: Lyophilized **tetanus toxoid vaccines** exhibit high stability under diverse environmental conditions.

2. Live-Attenuated Vaccines

- These vaccines, such as those for **yellow fever** and **polio**, benefit significantly from lyophilization, which preserves the viability of attenuated pathogens.

3. mRNA and DNA Vaccines

- Lyophilization is being explored to stabilize sensitive nucleic acids, reducing the need for ultra-cold storage.
- Example: Experimental **mRNA COVID-19 vaccines** have demonstrated stability at 4°C for months after lyophilization.

Formulation Considerations

The success of lyophilization depends on the careful formulation of the vaccine, which often includes stabilizing agents to protect biological components during the drying process.

1. **Cryoprotectants**:

   - Compounds like **sucrose, trehalose**, and **mannitol** prevent ice crystal formation and stabilize proteins and lipids.

2. **Buffer Systems**:

   - Buffers maintain pH stability during freezing and drying.

3. **Bulking Agents**:

   - Substances like **lactose** or **glycine** improve the physical structure of the lyophilized cake, ensuring ease of reconstitution.

Challenges in Lyophilization

1. **Cost-Intensive Process**:

- Lyophilization requires specialized equipment and significant energy input, increasing production costs.

2. **Reconstitution Complexity**:

- The need for reconstitution at the point of use adds an extra step in vaccine administration, requiring trained personnel.

3. **Process Optimization**:

- Ensuring uniform drying and minimizing residual moisture require precise control over freeze-drying parameters.

4. **Thermal Sensitivity**:

- Heat-sensitive components can degrade during secondary drying if the temperature is not carefully controlled.

Case Studies: Lyophilization Successes
1. Lyophilized Measles Vaccine

- **Problem**: Liquid formulations of the measles vaccine degraded rapidly at ambient temperatures, limiting their use in remote areas.
- **Solution**: Lyophilization enabled the vaccine to retain potency for up to two years when stored below 25°C, facilitating immunization campaigns in low-resource settings.

2. Experimental Lyophilized mRNA Vaccines

- **Problem**: mRNA vaccines for COVID-19 required ultra-cold storage (-70°C), complicating global distribution.
- **Solution**: Lyophilized mRNA formulations demonstrated stability at 4°C for up to six months, significantly reducing cold-chain dependencies.

Future Directions in Lyophilization

1. **Integration with Novel Delivery Platforms**:

- Combining lyophilization with microneedle patches or nanoparticles to create stable, easy-to-administer vaccines.

2. **Room-Temperature Stability**:

- Advances in cryoprotectants and drying techniques aim to produce lyophilized vaccines that remain stable at room temperature.

3. **Process Automation**:

- Incorporating AI and machine learning to optimize lyophilization cycles for cost-efficiency and uniformity.

4. **Sustainability in Manufacturing**:

- Developing energy-efficient freeze-dryers to reduce the environmental impact of lyophilization processes.

8.2.2 Spray-Drying and Powder Formulations

Spray-drying is an innovative and versatile technique for stabilizing vaccines by converting liquid formulations into dry powders. This process involves atomizing a liquid vaccine solution into fine droplets and rapidly drying them using heated air. The resulting powder formulations offer several advantages, including enhanced stability, simplified storage, and potential for alternative delivery methods, such as inhalation or microneedle patches. Spray-drying is increasingly recognized as a valuable alternative to freeze-drying, particularly for temperature-sensitive vaccines.

Process of Spray-Drying

Spray-drying transforms liquid vaccine formulations into a fine, dry powder through three sequential steps:

1. Atomization

- The liquid vaccine is converted into tiny droplets using a **nozzle** or **rotary atomizer**.
- Atomization ensures uniform particle size, which is crucial for consistent drying and stability.

2. Drying

- The droplets are exposed to a stream of hot air in a **spray-drying chamber**, causing rapid evaporation of water.
- This rapid drying process minimizes thermal degradation of sensitive vaccine components.

3. Collection

- The dried particles are collected using **cyclones** or **filters** and stored as a powder for further processing or packaging.

Advantages of Spray-Drying
1. Enhanced Stability

- Spray-dried powders are inherently more stable than liquid formulations, reducing the reliance on cold-chain logistics.
- Example: Spray-dried rotavirus vaccines demonstrated stability at temperatures up to 40°C for several months.

2. Scalability and Efficiency

- The spray-drying process is highly scalable, allowing large volumes of vaccines to be processed rapidly.

3. Compatibility with Alternative Delivery Routes

- Spray-dried powders can be formulated for non-invasive delivery methods, such as **inhalation** or **microneedle patches**, improving patient compliance.

4. Simplified Handling and Transportation

- The lightweight and compact nature of spray-dried powders reduces transportation costs and logistical challenges.

Applications in Vaccines
1. Protein-Based Vaccines

- Spray-drying protects proteins from denaturation by removing water rapidly and uniformly.
- Example: Spray-dried **hepatitis B vaccines** retain antigenicity under ambient conditions.

2. Live-Attenuated Vaccines

- This technique preserves the viability of live pathogens used in vaccines while enhancing their thermal stability.
- Example: Spray-dried formulations of **measles** and **tuberculosis (BCG)** vaccines have shown excellent stability in preclinical studies.

3. mRNA and DNA Vaccines

- Spray-drying encapsulates nucleic acids within protective carriers, such as polymers or lipids, improving stability and delivery efficiency.

4. Thermostable Vaccines for Resource-Limited Areas

- Spray-drying facilitates the production of vaccines that remain effective under extreme environmental conditions, addressing challenges in low-resource settings.

Key Formulation Considerations

To ensure the success of spray-drying, vaccine formulations must be optimized with appropriate excipients and stabilizers:

1. **Protective Carriers**:

   - Polymers like **PLGA** or sugars like **trehalose** protect antigens and nucleic acids during drying.

2. **Buffer Systems**:

   - Buffers maintain pH stability, preventing chemical degradation.

3. **Bulking Agents**:

- Compounds like **mannitol** improve the physical properties of the powder, ensuring ease of handling.

4. **Surfactants**:

- Surfactants prevent aggregation of antigens or nanoparticles during spray-drying.

Challenges in Spray-Drying
1. Thermal Sensitivity

- The high temperatures used in spray-drying can degrade heat-sensitive vaccine components, such as proteins or lipids.
- **Solution**: Optimize drying conditions with lower inlet temperatures and rapid evaporation techniques.

2. Particle Size Uniformity

- Inconsistent particle size can lead to variations in vaccine dosing and delivery efficiency.
- **Solution**: Use advanced atomization techniques for precise control over particle size.

3. Formulation Complexity

- Spray-drying requires careful selection of excipients to maintain antigen integrity and functionality.

4. Equipment and Process Optimization

- Scaling up spray-drying systems for commercial production requires significant investment and technical expertise.

Case Studies: Successful Applications of Spray-Drying
1. Spray-Dried Rotavirus Vaccine
Problem: Liquid rotavirus vaccines required strict cold-chain storage, limiting their use in tropical regions.
Solution: Spray-dried formulations demonstrated multi-month stability at

40°C, enabling cost-effective distribution in resource-limited settings.

2. Spray-Dried Influenza Vaccine

Problem: Traditional influenza vaccines required refrigeration, complicating distribution during global flu campaigns.

Solution: Spray-dried influenza vaccines showed equivalent immunogenicity to liquid formulations while remaining stable at room temperature.

Emerging Innovations in Spray-Drying

1. Nano-Spray Drying

- Nano-spray drying allows the production of ultra-fine particles, enhancing bioavailability and delivery to specific tissues.
- Applications: Ideal for inhalable vaccines targeting respiratory pathogens, such as influenza or COVID-19.

2. Encapsulation with Polymers

- Encapsulating antigens or nucleic acids within polymeric carriers during spray-drying improves protection against environmental stress.
- Example: **PLGA nanoparticles** encapsulated during spray-drying have shown enhanced mRNA stability and delivery efficiency.

3. Combined Lyophilization and Spray-Drying Techniques

- Hybrid approaches leverage the strengths of both methods, producing powders with superior stability and ease of reconstitution.

Future Directions

1. **Thermostable Powder Vaccines**:

   - Continued innovation in spray-drying techniques and excipients to develop vaccines stable at extreme temperatures.

2. **Integration with Novel Delivery Platforms**:

   - Formulating spray-dried powders for use in microneedle patches or inhalers for painless and non-invasive administration.

3. **Sustainable Manufacturing Practices**:

   ○ Reducing energy consumption and environmental impact during large-scale spray-drying operations.

4. **Personalized Vaccine Formulations**:

   ○ Producing patient-specific vaccines using spray-drying for targeted cancer immunotherapy or rare genetic disorders.

8.3 Excipients in Vaccine Formulation
8.3.1 Role of Trehalose, Mannitol, and Dextran

Excipients are essential components of vaccine formulations, serving critical roles in stabilizing active ingredients, improving storage conditions, and enhancing vaccine delivery. Among the most widely used excipients in vaccine formulations are **trehalose**, **mannitol**, and **dextran**, each offering unique stabilizing and protective properties. These excipients help preserve the structural integrity of vaccines during manufacturing, storage, and administration, ensuring their efficacy and safety.

1. Trehalose

Trehalose, a disaccharide composed of two glucose molecules, is widely recognized for its superior stabilizing properties in pharmaceutical and vaccine formulations.

Key Roles of Trehalose in Vaccine Formulation
a. Protecting Biological Molecules from Thermal and Freeze Damage

- Trehalose stabilizes proteins, lipids, and nucleic acids by forming a protective glass-like matrix around them.
- During freeze-drying or spray-drying, trehalose prevents the formation of damaging ice crystals that can denature proteins or disrupt lipid nanoparticles.

b. Enhancing Long-Term Stability

- Trehalose reduces the mobility of water molecules, minimizing hydrolysis and oxidative damage during long-term storage.
- Vaccines stabilized with trehalose have demonstrated extended shelf lives, even under ambient conditions.

c. Compatibility with Diverse Vaccine Types

- Trehalose is particularly effective in stabilizing nucleic acid-based vaccines (e.g., mRNA, saRNA) and protein-based vaccines.

Applications in Vaccine Formulations

- **mRNA COVID-19 Vaccines**: Trehalose has been used in experimental formulations to enhance the stability of lipid nanoparticles encapsulating mRNA.
- **Lyophilized Vaccines**: Trehalose is a key excipient in lyophilized formulations of live-attenuated vaccines, such as those for **measles** and **rotavirus**.

Advantages of Trehalose

- Biocompatible and non-toxic.
- Effective across a wide range of vaccine platforms.

Challenges

- Requires precise formulation to avoid crystallization during drying processes.

2. Mannitol

Mannitol, a naturally occurring sugar alcohol, is extensively used in vaccine formulations for its bulking, cryoprotective, and osmotic properties.

Key Roles of Mannitol in Vaccine Formulation

a. Cryoprotectant During Freeze-Drying

- Mannitol prevents ice crystal formation, protecting delicate vaccine components during the freezing and drying stages of lyophilization.

b. Bulking Agent

- As a bulking agent, mannitol adds structural integrity to lyophilized vaccine cakes, making them easier to handle and reconstitute.

c. Osmotic Balance

- Mannitol helps maintain osmotic stability in liquid vaccine formulations, preventing cell lysis and enhancing the stability of live-attenuated vaccines.

Applications in Vaccine Formulations

- **Lyophilized Viral Vaccines**: Mannitol is used in the lyophilized formulations of vaccines like **influenza** and **yellow fever** to improve cake structure and reconstitution.
- **Subunit Vaccines**: Mannitol stabilizes protein subunits, preventing aggregation during storage.

Advantages of Mannitol

- Chemically stable under a wide range of conditions.
- Improves physical properties of both liquid and lyophilized formulations.

Challenges

- Potential for crystallization in certain formulations, which can reduce vaccine stability.

3. Dextran

Dextran, a complex branched polysaccharide, plays a crucial role in vaccine stabilization by protecting active components and improving delivery efficiency.

Key Roles of Dextran in Vaccine Formulation

a. Stabilizing Biological Molecules

- Dextran prevents protein aggregation and denaturation by forming a protective hydrophilic layer around the molecules.
- It also reduces mechanical stress during manufacturing processes, such as spray-drying or freezing.

b. Viscosity Modulation

- Dextran increases the viscosity of liquid vaccine formulations, which helps in maintaining homogeneity and ensuring accurate dosing.

c. Controlled Release in Delivery Systems

- Dextran can be used in vaccine delivery platforms, such as **microneedles** or **nanoparticles**, for controlled antigen release.

Applications in Vaccine Formulations

- **Polysaccharide Vaccines**: Dextran is used as a stabilizer in polysaccharide-based vaccines, such as those for **pneumococcal disease**.
- **Spray-Dried Vaccines**: Dextran enhances the stability of spray-dried vaccines by minimizing thermal degradation.

Advantages of Dextran

- Excellent biocompatibility and biodegradability.
- Versatile applications in both liquid and dry vaccine formulations.

Challenges

- Higher molecular weight forms of dextran may increase viscosity excessively, complicating processing and administration.

Excipient	Primary Role	Applications	Advantages	Challenges
Trehalose	Thermal and freeze-drying protection	mRNA, lyophilized, and protein vaccines	Superior stabilization, broad compatibility	Crystallization during drying
Mannitol	Cryoprotectant, bulking agent	Lyophilized viral and subunit vaccines	Improves physical structure, osmotic balance	Potential crystallization issues
Dextran	Protein stabilization, controlled release	Polysaccharide and spray-dried vaccines	Biocompatible, versatile	Excessive viscosity with high MW

Comparative Analysis of Trehalose, Mannitol, and Dextran

Case Studies: Excipients in Action

1. Trehalose in COVID-19 Vaccines

Problem: Ultra-cold storage requirements for mRNA vaccines limited global accessibility.

Solution: Trehalose-based formulations demonstrated enhanced mRNA stability, enabling short-term storage at 4°C.

2. Mannitol in Influenza Vaccines

Problem: Cracking of lyophilized cakes reduced the efficacy of influenza vaccines.

Solution: Mannitol improved cake structure and reconstitution efficiency, ensuring vaccine integrity.

3. Dextran in Pneumococcal Vaccines

Problem: Polysaccharide vaccines showed reduced stability under mechanical stress.

Solution: Dextran minimized aggregation and maintained vaccine potency during manufacturing and storage.

Future Directions

- **Synergistic Excipient Combinations**

  - Using combinations of trehalose, mannitol, and dextran to leverage their complementary properties for enhanced stability.

- **Nanotechnology Integration**

  - Developing nano-excipient systems, such as trehalose or dextran-coated nanoparticles, to stabilize vaccines and improve delivery.

- **Excipient Optimization for Room-Temperature Vaccines**

  - Advancing formulations that maintain vaccine efficacy under ambient conditions, reducing the need for cold-chain systems.

- **Sustainable Excipient Production**

  - Exploring bio-based and eco-friendly methods for producing excipients to align with global sustainability goals.

- **8.3.2 Protecting Antigen Integrity**

The integrity of antigens is critical to the efficacy and safety of vaccines, as these molecules trigger the immune response necessary for protection against diseases. During manufacturing, storage, and transportation, antigens are exposed to a variety of stressors, including temperature fluctuations, oxidation, and mechanical forces, all of which can compromise their structure and function. Protecting antigen integrity is a key goal in vaccine formulation, achieved through strategic use of stabilizers, excipients, and advanced formulation techniques.

Challenges in Maintaining Antigen Integrity

- **Thermal Instability**

  - Heat-sensitive proteins, peptides, and nucleic acids are prone to denaturation and degradation at elevated temperatures.
  - **Example**: Protein antigens in live-attenuated vaccines lose their conformation when exposed to temperatures above their stability threshold.

- **Oxidative Damage**

  - Reactive oxygen species (ROS) can oxidize amino acids in proteins, altering their immunogenic properties.
  - Lipids in lipid nanoparticles are particularly susceptible to peroxidation.

- **Freeze-Thaw Cycles**

  - Freezing and thawing can cause protein aggregation, loss of antigenicity, and structural disruption.

- **Shear Stress**

  - Mechanical forces during manufacturing or transportation can fragment nucleic acids or unfold proteins, reducing efficacy.

- **Hydrolysis and Moisture Exposure**

  - Nucleic acids and proteins are vulnerable to hydrolysis in high-moisture environments.

- **Strategies to Protect Antigen Integrity**
    ### 1. Use of Stabilizing Excipients
    Excipients play a vital role in shielding antigens from environmental stressors, ensuring structural and functional integrity.
    #### a. Trehalose
- Forms a glass-like matrix around proteins or nucleic acids, stabilizing their structure during thermal or freeze-drying processes.
- Prevents denaturation by replacing water molecules around the antigen.
- **b. Mannitol**
- Protects antigens during lyophilization by preventing ice crystal formation.
- Acts as a bulking agent, ensuring physical integrity during storage and reconstitution.
- **c. Dextran**
- Reduces protein aggregation by creating a hydrophilic protective layer around antigens.
- **d. Polysorbates (e.g., Polysorbate 80)**
- Surfactants that prevent aggregation and surface adsorption of proteins.
- **2. Encapsulation in Delivery Vehicles**
    Encapsulation provides physical protection to antigens, shielding them from enzymatic degradation and environmental factors.
    #### a. Lipid Nanoparticles (LNPs)
- Encapsulate mRNA or protein antigens, protecting them from enzymatic degradation and oxidative stress.
- Example: LNPs used in mRNA COVID-19 vaccines ensure safe delivery of antigens into target cells.
- **b. Polymer-Based Nanoparticles**
- Polymers like PLGA or chitosan encapsulate antigens, enabling controlled release and protecting them from shear stress.
- **c. Microparticles**
- Antigens are encapsulated in biodegradable microspheres, such as those made from polylactic acid (PLA), for sustained stability and release.
- **3. Lyophilization (Freeze-Drying)**
    Lyophilization stabilizes antigens by removing water, reducing the risk of hydrolysis and microbial contamination.
- **Key Additives**: Cryoprotectants like trehalose and mannitol enhance the stability of antigens during the freeze-drying process.

- **Applications**: Widely used in live-attenuated vaccines and protein-based vaccines to extend shelf life.
- **4. Spray-Drying**

  Spray-drying converts liquid formulations into powder, protecting antigens from environmental degradation while simplifying storage and transportation.
- **Protective Additives**: Sugars like dextran and trehalose form a stabilizing matrix around the antigens during drying.
- **5. Controlled Release Formulations**

  Controlled release technologies protect antigens during storage and deliver them effectively at the site of action.
- **Hydrogel Systems**: Encapsulate antigens in hydrogels, which release them gradually while maintaining their integrity.
- **Adjuvant-Integrated Delivery**: Adjuvants like aluminum hydroxide stabilize antigens while enhancing immune responses.
- **6. Optimization of pH and Buffer Systems**

  Maintaining an optimal pH environment is crucial for preserving antigen structure and function.
- Buffers like **phosphate-buffered saline (PBS)** ensure antigen stability during storage and administration.
- **7. Prevention of Oxidative Damage**

  Antioxidants are incorporated into vaccine formulations to prevent oxidative degradation.
- **Examples**: Ascorbic acid and glutathione neutralize ROS, protecting antigens from oxidative damage.
- **Case Studies: Protecting Antigen Integrity**
  - **1. mRNA COVID-19 Vaccines**
- **Challenge**: mRNA is highly susceptible to enzymatic degradation and thermal instability.
- **Solution**: Lipid nanoparticles encapsulating mRNA were stabilized with cryoprotectants like trehalose, ensuring long-term integrity during storage and transportation.
- **2. Hepatitis B Vaccines**
- **Challenge**: The protein antigen in hepatitis B vaccines was prone to aggregation during manufacturing.
- **Solution**: Addition of polysorbate 80 prevented aggregation and maintained antigenicity.
- **Future Directions**

- **Smart Delivery Systems**

  - Developing stimuli-responsive carriers that protect antigens during storage and release them at the target site in response to environmental cues like pH or temperature.

- **Room-Temperature Stabilization**

  - Advancing formulations to maintain antigen integrity at ambient temperatures, reducing reliance on cold-chain logistics.

- **Advanced Encapsulation Technologies**

  - Using hybrid nanoparticles combining lipids and polymers for enhanced stability and targeted delivery.

- **Integrated Stability Enhancers**
- Incorporating multifunctional excipients that simultaneously protect against thermal, oxidative, and mechanical stresses.

NINE

BIOMIMETIC AND CELL-BASED DELIVERY SYSTEMS

9.1 Biomimetic Approaches

9.1.1 Cell Membrane-Coated Nanoparticles

Cell membrane-coated nanoparticles (CMNPs) represent an innovative biomimetic delivery system that combines the functionality of synthetic nanoparticles with the natural properties of biological membranes. This hybrid approach is inspired by the ability of cell membranes to evade immune responses, target specific cells or tissues, and interact with the biological environment in a highly specialized manner. By leveraging these natural capabilities, CMNPs are emerging as a powerful tool for the delivery of therapeutic agents, including vaccines, drugs, and genetic material.

Structure and Design of Cell Membrane-Coated Nanoparticles

CMNPs consist of two key components:

1. **Core Nanoparticle**:

   - The core is typically composed of materials such as **lipid-based nanoparticles, polymeric nanoparticles**, or **inorganic nanoparticles (e.g., gold, silica)**.
   - The core serves as the carrier for therapeutic agents, including drugs, antigens, or nucleic acids.

2. **Cell Membrane Coating**:

   ○ The nanoparticle is coated with a layer of biological membranes derived from cells such as **red blood cells (RBCs), cancer cells, platelets**, or **immune cells**.
   ○ The membrane coating imparts biomimetic properties to the nanoparticle, enhancing its ability to navigate the body's immune system and target specific cells.

Mechanism of Action
1. Prolonged Circulation

- Membrane coatings derived from RBCs or platelets provide a natural "stealth" property, evading detection and clearance by the immune system.
- This prolonged circulation improves the therapeutic efficacy of encapsulated agents by increasing their bioavailability.

2. Targeted Delivery

- Membranes derived from specific cell types (e.g., cancer cells or immune cells) retain their surface proteins, enabling the nanoparticle to home in on target tissues or cells.
- Example: Cancer cell membrane-coated nanoparticles can specifically target tumors due to homotypic binding between cancer cells.

3. Biocompatibility and Immune Modulation

- Membrane coatings reduce the likelihood of immunogenicity and systemic side effects, improving the safety profile of therapeutics.

Production of Cell Membrane-Coated Nanoparticles
Step 1: Isolation of Cell Membranes

- Cell membranes are harvested from donor cells (e.g., RBCs or tumor cells) through processes like **sonication** and **centrifugation.**
- The harvested membranes are purified to remove intracellular components.

Step 2: Preparation of Nanoparticle Core

- Nanoparticles are synthesized using materials like lipids, polymers, or metals, with therapeutic agents encapsulated within.

Step 3: Coating Process

- The purified cell membranes are fused with the nanoparticle core through techniques like **extrusion**, **electrostatic interactions**, or **sonication**, creating a seamless coating.

Step 4: Characterization

- Techniques like **dynamic light scattering (DLS)** and **electron microscopy** are used to verify particle size, uniformity, and membrane coating integrity.

Applications of Cell Membrane-Coated Nanoparticles
1. Drug Delivery

- CMNPs improve the therapeutic index of drugs by enhancing their bioavailability and reducing off-target effects.
- **Example**: RBC-coated nanoparticles have been used to deliver anti-inflammatory drugs with reduced immunogenicity.

2. Cancer Therapy

- Cancer cell membrane-coated nanoparticles specifically target tumors, delivering chemotherapy agents directly to cancerous cells.
- **Example**: Nanoparticles coated with membrane fragments from breast cancer cells have shown high tumor-homing capabilities in preclinical studies.

3. Vaccine Delivery

- CMNPs encapsulating antigens or nucleic acids enhance immune responses by mimicking pathogen-like structures.

- **Example**: Bacterial membrane-coated nanoparticles have been explored for delivering antigens in infectious disease vaccines.

4. Immune Modulation

- Platelet-coated nanoparticles can target sites of vascular injury, modulating inflammation and promoting tissue repair.
- **Example**: In autoimmune diseases, CMNPs help deliver immunomodulators to specific tissues without triggering systemic immune activation.

Advantages of Cell Membrane-Coated Nanoparticles

1. **Immune Evasion**

   - The biomimetic coating reduces recognition by macrophages and the complement system, prolonging circulation time.

2. **Targeted Delivery**

   - Retention of cell-specific surface markers enables precise delivery to target cells or tissues.

3. **Reduced Toxicity**

   - CMNPs lower the likelihood of systemic side effects by preventing off-target interactions.

4. **Versatility**

   - Membranes from various cell types allow customization of CMNPs for different therapeutic applications.

Challenges in Developing Cell Membrane-Coated Nanoparticles
1. Source of Membranes

- Harvesting sufficient membranes from donor cells can be labor-intensive and expensive.

2. Standardization of Production

- Ensuring uniform coating and reproducibility during large-scale manufacturing is technically challenging.

3. Stability Issues

- Membrane coatings may degrade during storage or circulation, reducing the efficacy of CMNPs.

4. Regulatory Hurdles

- The complexity of biomimetic nanoparticles poses challenges for regulatory approval due to the need for extensive safety and efficacy testing.

Case Studies

1. RBC-Coated Nanoparticles for Drug Delivery

Problem: Conventional drug delivery systems were rapidly cleared by macrophages.

Solution: RBC-coated nanoparticles prolonged drug circulation time by evading immune recognition, enhancing therapeutic efficacy in inflammatory conditions.

2. Cancer Cell Membrane-Coated Nanoparticles for Tumor Targeting

Problem: Traditional chemotherapies had low specificity, causing systemic toxicity.

Solution: Cancer cell membrane-coated nanoparticles specifically targeted tumor cells through homotypic interactions, improving drug delivery efficiency.

Future Directions

1. **Hybrid Membrane Coatings**

    - Combining membranes from multiple cell types (e.g., RBCs and immune cells) to enhance functionality and targeting.

2. **Integration with Advanced Therapeutics**

○ Developing CMNPs for delivering CRISPR-Cas9 systems, mRNA vaccines, and other cutting-edge therapies.

3. **Real-Time Monitoring Systems**

○ Incorporating biosensors within CMNPs for real-time tracking of nanoparticle delivery and therapeutic outcomes.

4. **Scalable Manufacturing Techniques**

○ Advancing production methods to enable large-scale, cost-effective manufacturing of CMNPs.

9.1.2 Artificial Antigen-Presenting Cells

Artificial antigen-presenting cells (aAPCs) are a revolutionary biomimetic approach designed to mimic the natural function of antigen-presenting cells (APCs) in the immune system. APCs, such as dendritic cells, play a critical role in initiating and regulating immune responses by presenting antigens to T cells. By replicating these processes, aAPCs offer a controlled and customizable platform for modulating the immune system, making them a powerful tool in immunotherapy, vaccine development, and immune modulation.

Structure and Design of Artificial Antigen-Presenting Cells

Artificial antigen-presenting cells are engineered platforms that simulate the functions of natural APCs. They are typically constructed using synthetic or biological materials to display antigenic and co-stimulatory signals.

1. Core Structure

- The core serves as the base material for aAPCs and can be composed of:

  ○ **Polymeric nanoparticles**: Biodegradable materials like PLGA.
  ○ **Lipid-based platforms**: Liposomes or lipid nanoparticles.
  ○ **Magnetic beads**: Micron- or nano-sized particles used in research and therapy.
  ○ **Cell-mimicking scaffolds**: Synthetic structures that imitate the size and surface properties of cells.

2. Functional Coatings

The surface of aAPCs is functionalized with biomolecules that replicate the key features of natural APCs:

- **Antigenic Peptides**: Specific epitopes from pathogens, tumors, or other targets presented on major histocompatibility complexes (MHC-I and MHC-II).
- **Co-Stimulatory Molecules**: Proteins like **CD80** and **CD86**, which are essential for T-cell activation.
- **Adhesion Molecules**: Facilitate stable interactions with T cells, such as **ICAM-1.**
- **Cytokines**: Interleukin-2 (IL-2) or IL-12 can be attached to enhance immune activation.

3. Tunable Design

- aAPCs can be tailored to elicit specific immune responses, such as activating cytotoxic T cells (CTLs) or promoting regulatory T cell (Treg) development.

Mechanism of Action

1. **Antigen Presentation**

   - aAPCs present peptide antigens bound to MHC molecules, mimicking the way natural APCs present antigens to T-cell receptors (TCRs).

2. **Co-Stimulation**

   - Co-stimulatory signals ensure the activation of naïve T cells and prevent anergy (immune tolerance).

3. **Cytokine Delivery**

   - Surface-bound cytokines or soluble factors released by aAPCs direct T-cell differentiation and proliferation.

4. **Targeted Immune Modulation**

- By controlling the type of antigen and co-stimulatory signals, aAPCs can either enhance immune activation (e.g., for cancer immunotherapy) or suppress immune responses (e.g., for autoimmune diseases).

Applications of Artificial Antigen-Presenting Cells

1. Cancer Immunotherapy

aAPCs are being developed to stimulate robust T-cell responses against tumor antigens, enhancing the efficacy of cancer treatments.

Example: aAPCs presenting tumor-specific antigens like **HER2** or **neoantigens** have demonstrated improved CTL activation in preclinical models of melanoma and breast cancer.

2. Vaccine Development

aAPCs are used to deliver antigens from infectious pathogens, promoting strong and durable immune responses.

Example: aAPCs loaded with viral antigens from **HIV** or **influenza** have shown promise in eliciting protective immunity in preclinical studies.

3. Autoimmune Disease Management

By presenting autoantigens in the absence of co-stimulatory signals, aAPCs can induce immune tolerance and suppress autoimmunity.

Example: aAPCs presenting **myelin basic protein (MBP)** epitopes are being explored for treating **multiple sclerosis**.

4. Infectious Disease Therapy

aAPCs can help in the targeted activation of immune cells to fight chronic infections, such as **HIV**, **hepatitis B**, or **tuberculosis**.

5. Transplant Immunology

aAPCs can promote tolerance toward donor antigens, reducing the risk of graft rejection in organ transplants.

Advantages of Artificial Antigen-Presenting Cells

1. **Customizability**

   - aAPCs can be engineered to target specific antigens and fine-tune immune responses based on therapeutic needs.

2. **Scalability**

- aAPCs can be produced synthetically, enabling large-scale manufacturing for widespread applications.

3. **Reduced Immunogenicity**

- Unlike natural APCs, aAPCs eliminate the risk of immune rejection or off-target effects.

4. **Enhanced Control**

- Their modular design allows for precise control over antigen presentation, co-stimulation, and cytokine signaling.

Challenges in Developing Artificial Antigen-Presenting Cells

1. **Complexity in Design**

- Achieving a balance between antigen presentation, co-stimulation, and cytokine delivery requires intricate engineering.

2. **Manufacturing Costs**

- High costs associated with the synthesis and functionalization of aAPCs may limit accessibility.

3. **In Vivo Stability**

- Ensuring that aAPCs remain functional and stable in the biological environment is challenging.

4. **Regulatory Approval**

- The novel nature of aAPCs necessitates extensive preclinical and clinical studies to demonstrate safety and efficacy.

Case Studies
1. aAPCs for Melanoma Immunotherapy

- **Objective**: Stimulate T cells against melanoma-specific antigens.
- **Approach**: aAPCs were functionalized with MHC-I molecules presenting melanoma antigens and co-stimulatory molecules like CD80.
- **Outcome**: Enhanced activation of cytotoxic T cells led to significant tumor regression in mouse models.

2. aAPCs in HIV Vaccine Research

- **Objective**: Elicit strong CD8+ T-cell responses to control HIV replication.
- **Approach**: aAPCs loaded with HIV-specific antigens were tested in preclinical studies.
- **Outcome**: Improved viral suppression and immune memory compared to traditional vaccine platforms.

Future Directions

1. **Integration with Advanced Delivery Systems**

   - Combining aAPCs with lipid nanoparticles or hydrogels for targeted delivery and sustained release.

2. **Personalized aAPCs**

   - Developing patient-specific aAPCs loaded with tumor neoantigens or autoantigens for precision medicine.

3. **In Vivo aAPCs**

   - Engineering nanoparticles that function as aAPCs directly in the patient's body, bypassing the need for ex vivo manipulation.

4. **Combination Therapies**

   - Using aAPCs in conjunction with immune checkpoint inhibitors, CAR-T cells, or cytokine therapies for enhanced efficacy.

9.2 Applications in Cancer and Infectious Diseases
9.2.1 Therapeutic Vaccines for Oncology

Therapeutic vaccines for oncology represent a significant advancement in cancer immunotherapy. Unlike preventive vaccines, which aim to prevent diseases, therapeutic cancer vaccines are designed to stimulate the immune system to recognize and attack existing cancer cells. These vaccines utilize tumor-specific antigens or neoantigens to elicit robust immune responses, targeting cancer cells while sparing healthy tissues. With advancements in biomimetic and cell-based delivery systems, therapeutic cancer vaccines are becoming increasingly precise and effective, offering new hope for treating a wide range of malignancies.

Principles of Therapeutic Cancer Vaccines

1. **Antigen Presentation**

   - Cancer vaccines introduce tumor antigens to antigen-presenting cells (APCs), such as dendritic cells, which present these antigens to T cells.

2. **Immune Activation**

   - The interaction between APCs and T cells activates cytotoxic T lymphocytes (CTLs), which recognize and destroy tumor cells expressing the target antigen.

3. **Memory Response**

   - Vaccines promote the formation of memory T cells, providing long-term immunity against tumor recurrence.

Types of Antigens Used in Cancer Vaccines

1. **Tumor-Associated Antigens (TAAs)**

   - Antigens expressed in both normal and tumor cells but overexpressed in cancer.
   - **Examples**: HER2, MUC1, carcinoembryonic antigen (CEA).

2. **Tumor-Specific Antigens (TSAs)**

   - Antigens expressed exclusively by tumor cells.

- ○ **Examples**: Mutant p53, Ras proteins, and fusion proteins in specific cancers.

3. **Neoantigens**

- ○ Antigens arising from tumor-specific mutations, unique to each patient's cancer.
- ○ **Examples**: Mutated epidermal growth factor receptor (EGFRvIII) in glioblastoma.

Types of Therapeutic Cancer Vaccines
1. Peptide-Based Vaccines

- Short synthetic peptides mimicking tumor antigens are used to activate T cells.
- **Advantages**: Simple to manufacture and customize.
- **Limitations**: Limited immunogenicity; often requires adjuvants or delivery platforms.

Example: A vaccine targeting **HER2 peptides** is in clinical trials for HER2-positive breast cancer.
2. DNA and RNA Vaccines

- These vaccines deliver genetic material encoding tumor antigens to host cells, which then produce the antigens.
- **Advantages**: Rapid production and scalability.
- **Limitations**: Requires effective delivery systems to ensure intracellular uptake.

Example: RNA-based cancer vaccines targeting **KRAS mutations** in lung cancer are under development.
3. Dendritic Cell Vaccines

- Patient-derived dendritic cells are loaded with tumor antigens ex vivo and reinfused into the patient to stimulate T cells.
- **Advantages**: High specificity and potent immune activation.
- **Limitations**: Labor-intensive and expensive to produce.

Example: **Sipuleucel-T**, the first FDA-approved cancer vaccine, is used to treat metastatic prostate cancer.

4. Oncolytic Virus-Based Vaccines

- Engineered viruses selectively infect and kill tumor cells while expressing tumor antigens to stimulate immunity.
- **Advantages**: Dual action of direct tumor lysis and immune activation.
- **Limitations**: Potential for systemic inflammation.

Example: **Talimogene laherparepvec (T-VEC)**, an oncolytic virus vaccine for melanoma.

5. Nanoparticle-Based Vaccines

- Nanoparticles encapsulate tumor antigens, adjuvants, and cytokines for targeted delivery.
- **Advantages**: Enhanced stability, immune activation, and controlled release.
- **Limitations**: Complex manufacturing processes.

Example: Lipid nanoparticle vaccines delivering neoantigens for personalized cancer treatment.

Delivery Platforms for Cancer Vaccines

The efficacy of cancer vaccines heavily depends on the delivery system, which ensures antigen stability, targeting, and immune activation.

1. **Liposomes and Lipid Nanoparticles**

   - Encapsulate and protect antigens, ensuring efficient delivery to APCs.
   - Widely used in mRNA-based vaccines.

2. **Microneedles**

   - Deliver antigens directly to the skin's immune-rich environment, enhancing vaccine efficacy.

3. **Hydrogels**

   - Act as a depot for sustained antigen release at the injection site.

4. **Cell-Mimetic Systems**

   - Artificial antigen-presenting cells (aAPCs) and cell membrane-coated nanoparticles simulate natural APCs to optimize immune responses.

Adjuvants in Cancer Vaccines
Adjuvants are critical for enhancing the immune response to cancer vaccines.

1. **Toll-Like Receptor (TLR) Agonists**

   - Stimulate innate immunity to enhance T-cell activation.
   - **Example**: CpG oligodeoxynucleotides (TLR9 agonists).

2. **Cytokines**

   - IL-2 and GM-CSF are used to boost T-cell proliferation and activation.

3. **Aluminum Salts**

   - Stabilize antigens and promote long-term immune responses.

Applications in Specific Cancers
1. Melanoma

- Vaccines targeting neoantigens unique to melanoma have demonstrated enhanced immune responses in clinical trials.

2. Prostate Cancer

- **Sipuleucel-T**, an autologous dendritic cell vaccine, extends survival in patients with metastatic castration-resistant prostate cancer.

3. Lung Cancer

- mRNA vaccines targeting KRAS mutations are under development for non-small cell lung cancer.

4. Breast Cancer

- Vaccines targeting HER2 and MUC1 antigens are being explored for HER2-positive and triple-negative breast cancers.

Challenges in Therapeutic Cancer Vaccines

1. Tumor Microenvironment

- Immunosuppressive factors in the tumor microenvironment, such as regulatory T cells and myeloid-derived suppressor cells, reduce vaccine efficacy.

2. Antigen Selection

- Identifying universal or patient-specific tumor antigens remains a challenge.

3. Delivery Efficiency

- Ensuring that antigens reach APCs and elicit robust immune responses is critical.

4. Personalization Costs

- Personalized vaccines, such as those based on neoantigens, are expensive to develop and manufacture.

Case Studies
1. Neoantigen Vaccines for Melanoma

- **Objective**: Stimulate T cells against tumor-specific neoantigens.
- **Approach**: Personalized mRNA vaccines encoding unique neoantigens were administered to patients.
- **Outcome**: Enhanced T-cell responses and reduced tumor progression in several patients.

2. Sipuleucel-T for Prostate Cancer

- **Objective**: Prolong survival in metastatic prostate cancer patients.
- **Approach**: Patient-derived dendritic cells were loaded with a prostate cancer antigen (PAP) and reinfused.
- **Outcome**: Median survival increased by 4.1 months compared to standard therapy.

Future Directions

1. **Integration with Immune Checkpoint Inhibitors**

   - Combining vaccines with inhibitors like anti-PD-1 or anti-CTLA-4 enhances immune responses by overcoming tumor-induced immunosuppression.

2. **Personalized Vaccine Development**

   - Advances in genomics and proteomics will enable rapid identification of patient-specific neoantigens for tailored therapies.

3. **Delivery Innovations**

   - Microneedle patches, lipid nanoparticles, and hydrogels will improve antigen delivery and vaccine efficacy.

4. **Multi-Antigen Vaccines**

   - Vaccines targeting multiple antigens simultaneously will address tumor heterogeneity and prevent immune escape.

9.2.2 Targeting Mutating Pathogens

Targeting mutating pathogens presents one of the greatest challenges in infectious disease management and vaccine development. Pathogens such as **viruses**, **bacteria**, and even **parasites** possess the ability to evolve rapidly, often altering their genetic or protein structures to evade the immune system. These mutations, driven by natural selection, enable pathogens to escape vaccine-induced immunity or drug treatments, making it imperative to develop adaptive and robust strategies to combat them.

Mechanisms of Pathogen Mutation

1. **Antigenic Drift**

   - Small, gradual changes in the pathogen's surface proteins due to replication errors.
   - **Example**: Seasonal changes in **influenza virus hemagglutinin (HA)** and neuraminidase (NA) proteins.

2. **Antigenic Shift**

   - Abrupt, major genetic reassortments that result in novel surface proteins.
   - **Example**: The emergence of pandemic influenza strains.

3. **Selective Pressure**

   - Immune responses, vaccines, or antimicrobial drugs impose selective pressure, encouraging the survival of resistant strains.
   - **Example**: Antibiotic-resistant bacteria like **methicillin-resistant Staphylococcus aureus (MRSA)**.

4. **High Mutation Rates**

   - Certain pathogens, such as RNA viruses, exhibit high mutation rates due to error-prone replication mechanisms.
   - **Example**: HIV mutates rapidly, creating diverse quasispecies.

5. **Recombination and Horizontal Gene Transfer**

   - Exchange of genetic material between pathogens or acquisition of genes from the host.
   - **Example**: Bacteria acquiring resistance genes through plasmids.

Strategies for Targeting Mutating Pathogens
1. Broadly Neutralizing Antibodies (bnAbs)
Broadly neutralizing antibodies target conserved regions of pathogens that remain unchanged despite mutations.
Applications:

- bnAbs targeting the conserved **stem region of influenza HA** are being developed to provide universal flu protection.
- HIV research focuses on bnAbs that target conserved epitopes on the **gp120** envelope glycoprotein.

2. Multivalent Vaccines

Multivalent vaccines incorporate multiple antigens or epitopes to provide broad protection against diverse strains of a pathogen.

Examples:

- **Quadrivalent influenza vaccines** protect against two influenza A strains and two influenza B strains.
- **Pneumococcal conjugate vaccines (PCVs)** target up to 23 serotypes of *Streptococcus pneumoniae*.

3. Universal Vaccines

Universal vaccines focus on conserved antigens shared across all strains of a mutating pathogen.

Examples:

- Universal flu vaccines target conserved regions of HA and NA to provide long-lasting immunity against all influenza strains.
- Efforts are underway to develop a universal **coronavirus vaccine** targeting conserved regions of the spike protein.

4. Adaptive Vaccine Platforms

Adaptive platforms allow for rapid modification of vaccine components in response to emerging mutations.

Examples:

- **mRNA vaccines** for COVID-19 (Pfizer-BioNTech and Moderna) were quickly adapted to address variants like Delta and Omicron.
- DNA vaccines offer a flexible approach for encoding antigens of newly mutated strains.

5. Epitope-Based Vaccines

Epitope-based vaccines focus on immunodominant regions of antigens that are less likely to mutate.

- Computational tools are used to identify conserved epitopes for vaccine design.
- **Example**: Epitope-based HIV vaccines are being explored to elicit robust T-cell responses.

6. Cross-Reactive Immune Responses

Stimulating cross-reactive T cells that can recognize diverse pathogen strains helps overcome the effects of mutation.

- **Example**: T-cell responses targeting conserved internal proteins of influenza viruses have shown promise in preclinical studies.

7. Combination Therapies

Using vaccines in combination with antiviral or antimicrobial drugs reduces the likelihood of resistance and improves efficacy.
Example:

- Combining antiretroviral therapy (ART) with therapeutic HIV vaccines.

8. Nanoparticle-Based Delivery Systems

Nanoparticles can present multiple antigens simultaneously or mimic pathogen structures to elicit broad immune responses.
Example:

- Multivalent nanoparticle vaccines displaying different influenza HA epitopes have shown broad protection in animal models.

Challenges in Targeting Mutating Pathogens

1. **Rapid Evolution**

   - High mutation rates in RNA viruses, such as HIV and influenza, make it difficult to develop long-lasting vaccines.

2. **Antigenic Variation**

   - Pathogens like *Plasmodium falciparum* (malaria) and *Neisseria gonorrhoeae* frequently change surface antigens to evade immunity.

3. **Resistance Development**

   - Drug and vaccine resistance in bacteria, such as **multidrug-resistant tuberculosis (MDR-TB)**, complicates treatment strategies.

4. **Immune Evasion**

   - HIV integrates into host DNA and evades immune responses, making it a challenging target.

5. **Global Surveillance**

   - Monitoring emerging mutations in real-time is resource-intensive, particularly in low-resource settings.

Case Studies
1. Influenza Virus

- **Challenge**: Antigenic drift necessitates annual vaccine updates.
- **Solution**: Universal flu vaccines targeting conserved HA regions are under development, aiming for long-term immunity.

2. SARS-CoV-2

- **Challenge**: Variants like Delta and Omicron reduce vaccine efficacy.
- **Solution**: mRNA vaccines were rapidly updated to include spike protein mutations, maintaining effectiveness against new variants.

3. HIV

- **Challenge**: High mutation rates create diverse viral populations within a single patient.
- **Solution**: bnAbs targeting conserved epitopes on the HIV envelope glycoprotein are in advanced clinical trials.

Future Directions

1. **AI-Driven Antigen Discovery**

- Artificial intelligence can identify conserved and immunogenic epitopes for vaccine design against mutating pathogens.

2. **Universal Vaccine Development**

- Focused efforts on universal vaccines for influenza, coronaviruses, and HIV hold promise for long-term immunity.

3. **Integrated Global Surveillance Systems**

- Enhanced pathogen sequencing and data sharing will enable faster responses to emerging mutations.

4. **Next-Generation Adjuvants**

- Advanced adjuvants capable of boosting cross-reactive immune responses against diverse pathogen strains.

5. **Personalized Vaccination**

- Tailoring vaccines based on individual immune profiles and regional pathogen variants.

TEN

REGULATORY, ETHICAL, AND GLOBAL PERSPECTIVES

10.1 Regulatory Pathways

10.1.1 Approval Processes for Novel Platforms

The rapid advancement of novel therapeutic platforms, such as **mRNA vaccines**, **gene therapies**, and **nanoparticle-based delivery systems**, presents unique challenges for regulatory approval. Traditional approval processes often struggle to accommodate these cutting-edge technologies due to their complexity, limited historical data, and innovative mechanisms of action. Regulatory agencies, including the **FDA (Food and Drug Administration)**, **EMA (European Medicines Agency)**, and **WHO**, have established specialized frameworks to streamline the approval of novel platforms while ensuring their safety, efficacy, and quality.

1. Regulatory Frameworks for Novel Platforms

1.1. Fast-Track Designations

Fast-track programs aim to accelerate the review and approval of therapies addressing unmet medical needs.

- **FDA's Fast Track**: Allows sponsors to submit data on a rolling basis and gain priority review.
- **EMA's PRIME (PRIority Medicines)**: Offers early dialogue with regulators to expedite approval.

1.2. Breakthrough Therapy Designation

Reserved for treatments showing substantial improvement over existing therapies in early clinical trials.

- **Example**: mRNA-based COVID-19 vaccines received expedited review due to their potential to address the pandemic.

1.3. Adaptive Pathways

Adaptive regulatory approaches allow conditional approval based on early evidence, with post-approval data collection.

- **EMA Adaptive Pathway**: Ideal for novel vaccines or gene therapies targeting rare diseases.

1.4. Accelerated Approval

Grants approval based on surrogate endpoints (e.g., biomarker data) rather than long-term clinical outcomes.

- **Example**: The approval of certain mRNA vaccines was based on immunogenicity endpoints rather than years-long efficacy studies.

2. Key Steps in the Approval Process
2.1. Preclinical Studies

- Evaluate the safety, immunogenicity, and mechanism of action in **in vitro** and **animal models**.
- **Challenge for Novel Platforms**: Establishing new standards for testing unconventional delivery systems like lipid nanoparticles (LNPs).

2.2. Investigational New Drug (IND) Application

- Submission to regulatory authorities seeking permission to initiate clinical trials.
- Includes **chemistry, manufacturing, and controls (CMC)** data, preclinical results, and a clinical trial plan.

2.3. Clinical Trials

- **Phase I**: Evaluate safety and dosing in a small group of healthy volunteers.
- **Phase II**: Assess efficacy and side effects in a larger group of patients.
- **Phase III**: Confirm efficacy and monitor adverse effects in thousands of participants.
- **Challenge**: Novel platforms often require unique endpoints or trial designs, such as real-world evidence collection for personalized therapies.

2.4. Biologics License Application (BLA) or Marketing Authorization Application (MAA)

- Submission of complete clinical, preclinical, and manufacturing data for final review.

3. Regulatory Considerations for Novel Platforms
3.1. Safety Assessment

- Novel platforms may involve unknown risks, such as unexpected immune responses or long-term effects.
- **Example**: For mRNA vaccines, LNPs raised concerns about reactogenicity and systemic inflammation.

3.2. Manufacturing Challenges

- Ensuring consistent quality for complex platforms like gene therapies or mRNA vaccines requires advanced technologies.
- **Regulatory Standard**: Agencies demand detailed **Good Manufacturing Practices (GMP)** documentation.

3.3. Long-Term Monitoring

- Novel therapies often require extensive post-approval surveillance to track long-term safety and effectiveness.
- **Example**: Conditional approvals may mandate Phase IV studies or real-world evidence collection.

3.4. Ethical Concerns

- Balancing accelerated approval with patient safety is critical, especially during public health emergencies.

4. Case Studies: Regulatory Approval of Novel Platforms
4.1. mRNA-Based COVID-19 Vaccines

- **Background**: Pfizer-BioNTech and Moderna's vaccines were the first mRNA vaccines approved for widespread use.
- **Regulatory Strategy**:

  - Leveraged emergency use authorization (EUA) to expedite approval.
  - Demonstrated safety and efficacy through large-scale Phase III trials within a compressed timeline.
  - Post-approval commitments included real-world data collection for safety and durability of protection.

4.2. CAR-T Cell Therapies

- **Background**: CAR-T therapies, such as Kymriah (Novartis), represent a breakthrough in cell-based cancer immunotherapy.
- **Regulatory Challenges**:

  - Demonstrating the long-term safety of genetically modified cells.
  - Establishing robust manufacturing and quality controls for patient-specific therapies.

4.3. Gene Therapy for Rare Diseases

- **Background**: Zolgensma (Novartis), a gene therapy for spinal muscular atrophy, highlighted the complexities of approving one-time treatments.
- **Regulatory Innovations**:

  - Leveraged accelerated approval based on surrogate endpoints like biomarker improvements.
  - Required extensive post-market safety monitoring.

5. Challenges in Regulatory Pathways
5.1. Lack of Historical Data

- Novel platforms often lack prior regulatory precedents, making standardization difficult.

5.2. Cost and Complexity

- High costs of developing and validating novel therapies create barriers for small-scale innovators.

5.3. Public Perception and Trust

- The rapid approval of novel platforms, such as COVID-19 vaccines, raised concerns about safety and transparency.

5.4. Global Regulatory Harmonization

- Divergent requirements across regulatory agencies complicate global market access for novel therapies.

6. Future Directions in Regulatory Pathways

1. **Digital Tools for Regulatory Review**

   - AI and machine learning for analyzing clinical data and identifying safety signals.

2. **Adaptive Trial Designs**

   - Seamless Phase I/II/III trials for faster decision-making without compromising safety.

3. **Global Collaboration**

   - Joint reviews and approvals through international frameworks, such as the **International Council for Harmonisation (ICH)**.

4. **Real-World Evidence Integration**

○ Incorporating real-world data into regulatory decision-making to supplement traditional clinical trials.

5. **Patient-Centered Approaches**

○ Engaging patients in the design and evaluation of novel therapies to align regulatory decisions with patient needs.

10.1.2 Harmonizing Global Regulatory Standards

Harmonizing global regulatory standards is essential in today's interconnected world to facilitate the development, approval, and distribution of medicines, vaccines, and novel therapeutic platforms across multiple regions. Divergent regulatory frameworks, guidelines, and processes among countries pose significant challenges for pharmaceutical companies, resulting in delays, increased costs, and inconsistent access to life-saving treatments. Achieving regulatory harmonization ensures that products meet consistent safety, efficacy, and quality standards worldwide, enabling efficient market access and equitable healthcare delivery.

Importance of Harmonization

1. **Streamlining Development**

○ Unified standards reduce the need for redundant studies, saving time and resources.
○ Example: Standardized clinical trial requirements eliminate the need for separate trials in different regions.

2. **Improving Access**

○ Harmonization accelerates product registration in multiple countries, ensuring timely access to essential medicines.

3. **Facilitating Global Trade**

○ Consistent regulatory requirements simplify cross-border trade, promoting global health equity.

4. **Enhancing Safety and Quality**

- ○ Uniform guidelines ensure that all products meet the same stringent safety and quality criteria, protecting public health.

Key Challenges in Harmonizing Regulatory Standards
1. Diverse Regulatory Requirements

- Different countries have unique guidelines for clinical trials, approval processes, and post-market surveillance.
- Example: Variations in dossier requirements between the FDA, EMA, and regulatory agencies in emerging markets.

2. Resource Disparities

- Developing countries may lack the infrastructure, expertise, or resources to implement stringent regulatory frameworks.

3. Rapid Technological Advances

- Novel platforms like mRNA vaccines or CAR-T therapies often outpace existing regulatory guidelines, creating discrepancies.

4. Intellectual Property and Data Protection

- Differing policies on patent rights and data exclusivity impact how products are evaluated and approved.

5. Political and Economic Barriers

- Conflicting priorities among nations can slow the adoption of harmonized standards.

Organizations Driving Global Harmonization
1. International Council for Harmonisation (ICH)

- Focus: Harmonizing technical guidelines for pharmaceutical product development and registration.
- Key Areas:

- **Quality**: Guidelines for Good Manufacturing Practices (ICH Q series).
- **Safety**: Toxicology testing and risk assessments (ICH S series).
- **Efficacy**: Clinical trial design and pharmacovigilance (ICH E series).

2. World Health Organization (WHO)

- Focus: Establishing global health standards, particularly for low- and middle-income countries.
- Key Initiatives:

  - **Prequalification Program**: Ensures that medicines and vaccines meet international standards for global procurement.
  - Guidelines for biosimilars, vaccines, and traditional medicines.

3. Pharmaceutical Inspection Co-operation Scheme (PIC/S)

- Focus: Harmonizing Good Manufacturing Practice (GMP) standards globally.
- Members: Over 50 regulatory agencies collaborate to ensure consistent inspection practices.

4. ASEAN and African Medicines Regulatory Harmonization (AMRH)

- Focus: Regional harmonization initiatives in Southeast Asia and Africa to streamline approvals and improve access to medicines.

Steps Toward Harmonization
1. Standardized Dossier Submissions

- Adoption of the **Common Technical Document (CTD)** format, developed by ICH, simplifies applications across multiple regions.
- **Example**: The CTD is now mandatory in the EU, Japan, and the USA.

2. Mutual Recognition Agreements (MRAs)

- Regulatory authorities recognize each other's evaluations, reducing duplication.
- **Example**: The EU and FDA have an MRA for GMP inspections.

3. Collaborative Reviews

- Joint reviews of dossiers by multiple regulatory authorities improve efficiency.
- **Example**: WHO's collaborative registration procedure accelerates access to vaccines in developing countries.

4. Capacity Building in Developing Regions

- Training programs and resource sharing help emerging regulatory agencies adopt harmonized standards.
- **Example**: WHO and ICH provide technical support for regulatory strengthening in Africa.

Case Studies
1. COVID-19 Vaccine Approvals

- **Challenge**: The urgent need for vaccines highlighted the lack of harmonized processes, leading to delays in global access.
- **Solution**: WHO's emergency use listing (EUL) process enabled faster approval in low- and middle-income countries by leveraging evaluations from stringent regulatory authorities (SRAs).

2. ICH Q8-Q11 Guidelines on Quality by Design (QbD)

- **Impact**: Harmonized QbD guidelines streamlined manufacturing processes globally, ensuring consistent product quality.

Benefits of Harmonized Standards

1. **Faster Access to Innovations**

   - Patients in all regions benefit from timely access to new treatments.

2. **Cost Efficiency**

   - Reduces duplicative testing and submission processes for manufacturers.

3. **Improved Global Health Outcomes**

   - Consistent safety and efficacy standards protect patients worldwide.

Future Directions
1. Digital Integration

- Leveraging blockchain and AI to create global databases for regulatory submissions, pharmacovigilance, and inspections.

2. Expanded Regional Harmonization

- Expanding initiatives like AMRH to other regions, such as Latin America.

3. Real-World Evidence (RWE)

- Incorporating global real-world data into regulatory decision-making.

4. Inclusive Global Frameworks

- Bridging resource gaps to ensure that developing countries can participate fully in harmonized systems.

10.2 Ethical Challenges
10.2.1 Vaccine Equity and Access
Vaccine equity and access are critical ethical challenges in global public health. The disparity in the availability, affordability, and distribution of vaccines between high-income and low- to middle-income countries has long been a persistent issue. The COVID-19 pandemic brought this inequity into stark focus, with wealthier nations gaining faster and wider access to life-saving vaccines while poorer regions struggled with shortages. Ensuring equitable access to vaccines is not only a matter of ethics but also a practical necessity for achieving global health security.
Dimensions of Vaccine Inequity
1. Economic Disparities

- High-income countries often dominate vaccine procurement due to their ability to negotiate advanced purchase agreements and pay premium prices.

- Example: During the COVID-19 pandemic, wealthier nations secured the majority of vaccine supplies early, leaving low-income countries with limited access.

2. Infrastructure Limitations

- Inadequate cold-chain systems and healthcare infrastructure in low-income countries hinder vaccine storage and distribution.
- Example: Ultra-cold storage requirements for mRNA vaccines like Pfizer-BioNTech's made distribution difficult in resource-limited settings.

3. Intellectual Property (IP) Barriers

- Patents and proprietary manufacturing processes limit the ability of developing countries to produce vaccines locally.
- Example: Advocacy for IP waivers under the World Trade Organization's TRIPS agreement highlighted the need for knowledge-sharing.

4. Geopolitical Influences

- Vaccine nationalism and export restrictions imposed by some nations disrupted global supply chains.
- Example: Export bans by vaccine-producing countries during the COVID-19 crisis delayed deliveries to other regions.

5. Vaccine Hesitancy

- Misinformation, cultural beliefs, and distrust in healthcare systems contribute to lower vaccination rates in underserved communities, even when vaccines are available.

Ethical Principles for Vaccine Equity

1. **Justice**

   - Ensuring fair allocation of resources based on need rather than wealth or political power.

2. **Solidarity**

   - Recognizing the interconnectedness of global health and the shared responsibility to protect vulnerable populations.

3. **Beneficence**

   - Prioritizing actions that maximize benefits and reduce harm, particularly for disadvantaged groups.

4. **Transparency**

   - Promoting openness in decision-making processes related to vaccine allocation and distribution.

Global Initiatives Addressing Vaccine Equity
1. COVAX (COVID-19 Vaccines Global Access Facility)

- **Objective**: Ensure equitable access to COVID-19 vaccines for all countries, regardless of income level.
- **Mechanism**: Pooled procurement and distribution of vaccines to participating countries.
- **Challenges**: Funding shortfalls and supply chain issues limited the program's ability to meet global demand.

2. GAVI, The Vaccine Alliance

- **Objective**: Increase access to vaccines in low-income countries through financial support and infrastructure development.
- **Impact**: GAVI has facilitated the delivery of billions of vaccine doses, including for diseases like polio, measles, and pneumonia.

3. WHO's Fair Allocation Framework

- **Objective**: Provide a systematic approach to prioritize vaccine distribution based on risk and healthcare capacity.
- **Application**: Guidelines for COVID-19 vaccine allocation aimed at ensuring frontline workers and high-risk populations were vaccinated

first.

Key Strategies for Promoting Vaccine Equity
1. Increasing Global Manufacturing Capacity

- Partnerships between pharmaceutical companies and developing nations can expand vaccine production.
- Example: Initiatives like the mRNA vaccine technology transfer hub established by WHO in South Africa aim to build local manufacturing capacity.

2. Waiving Intellectual Property Protections

- Temporarily suspending IP rights for critical vaccines can enable broader production.
- **Debate**: Proponents argue it accelerates access; opponents cite potential risks to innovation.

3. Strengthening Supply Chains

- Investment in cold-chain logistics, storage facilities, and healthcare worker training is essential for vaccine delivery in resource-limited areas.

4. Funding and Donations

- High-income countries can support vaccine equity through financial contributions and surplus dose donations.
- Example: Several G7 nations pledged doses to COVAX, although actual deliveries often fell short of commitments.

5. Addressing Vaccine Hesitancy

- Community engagement, culturally sensitive education campaigns, and combating misinformation are critical to increasing vaccine acceptance.

Case Studies
1. COVID-19 Vaccine Distribution in Africa

- **Challenge**: Africa received only 2% of global COVID-19 vaccine supplies in the early phases of the pandemic.
- **Solution**: Programs like COVAX and regional partnerships, such as the African Vaccine Acquisition Trust (AVAT), improved distribution and local production capacity.

2. HPV Vaccines in Low-Income Countries

- **Challenge**: The high cost of HPV vaccines limited access in low-income regions, where cervical cancer rates are highest.
- **Solution**: GAVI negotiated reduced prices with manufacturers, increasing vaccine availability in over 40 countries.

Ethical Debates in Vaccine Equity
1. Prioritizing Healthcare Workers vs. Vulnerable Populations

- Ethical dilemmas arise in balancing the vaccination of frontline workers, who are at higher exposure risk, with older adults, who face severe outcomes.

2. National Interest vs. Global Solidarity

- Should countries prioritize their own populations before donating surplus doses? Critics argue this approach undermines global health efforts.

3. Affordability vs. Innovation

- Balancing affordable vaccine access with incentivizing pharmaceutical innovation through profit-driven models remains contentious.

Future Directions

1. **Global Health Partnerships**

   - Expanding collaborations between governments, NGOs, and private sectors to improve vaccine access.

2. **Sustainable Local Manufacturing**

   - Investing in vaccine production facilities in low- and middle-income countries to reduce dependency on imports.

3. **Dynamic Allocation Models**

   - Real-time monitoring systems to ensure vaccines are distributed where they are most needed.

4. **Comprehensive Education Campaigns**

   - Combating vaccine hesitancy through evidence-based and culturally tailored communication strategies.

10.2.2 Addressing Vaccine Hesitancy

Vaccine hesitancy, defined as the delay in acceptance or refusal of vaccines despite availability, is a significant global public health challenge. It is influenced by a complex interplay of factors, including misinformation, mistrust in healthcare systems, cultural beliefs, and individual perceptions of risk and benefit. Addressing vaccine hesitancy is critical for achieving high vaccination coverage and ensuring the success of immunization programs, particularly in the context of emerging infectious diseases and pandemics.

Understanding the Drivers of Vaccine Hesitancy

1. Misinformation and Lack of Awareness

- Widespread misinformation about vaccine safety, efficacy, and side effects fosters fear and reluctance.
- Example: Myths linking vaccines to autism have been widely debunked but continue to circulate.

2. Trust Deficits in Healthcare Systems

- A lack of trust in government and healthcare institutions, often fueled by past unethical practices, leads to skepticism.
- Example: Historical unethical experiments, such as the Tuskegee Syphilis Study, have contributed to mistrust among marginalized communities.

3. Perceived Risk vs. Benefit

- Low perception of disease severity or susceptibility reduces the perceived need for vaccination.
- Example: Younger individuals may undervalue the importance of COVID-19 vaccines due to a perceived low risk of severe outcomes.

4. Cultural and Religious Beliefs

- Some cultural or religious groups oppose vaccines due to concerns about their ingredients or perceived interference with divine will.

5. Fear of Adverse Effects

- Concerns about rare side effects, often amplified by media coverage, discourage vaccination.
- Example: Reports of myocarditis following mRNA COVID-19 vaccination created fear despite its rarity.

Strategies to Address Vaccine Hesitancy
1. Enhancing Communication and Education
Effective communication strategies are essential for building trust and dispelling misinformation.
a. Transparent Messaging

- Provide clear, evidence-based information about vaccine benefits and risks.
- **Example**: Campaigns explaining the science behind mRNA vaccines reduced hesitancy during the COVID-19 pandemic.

b. Leveraging Trusted Voices

- Engage community leaders, religious figures, and local influencers to advocate for vaccination.
- **Example**: Religious leaders endorsing polio vaccines improved uptake in resistant communities.

c. Targeted Campaigns

- Tailor messages to address specific concerns of different demographic groups.
- **Example**: Multilingual campaigns to reach non-native speakers in diverse populations.

2. Building Trust in Healthcare Systems

Restoring and maintaining trust in healthcare institutions is vital for addressing hesitancy.

a. Community Engagement

- Involve local communities in planning and implementing vaccination programs to foster ownership and trust.

b. Ethical Practices

- Ensure transparency and fairness in vaccine distribution to avoid perceptions of inequality.

c. Accessible Healthcare

- Improve access to vaccines by reducing logistical barriers, such as distance to clinics and costs.

3. Combating Misinformation

Misinformation can be effectively countered through proactive measures.

a. Social Media Monitoring

- Identify and address misinformation on social media platforms in real time.
- **Example**: Fact-checking organizations debunking viral vaccine myths during the COVID-19 pandemic.

b. Digital Literacy Programs

- Educate communities on how to critically evaluate online information sources.

c. Partnering with Technology Companies

- Collaborate with platforms like Facebook, Twitter, and YouTube to limit the spread of false information.

4. Addressing Cultural and Religious Concerns

Respecting and understanding cultural and religious contexts is crucial.

a. Collaborative Dialogue

- Engage with cultural and religious leaders to address vaccine-related concerns within their communities.
- **Example**: Islamic scholars endorsing vaccines containing halal ingredients.

b. Inclusive Practices

- Develop culturally sensitive materials and training programs for healthcare workers.

5. Ensuring Vaccine Safety

Public confidence in vaccines relies on demonstrating their safety.

a. Transparent Reporting of Adverse Events

- Provide accurate information about side effects and their frequency.
- **Example**: Communication about the rare risk of blood clots associated with adenovirus vaccines.

b. Strengthening Post-Marketing Surveillance

- Monitor vaccine safety through real-world data collection and promptly address safety concerns.

Case Studies

1. Polio Eradication in Nigeria

- **Challenge**: Misinformation and religious opposition led to low vaccination rates.

- **Solution**: Community engagement, religious leader endorsements, and culturally tailored messaging significantly improved vaccine uptake.

2. COVID-19 Vaccine Rollout in Rural India

- **Challenge**: Hesitancy due to mistrust and lack of awareness in rural areas.
- **Solution**: Door-to-door campaigns by local healthcare workers educated communities and addressed concerns, leading to higher coverage.

Challenges in Addressing Vaccine Hesitancy

1. **Misinformation Proliferation**

   - Social media platforms amplify misinformation at an unprecedented scale.

2. **Resource Limitations**

   - Low-income regions may lack funding for education campaigns and healthcare worker training.

3. **Persistent Distrust**

   - Long-standing mistrust in healthcare systems and governments is difficult to overcome.

4. **Rapidly Evolving Vaccines**

   - The development of novel platforms like mRNA vaccines can introduce additional uncertainty.

Future Directions

1. **AI-Driven Communication Tools**

   - Utilize AI to monitor and counter misinformation in real time.

2. **Global Vaccine Literacy Programs**

   ○ Establish universal education programs to improve understanding of vaccines and their benefits.

3. **Integrated Community Health Initiatives**

   ○ Combine vaccination efforts with other health services to build trust and reduce hesitancy.

4. **Personalized Outreach**

   ○ Use data analytics to identify and address hesitancy in specific populations.

10.3 Global Health and Pandemic Preparedness
10.3.1 Lessons from SARS, MERS, and COVID-19

The global outbreaks of **Severe Acute Respiratory Syndrome (SARS)** in 2003, **Middle East Respiratory Syndrome (MERS)** in 2012, and the ongoing **COVID-19** pandemic have profoundly reshaped global health strategies and pandemic preparedness. These coronaviruses revealed vulnerabilities in healthcare systems, the critical importance of coordinated international responses, and the need for proactive measures to mitigate future pandemics. Each outbreak has contributed valuable lessons, driving innovations in disease surveillance, vaccine development, and global health governance.

1. Understanding the Epidemics
1.1 SARS (Severe Acute Respiratory Syndrome)

- **Outbreak**: 2003; caused by SARS-CoV-1.
- **Global Impact**: Spread to 29 countries, infecting over 8,000 people with a mortality rate of ~10%.
- **Transmission**: Zoonotic origin, spread via respiratory droplets.
- **Control Measures**: Quarantine, travel restrictions, and public health campaigns successfully halted transmission within months.

1.2 MERS (Middle East Respiratory Syndrome)

- **Outbreak**: 2012; caused by MERS-CoV.
- **Global Impact**: Limited outbreaks primarily in the Middle East, with a mortality rate of ~35%.
- **Transmission**: Zoonotic origin (camels), with occasional human-to-human spread.
- **Control Measures**: Infection prevention protocols in healthcare settings were critical to containment.

1.3 COVID-19

- **Outbreak**: Declared a pandemic in 2020; caused by SARS-CoV-2.
- **Global Impact**: Over 600 million infections and more than 6 million deaths worldwide (as of 2024).
- **Transmission**: Zoonotic origin, with efficient human-to-human spread via respiratory droplets, aerosols, and surfaces.
- **Control Measures**: Vaccination campaigns, social distancing, mask mandates, and public health policies varied widely in effectiveness.

2. Key Lessons Learned
2.1 Early Detection and Surveillance

- **SARS** demonstrated the need for rapid identification of emerging infectious diseases to prevent global spread.
- **MERS** highlighted the importance of zoonotic disease monitoring and understanding animal reservoirs.
- **COVID-19** underscored the role of real-time genomic sequencing in tracking virus evolution and detecting variants.
- **Lesson**: Strengthening global disease surveillance systems is essential for early detection and containment.

2.2 Global Collaboration

- **SARS**: International cooperation through WHO-led efforts enabled rapid containment.
- **MERS**: Limited international spread emphasized the need for global vigilance even in localized outbreaks.
- **COVID-19**: Variations in pandemic responses exposed disparities in global preparedness and coordination.

- **Lesson**: Collaborative frameworks, such as WHO's International Health Regulations (IHR), need to be consistently implemented and updated.

2.3 Vaccine Development

- **SARS**: Efforts to develop vaccines were abandoned as the outbreak ended, leaving no vaccine ready for future coronavirus threats.
- **MERS**: Vaccines remain in development but have yet to reach widespread use due to the disease's sporadic nature.
- **COVID-19**: mRNA vaccines were rapidly developed and deployed, marking a milestone in vaccine technology.
- **Lesson**: Continued investment in platform technologies (e.g., mRNA, viral vectors) ensures readiness for rapid vaccine production.

2.4 Healthcare Infrastructure

- **SARS**: Healthcare systems struggled with surges in cases, revealing gaps in infection control practices.
- **MERS**: Outbreaks in hospitals highlighted the need for stringent infection prevention measures.
- **COVID-19**: Overwhelmed hospitals and supply shortages demonstrated the importance of surge capacity and stockpiles of medical supplies.
- **Lesson**: Strengthening healthcare infrastructure and training is critical to pandemic resilience.

2.5 Communication and Public Trust

- **SARS**: Transparent communication helped reduce public fear and improve compliance with public health measures.
- **MERS**: Misinformation and limited awareness in affected regions slowed response efforts.
- **COVID-19**: Mixed messaging, politicization, and misinformation undermined trust in public health institutions.
- **Lesson**: Clear, consistent, and science-based communication is vital for effective pandemic management.

2.6 Addressing Inequities

- **SARS**: Affected primarily high-income regions, limiting lessons on equity.
- **MERS**: Unequal access to diagnostics and treatments in low-resource settings hampered response efforts.
- **COVID-19**: Vaccine inequity between high-income and low-income countries prolonged the pandemic globally.
- **Lesson**: Equitable access to diagnostics, treatments, and vaccines is necessary to control pandemics and protect vulnerable populations.

3. Innovations and Advances
3.1 Genomic Surveillance

- Real-time sequencing, pioneered during COVID-19, allows for rapid identification of variants, aiding in vaccine updates and public health interventions.

3.2 Digital Health Technologies

- Mobile applications for contact tracing and symptom monitoring were widely adopted during COVID-19, revolutionizing public health surveillance.

3.3 Vaccine Platforms

- mRNA vaccines demonstrated unprecedented speed and adaptability, paving the way for future pandemic vaccines.

3.4 Global Stockpiles

- Strategic reserves of personal protective equipment (PPE) and medical supplies have become a priority for pandemic preparedness.

4. Ongoing Challenges
4.1 Political and Economic Barriers

- Disparities in resource allocation and geopolitical tensions hinder unified global responses.

4.2 Vaccine Hesitancy

- Resistance to vaccination, fueled by misinformation, remains a significant obstacle to achieving herd immunity.

4.3 Zoonotic Spillover

- Human encroachment into wildlife habitats increases the risk of zoonotic diseases. Strengthening One Health approaches, integrating human, animal, and environmental health, is essential.

4.4 Antimicrobial Resistance (AMR)

- Secondary bacterial infections during pandemics exacerbate AMR, complicating treatment options.

5. Recommendations for Future Preparedness

1. **Global Surveillance Networks**

   - Expand and integrate real-time disease monitoring systems across regions to detect outbreaks early.

2. **Sustainable Vaccine Platforms**

   - Maintain investment in adaptable platforms like mRNA to ensure rapid response capabilities.

3. **Equitable Access Mechanisms**

   - Strengthen initiatives like COVAX to ensure low-income countries have fair access to vaccines and treatments.

4. **Healthcare System Resilience**

   - Build capacity for surge scenarios, including training healthcare workers and stockpiling critical supplies.

5. **Strengthened International Collaboration**

   ○ Enhance adherence to WHO's International Health Regulations and promote cooperative research initiatives.

6. **Public Health Communication**

   ○ Develop frameworks for transparent, consistent, and evidence-based messaging to build trust and counter misinformation.

7. **Zoonotic Disease Prevention**

   ○ Implement One Health strategies to reduce the risk of spillover events by monitoring wildlife and addressing environmental factors.

10.3.2 Building Resilient Vaccine Supply Chains

The COVID-19 pandemic underscored the critical importance of resilient vaccine supply chains in ensuring global health security. Disruptions to vaccine manufacturing, distribution, and logistics revealed vulnerabilities in supply chain systems, particularly for low- and middle-income countries. Building robust, adaptable, and equitable vaccine supply chains is essential to meet current immunization demands and prepare for future public health emergencies.

Key Components of Vaccine Supply Chains
1. Manufacturing and Production

- Vaccine manufacturing involves highly complex processes requiring stringent quality controls, advanced technologies, and trained personnel.
- **Bottlenecks**: Dependence on limited facilities for critical components, such as lipid nanoparticles for mRNA vaccines, can delay production.

2. Storage and Distribution

- Vaccines often require specific temperature conditions (e.g., cold or ultra-cold chains) for storage and transport.
- **Challenges**: Limited cold-chain infrastructure in resource-limited settings hinders distribution.

3. Regulatory Approvals

- Delays in international regulatory harmonization and cross-border approvals slow vaccine deployment.

4. Last-Mile Delivery

- The final leg of vaccine delivery involves reaching remote or underserved populations.
- **Issues**: Geographic barriers, workforce shortages, and lack of transportation can impede delivery.

Challenges in Vaccine Supply Chains
1. Limited Manufacturing Capacity

- Concentration of vaccine production in a few countries creates supply bottlenecks during global demand surges.

2. Raw Material Shortages

- Dependencies on a limited number of suppliers for essential raw materials disrupt production schedules.
- **Example**: Shortages of vials, syringes, and lipid nanoparticles during the COVID-19 pandemic.

3. Cold-Chain Logistics

- Many vaccines, particularly mRNA vaccines, require ultra-cold storage (-70°C), which is not feasible in many low-resource regions.

4. Geopolitical Tensions

- Export bans, trade restrictions, and vaccine nationalism exacerbate inequities and disrupt supply chains.

5. Misinformation and Vaccine Hesitancy

- Resistance to vaccination can lead to wasted doses and logistical inefficiencies.

Strategies to Build Resilient Vaccine Supply Chains
1. Diversifying Manufacturing Capacity

- Establishing decentralized production facilities reduces dependency on a few regions.
- **Example**: WHO's mRNA vaccine technology transfer hub in South Africa aims to empower local manufacturing.

2. Strengthening Cold-Chain Infrastructure

- Investing in advanced cold-chain systems ensures the safe storage and transport of temperature-sensitive vaccines.
- **Technologies**: Solar-powered refrigerators, phase-change materials for passive cooling, and mobile cold units.

3. Enhancing Raw Material Supply Chains

- Securing diversified sources for critical raw materials prevents production delays.
- Encouraging local production of components, such as glass vials and adjuvants, can mitigate shortages.

4. Streamlining Regulatory Processes

- Harmonizing regulatory standards across countries accelerates vaccine approvals and distribution.
- **Example**: WHO's collaborative registration procedures reduce delays in low-income countries.

5. Leveraging Digital Technology

- Real-time tracking and monitoring systems improve supply chain transparency and efficiency.
- **Applications**: Blockchain for tracking vaccine batches, IoT sensors for cold-chain monitoring, and AI for demand forecasting.

6. Building Regional Distribution Hubs

- Regional hubs enhance timely vaccine distribution by reducing dependency on long-distance supply chains.
- **Example**: The African Vaccine Acquisition Trust (AVAT) facilitates equitable distribution across Africa.

7. Preparing for Surge Demand

- Strategic stockpiles of vaccines and critical materials enable rapid response during emergencies.
- Establishing flexible production lines that can be repurposed for different vaccines helps address sudden demand spikes.

Case Studies
1. Pfizer-BioNTech mRNA Vaccine Supply Chain

- **Challenges**: Ultra-cold storage requirements limited distribution in low-resource settings.
- **Solutions**: Partnerships with logistics companies to deploy mobile cold storage units and distribute vaccines globally.

2. India's COVID-19 Vaccine Production

- **Challenges**: High domestic demand and raw material shortages impacted global exports.
- **Solutions**: Diversified manufacturing (e.g., Serum Institute of India producing multiple vaccines) and government funding to expand capacity.

3. Ebola Vaccine Distribution

- **Challenges**: Remote and conflict-affected regions posed significant logistical barriers.
- **Solutions**: Use of portable cold-chain technology and community engagement to ensure vaccine access.

Innovations in Supply Chain Resilience

1. Modular Manufacturing Units

- Portable vaccine manufacturing units can be deployed in regions lacking production capacity.
- **Example**: BioNTech's modular mRNA factories for deployment in Africa.

2. Predictive Analytics

- AI-driven tools forecast demand and identify potential bottlenecks, allowing proactive adjustments.

3. Advanced Cold-Chain Technologies

- Innovations like nanomaterials for insulation and portable cryogenic containers reduce reliance on traditional cold-chain systems.

4. Cross-Sector Collaboration

- Public-private partnerships enable resource sharing and improve scalability.
- **Example**: COVAX collaboration among governments, manufacturers, and NGOs.

Future Directions

1. **Sustainable Vaccine Manufacturing**

   - Incorporating renewable energy sources in production and logistics to reduce the environmental impact of supply chains.

2. **Global Equity Frameworks**

   - Establishing binding agreements to ensure equitable vaccine allocation during pandemics.

3. **Decentralized Supply Chains**

- Expanding regional manufacturing and distribution hubs to reduce dependency on global logistics.

4. One Health Integration

- Combining human, animal, and environmental health considerations to ensure preparedness for zoonotic disease outbreaks.

ELEVEN

NEW DEVELOPMENTS IN VACCINE DELIVERY

11.1 AI and Personalized Vaccines

11.1.1 Role of Machine Learning in Antigen Selection

Machine learning (ML), a subset of artificial intelligence (AI), is revolutionizing vaccine development by enabling the efficient and precise selection of antigens. Antigen selection, the process of identifying target molecules capable of eliciting an immune response, is critical to vaccine efficacy. Traditional methods of antigen discovery are labor-intensive and time-consuming. Machine learning leverages large-scale biological data to identify promising antigens rapidly, enhancing vaccine design, especially for complex or mutating pathogens.

1. Importance of Antigen Selection in Vaccine Development

The effectiveness of a vaccine hinges on its ability to target specific antigens that stimulate robust and protective immune responses.

- **Challenges**:

  - Pathogen complexity (e.g., diverse antigenic variations in viruses like HIV and influenza).
  - Identification of conserved epitopes to overcome mutation-related vaccine resistance.

- **Applications**:

○ Machine learning facilitates the discovery of epitopes for emerging infectious diseases, cancer vaccines, and autoimmune therapies.

2. How Machine Learning Transforms Antigen Selection

Machine learning applies computational models to analyze biological data, predict immunogenicity, and prioritize antigens.

2.1 Data Sources for Machine Learning

Machine learning models rely on diverse datasets to identify potential antigens:

- **Genomic Data**: Pathogen genomes sequenced to identify antigenic regions.
- **Proteomic Data**: Analysis of pathogen proteins to discover immunodominant regions.
- **Epitope Databases**: Existing knowledge of immune system interactions with known antigens (e.g., IEDB, ImmPort).
- **Patient Immune Responses**: Data from infected or vaccinated individuals revealing effective antigenic targets.

2.2 Machine Learning Approaches
a. Supervised Learning

- Trains models using labeled data, such as known epitopes, to predict new immunogenic regions.
- **Example**: Predicting binding affinities of pathogen peptides to Major Histocompatibility Complex (MHC) molecules.

b. Unsupervised Learning

- Identifies patterns in unlabeled data, such as conserved sequences across pathogen variants.
- **Example**: Clustering proteins to find conserved epitopes.

c. Deep Learning

- Uses neural networks to analyze complex, high-dimensional data like protein structures.

- **Example**: Predicting 3D folding of antigens to identify surface-accessible regions.

d. Reinforcement Learning

- Continuously optimizes antigen prediction models based on feedback from experimental outcomes.
- **Example**: Improving models with experimental validation of immunogenicity.

3. Applications of Machine Learning in Antigen Selection
3.1 Predicting Immunogenic Epitopes

- ML models analyze pathogen genomes to identify peptides likely to bind MHC molecules, a prerequisite for T-cell activation.
- **Example**: Neural networks predict Class I and Class II MHC-peptide binding for SARS-CoV-2 vaccines.

3.2 Prioritizing Conserved Antigens

- Identifying conserved regions in rapidly mutating pathogens like influenza or HIV helps create universal vaccines.
- **Example**: Machine learning identified conserved epitopes in the HA stem of influenza viruses.

3.3 Designing Multivalent Vaccines

- Predicts combinations of antigens to maximize coverage against diverse pathogen strains.
- **Example**: Multivalent nanoparticle vaccines targeting multiple dengue virus serotypes.

3.4 Cancer Vaccine Development

- Machine learning identifies tumor neoantigens (mutations specific to cancer cells) for personalized cancer vaccines.
- **Example**: Models analyzing mutational data to predict neoantigens in melanoma.

3.5 Detecting Emerging Pathogens

- Real-time analysis of pathogen genomic data during outbreaks can identify antigens for rapid vaccine development.
- **Example**: ML tools predicted immunogenic antigens for Zika and Ebola viruses.

4. Advantages of Machine Learning in Antigen Selection

1. **Speed**

   - Machine learning accelerates antigen discovery, reducing vaccine development timelines.
   - **Example**: Rapid antigen prediction for SARS-CoV-2 vaccines helped expedite mRNA vaccine development.

2. **Accuracy**

   - Predictive models minimize trial-and-error, focusing on highly immunogenic antigens.

3. **Personalization**

   - Machine learning facilitates patient-specific antigen selection for personalized vaccines, particularly in oncology.

4. **Scalability**

   - Capable of analyzing vast datasets, enabling global monitoring of antigenic changes in pathogens.

5. **Cost Efficiency**

   - Reduces the need for extensive experimental testing by narrowing antigen candidates computationally.

5. Challenges and Limitations

1. **Data Quality and Bias**

    ○ Incomplete or biased datasets can lead to inaccurate predictions.
    ○ **Solution**: Standardize data collection and integrate diverse datasets.

2. **Interpretability of Models**

    ○ Complex ML models like deep learning can act as "black boxes," making it hard to explain predictions.
    ○ **Solution**: Develop interpretable models and validate predictions experimentally.

3. **Computational Resource Requirements**

    ○ High-dimensional data analysis requires significant computational power.
    ○ **Solution**: Cloud-based platforms and advances in quantum computing.

4. **Integration with Experimental Validation**

    ○ Predicted antigens require rigorous validation in preclinical and clinical settings.

6. Case Studies
6.1 COVID-19 Vaccine Development

- **Objective**: Rapidly identify immunogenic epitopes for SARS-CoV-2.
- **Approach**: Machine learning models analyzed viral genomes and identified spike protein regions for inclusion in mRNA vaccines.
- **Outcome**: Enabled accelerated vaccine development timelines.

6.2 Neoantigen Prediction in Cancer Vaccines

- **Objective**: Develop personalized vaccines targeting tumor-specific mutations.
- **Approach**: Machine learning predicted patient-specific neoantigens from mutational data in melanoma.

- **Outcome**: Successful stimulation of T-cell responses in clinical trials.

7. Future Directions

1. **Integrated AI Pipelines**

   - Developing AI systems that combine antigen discovery, immune response modeling, and vaccine delivery optimization.

2. **Real-Time Outbreak Monitoring**

   - Using machine learning to analyze genomic data from emerging pathogens for immediate antigen identification.

3. **AI-Powered Personalized Vaccines**

   - Leveraging patient-specific data for tailored vaccines in oncology and autoimmunity.

4. **Collaborative Platforms**

   - Establishing global databases and collaborative AI models to enhance antigen prediction accuracy.

5. **Quantum Computing in ML**

   - Using quantum algorithms to analyze complex antigenic interactions for faster and more accurate predictions.

11.1.2 Tailored Vaccines for Specific Populations
Tailoring vaccines for specific populations is a transformative approach in immunization science, leveraging advances in **genomics, epidemiology,** and **personalized medicine.** These vaccines are designed to meet the unique biological, genetic, and environmental needs of particular groups, enhancing safety, efficacy, and accessibility. From age-based formulations to vaccines targeting region-specific pathogens, tailoring vaccination strategies has the potential to revolutionize public health and improve outcomes across diverse populations.

1. The Need for Tailored Vaccines
1.1 Variability in Immune Responses

- Factors such as **age**, **genetics**, and **comorbidities** influence vaccine-induced immunity.
- **Example**: Elderly individuals often exhibit weaker responses due to immunosenescence, while infants have immature immune systems.

1.2 Epidemiological Differences

- Regional prevalence of pathogens and strain variations necessitate customized vaccine formulations.
- **Example**: The malaria vaccine RTS,S targets *Plasmodium falciparum*, predominant in sub-Saharan Africa.

1.3 Safety Concerns

- Rare adverse reactions in certain populations, such as autoimmune conditions or allergies, highlight the importance of tailored vaccines.

2. Strategies for Tailored Vaccines
2.1 Age-Specific Vaccines
a. Pediatric Vaccines

- Designed for the developing immune systems of infants and children.
- **Example**: Rotavirus vaccines are formulated for early administration to infants, preventing severe diarrheal diseases.

b. Vaccines for the Elderly

- Enhanced formulations with adjuvants or higher antigen doses address weakened immune responses.
- **Example**: High-dose influenza vaccines like Fluzone High-Dose improve efficacy in individuals over 65 years old.

2.2 Genetic and Epigenetic Profiling

- Leveraging genomic data allows the design of vaccines tailored to genetic susceptibilities.
- **Example**: Personalized cancer vaccines identify tumor neoantigens based on individual genomic profiles.

2.3 Region-Specific Vaccines

- Address the unique pathogen profiles and environmental conditions of specific areas.
- **Example**: Dengue vaccines (e.g., Dengvaxia) are tailored to regions with high dengue virus prevalence.

2.4 Comorbidity-Based Customization

- Developing vaccines for individuals with chronic conditions, such as diabetes or cardiovascular diseases, ensures safety and efficacy.
- **Example**: COVID-19 vaccines have been evaluated specifically for patients with underlying health risks.

2.5 Maternal and Neonatal Vaccines

- Vaccines administered during pregnancy protect both the mother and the newborn through passive immunity.
- **Example**: Tdap (tetanus, diphtheria, and pertussis) vaccines are given during pregnancy to protect infants from pertussis.

3. Advances Enabling Tailored Vaccines
3.1 Genomic and Proteomic Insights

- High-throughput sequencing and proteomic analyses identify population-specific epitopes for inclusion in vaccines.
- **Example**: HLA typing is used to predict immune responses in different genetic populations.

3.2 Artificial Intelligence and Machine Learning

- AI tools analyze vast datasets to predict immunogenic targets for diverse populations.

- **Example**: AI-driven models have accelerated the development of vaccines for emerging infectious diseases.

3.3 Adjuvant Technologies

- Novel adjuvants enhance immune responses in populations with weaker immunity, such as the elderly.
- **Example**: MF59, an oil-in-water emulsion adjuvant, is used in influenza vaccines for older adults.

3.4 Delivery Innovations

- Technologies like microneedles and lipid nanoparticles facilitate targeted delivery for specific groups.
- **Example**: Microneedle patches enable pain-free vaccination for children.

4. Applications of Tailored Vaccines
4.1 Influenza Vaccines

- Tailored formulations target specific strains predicted to circulate in different hemispheres annually.

4.2 Cancer Vaccines

- Neoantigen-based vaccines are customized for individual patients, targeting mutations unique to their tumors.

4.3 Malaria Vaccines

- RTS,S is optimized for regions with high *Plasmodium falciparum* transmission, focusing on endemic zones.

4.4 HIV Vaccines

- Experimental HIV vaccines are designed for genetic variations in populations disproportionately affected by the virus, such as sub-Saharan Africa.

5. Challenges in Developing Tailored Vaccines
5.1 Cost and Scalability

- Personalization and regional customization increase production complexity and costs.
- **Solution**: Advancing manufacturing technologies like modular facilities and mRNA platforms can reduce costs.

5.2 Data Gaps

- Limited genomic and epidemiological data from underrepresented populations hinder vaccine design.
- **Solution**: Expanding genomic research initiatives in low- and middle-income countries.

5.3 Regulatory Barriers

- Approval processes vary by region, complicating the deployment of tailored vaccines globally.
- **Solution**: Harmonizing international regulatory frameworks.

6. Case Studies
6.1 Dengue Vaccine (Dengvaxia)

- Tailored for populations in dengue-endemic regions, targeting all four serotypes of the dengue virus.
- **Impact**: Provides partial immunity but highlights challenges in designing vaccines for variable immune responses.

6.2 Neoantigen Cancer Vaccines

- **Example**: Personalized vaccines for melanoma patients demonstrated significant immune activation in clinical trials.
- **Outcome**: Customized therapies are improving survival rates in hard-to-treat cancers.

6.3 Malaria Vaccine (RTS,S)

- Tailored for African regions with high malaria transmission, focusing on children under five.
- **Impact**: Demonstrates the feasibility of region-specific vaccine strategies.

7. Future Directions
7.1 Integration of Multi-Omics Data

- Combining genomics, proteomics, and metabolomics to design hyper-personalized vaccines.

7.2 AI-Driven Personalization

- Using AI to create dynamic vaccine formulations tailored to individual or population-specific needs.

7.3 Decentralized Manufacturing

- Local production facilities can produce region-specific vaccines rapidly, reducing reliance on global supply chains.

7.4 Expanding Vaccine Equity

- Tailored vaccines must be accessible and affordable for all populations to achieve global health equity.

11.2 Interdisciplinary Collaboration
11.2.1 Bridging Academia, Industry, and Governments

Effective vaccine development and delivery hinge on robust collaboration among academia, industry, and governments. These three sectors bring complementary strengths to the table: academia excels in foundational research, industry drives product development and scaling, and governments ensure regulatory oversight and equitable distribution. By fostering interdisciplinary partnerships, this tripartite collaboration can address global health challenges more efficiently, from responding to emerging diseases to improving vaccine accessibility.

1. The Role of Each Stakeholder
1.1 Academia

- **Primary Role**: Conduct basic and translational research, discovering antigens, delivery methods, and immune mechanisms.
- **Strengths**:

  - Expertise in immunology, virology, and molecular biology.
  - Access to public funding and global research networks.
  - Independent validation of safety and efficacy.

- **Challenges**:

  - Limited resources for large-scale development and clinical trials.
  - Difficulty transitioning research discoveries to market-ready products.

1.2 Industry

- **Primary Role**: Develop, manufacture, and commercialize vaccines.
- **Strengths**:

  - Advanced production capabilities and scalability.
  - Expertise in clinical trial design, regulatory submissions, and global distribution.
  - Financial investment in rapid product development.

- **Challenges**:

  - Profit-driven motives may deprioritize low-income markets.
  - Limited capacity to conduct exploratory research without academic partnerships.

1.3 Governments

- **Primary Role**: Provide funding, regulate approval processes, and ensure equitable access.
- **Strengths**:

  - Oversight to enforce safety and efficacy standards.
  - Mechanisms for funding large-scale public health initiatives.

- ○ Authority to drive equitable vaccine distribution and mandate immunization programs.

- **Challenges**:

  - ○ Bureaucratic inefficiencies can delay approvals and funding.
  - ○ Balancing public health priorities with political and economic pressures.

2. Benefits of Bridging Academia, Industry, and Governments

1. **Accelerated Innovation**

   - ○ Academic research and industry expertise in commercialization expedite the transition from discovery to deployment.
   - ○ **Example**: mRNA vaccine platforms were developed through years of academic research and scaled rapidly by companies like Moderna and Pfizer-BioNTech.

2. **Shared Resources**

   - ○ Collaborative projects pool funding, facilities, and talent, reducing redundancy and fostering innovation.
   - ○ **Example**: Public-private partnerships during the COVID-19 pandemic mobilized global resources for vaccine development.

3. **Improved Public Trust**

   - ○ Transparent partnerships, supported by government oversight, enhance confidence in vaccines.

4. **Efficient Regulatory Pathways**

   - ○ Collaboration simplifies the navigation of complex regulatory processes, enabling faster approvals.
   - ○ **Example**: Emergency Use Authorizations (EUAs) during the COVID-19 pandemic were facilitated by joint efforts across sectors.

5. **Equitable Access**

   ◦ Governments and NGOs ensure that vaccines developed by academia and industry reach underserved populations.

3. Models of Effective Collaboration
3.1 Public-Private Partnerships (PPPs)

- **Definition**: Long-term collaborations between public entities (e.g., governments, universities) and private companies.
- **Example**: The Coalition for Epidemic Preparedness Innovations (CEPI) funds vaccine development for emerging infectious diseases, bridging academia, industry, and governments.

3.2 Collaborative R&D Programs

- **Definition**: Joint research initiatives funded by multiple stakeholders.
- **Example**: The NIH's Vaccine Research Center partnered with pharmaceutical companies to develop HIV vaccine candidates.

3.3 Advanced Market Commitments (AMCs)

- **Definition**: Agreements where governments or NGOs guarantee vaccine purchases to incentivize industry investments.
- **Example**: GAVI's AMC for pneumococcal vaccines increased access in low-income countries.

3.4 National and Regional Networks

- **Definition**: Government-led frameworks connecting academic institutions and industry within a country or region.
- **Example**: Operation Warp Speed (OWS) in the USA integrated academia, industry, and federal agencies to accelerate COVID-19 vaccine development.

4. Challenges in Bridging Sectors

1. **Differing Objectives**

- ◦ Academia focuses on knowledge generation, industry on profits, and governments on public welfare. Aligning these priorities requires negotiation and compromise.

2. **Intellectual Property (IP) Disputes**

   - ◦ IP rights often hinder collaboration, particularly in academic-industry partnerships.
   - ◦ **Solution**: Establish clear IP-sharing agreements upfront.

3. **Funding Inequities**

   - ◦ Research in low-income countries often lacks adequate funding, limiting their participation in global collaborations.
   - ◦ **Solution**: Global initiatives like COVAX ensure equitable funding distribution.

4. **Regulatory Complexity**

   - ◦ Diverse regulatory frameworks across countries slow multinational collaborations.
   - ◦ **Solution**: Harmonize global regulatory standards through initiatives like the International Council for Harmonisation (ICH).

5. Case Studies
5.1 COVID-19 Vaccine Development

- **Stakeholders**: Moderna (industry), NIH (academia), and Operation Warp Speed (government).
- **Outcome**: The partnership led to the rapid development, approval, and deployment of mRNA vaccines, highlighting the power of interdisciplinary collaboration.

5.2 Global Polio Eradication Initiative (GPEI)

- **Stakeholders**: WHO, CDC, UNICEF (governmental and intergovernmental), and vaccine manufacturers.

- **Outcome**: Collaborative funding and distribution efforts reduced polio cases worldwide by over 99%.

5.3 Malaria Vaccine (RTS,S)

- **Stakeholders**: GSK (industry), PATH (NGO), and African governments.
- **Outcome**: The vaccine was successfully piloted and deployed in sub-Saharan Africa through coordinated efforts.

TWELVE
CASE STUDIES

12.1 Success Stories

12.1.1 mRNA Vaccines for COVID-19

The development and deployment of **mRNA vaccines for COVID-19** mark a historic achievement in modern medicine. These vaccines, including the **Pfizer-BioNTech (Comirnaty)** and **Moderna (Spikevax)** vaccines, were the first of their kind to receive regulatory approval and have revolutionized the landscape of vaccine science. Their success showcases the power of interdisciplinary collaboration, cutting-edge technology, and global coordination in combating a pandemic.

1. Background on mRNA Technology

1.1 What are mRNA Vaccines?

- mRNA vaccines use synthetic messenger RNA (mRNA) to instruct cells to produce a harmless piece of the virus, typically a spike protein, which triggers an immune response.

1.2 Why mRNA for COVID-19?

- The SARS-CoV-2 virus required a rapid response, and mRNA technology allowed for faster design, testing, and production compared to traditional vaccine platforms.

1.3 Timeline

- **Pre-COVID-19 Research:** Decades of foundational work in RNA stability and delivery methods paved the way for the rapid development of mRNA vaccines.

- **2020 Acceleration**: The availability of SARS-CoV-2 genomic data in January 2020 enabled vaccine design within weeks.

2. Development Process
2.1 Collaboration and Funding

- **Pfizer-BioNTech**: A partnership between a global pharmaceutical giant (Pfizer) and a biotech company (BioNTech).
- **Moderna**: Supported by the U.S. government's Operation Warp Speed.
- **Funding Sources**: Public funding, private investments, and philanthropic contributions facilitated rapid progress.

2.2 Vaccine Design

- The vaccines were designed to encode the **SARS-CoV-2 spike protein**, critical for viral entry into human cells.

2.3 Clinical Trials

- Phases I–III were conducted in record time without compromising safety or efficacy standards:

  - Phase III trials involved over 30,000 participants for Moderna and 43,000 for Pfizer-BioNTech.
  - Efficacy rates: Approximately **94% (Moderna)** and **95% (Pfizer-BioNTech)** in preventing symptomatic COVID-19.

2.4 Regulatory Approval

- Emergency Use Authorizations (EUAs) were granted by regulatory agencies such as the **FDA**, **EMA**, and **WHO** within months of trial completion.

3. Success Factors
3.1 Rapid Innovation

- mRNA vaccines were developed within **less than a year** from the identification of the SARS-CoV-2 genome, a record-breaking timeline.

3.2 Flexible Technology

- mRNA platforms allowed for quick adjustments to incorporate new variants, such as Delta and Omicron.

3.3 Scalable Manufacturing

- The use of **lipid nanoparticles (LNPs)** for delivery enabled large-scale production without the need for traditional live-virus cultures.

3.4 Global Distribution

- Vaccines were distributed to billions of people worldwide through collaborative efforts like **COVAX** and bilateral agreements.

4. Real-World Impact
4.1 Pandemic Control

- mRNA vaccines were instrumental in reducing severe cases, hospitalizations, and deaths, particularly in high-risk populations.

4.2 Variant Adaptability

- Boosters targeting variants were rapidly developed, demonstrating the adaptability of mRNA platforms.

4.3 Economic Benefits

- Vaccination programs accelerated the reopening of economies, mitigating the pandemic's financial toll.

5. Challenges Encountered
5.1 Cold-Chain Logistics

- **Pfizer-BioNTech** required ultra-cold storage (-70°C), limiting distribution in low-resource settings.
- **Solution**: Investments in cold-chain infrastructure and the development of vaccines with less stringent storage requirements.

5.2 Vaccine Hesitancy

- Misinformation about mRNA technology led to hesitancy in some populations.
- **Solution**: Targeted education campaigns and transparent communication about vaccine safety.

5.3 Inequitable Access

- High-income countries initially dominated procurement, delaying access in low- and middle-income regions.
- **Solution**: Initiatives like COVAX and increased donations by wealthier nations improved equity.

6. Broader Implications for Vaccine Science
6.1 Platform Technology

- The success of mRNA vaccines has validated the platform for other diseases, including influenza, Zika, and cancer.

6.2 Research Integration

- Highlighted the importance of integrating academic research, industrial capabilities, and governmental support for rapid innovation.

6.3 Global Preparedness

- Demonstrated the need for proactive investments in vaccine platforms and global manufacturing capacity.

7. Future Directions
7.1 Universal Vaccines

- Research into universal coronavirus vaccines aims to provide protection against all variants and related viruses.

7.2 mRNA Applications Beyond COVID-19

- Expanded use of mRNA technology for therapeutic vaccines, such as cancer immunotherapy, and other infectious diseases.

7.3 Decentralized Manufacturing

- Building regional mRNA production facilities to ensure equitable access during future pandemics.

8. Case Study Summary
Pfizer-BioNTech Vaccine

- **Efficacy**: 95% during initial trials; significant real-world effectiveness in reducing severe outcomes.
- **Challenges**: Ultra-cold storage and initial access disparities.

Moderna Vaccine

- **Efficacy**: 94.1% in trials; effective against variants with updated boosters.
- **Challenges**: Cost and scalability for low-income regions.

COVAX Contribution

- Facilitated vaccine distribution to over 92 low- and middle-income countries, despite logistical hurdles.

12.1.2 Microneedle Systems for Flu

Microneedle systems represent a groundbreaking advancement in vaccine delivery, offering a minimally invasive, patient-friendly alternative to traditional injections. Their application for influenza (flu) vaccines has demonstrated significant potential in enhancing immunization programs by improving accessibility, patient compliance, and vaccine efficacy. Microneedle systems for flu vaccines exemplify how innovative delivery platforms can transform the landscape of preventive healthcare.

1. The Need for Improved Flu Vaccine Delivery
1.1 Limitations of Traditional Flu Vaccines

- **Pain and Fear of Needles**: Deterrents for many, particularly children and needle-phobic individuals.
- **Cold Chain Dependence**: Traditional vaccines often require strict cold storage, limiting distribution in low-resource settings.
- **Healthcare Infrastructure**: Intramuscular injections typically require trained professionals, increasing the burden on healthcare systems.

1.2 Influenza as a Global Health Concern

- Annual flu epidemics result in **3-5 million severe cases** and up to **650,000 deaths** worldwide.
- Seasonal vaccination is the most effective prevention strategy, but global coverage remains suboptimal.

2. Microneedle Technology for Flu Vaccines
2.1 How Microneedles Work

- Microneedles are tiny, skin-penetrating structures (typically 50–900 µm long) that deliver vaccines directly to the dermis and epidermis, where a high concentration of immune cells ensures robust immunogenic responses.

2.2 Types of Microneedle Systems

- **Solid Microneedles**: Pre-coated with flu vaccine antigens, dissolve upon skin application.
- **Dissolvable Microneedles**: Made from biodegradable polymers that encapsulate the vaccine, releasing it as the microneedles dissolve.
- **Hollow Microneedles**: Deliver liquid formulations into the skin.

3. Advantages of Microneedle Flu Vaccines
3.1 Enhanced Immune Response

- Targeting the skin's immune-rich layers results in stronger and more durable antibody responses.

3.2 Painless Administration

- Minimal penetration reduces discomfort, increasing acceptance among needle-phobic patients and children.

3.3 Simplified Distribution

- Heat-stable formulations in microneedles reduce cold-chain requirements, enabling broader access in remote areas.

3.4 Self-Administration

- Microneedle patches can be applied by patients themselves, reducing dependency on healthcare professionals.

3.5 Reduced Medical Waste

- Biodegradable microneedles minimize sharps waste, contributing to eco-friendly healthcare practices.

4. Development and Deployment of Microneedle Flu Vaccines
4.1 Preclinical Studies

- Animal models demonstrated enhanced immune responses with microneedle-delivered flu vaccines compared to intramuscular injections.
- **Example**: Mice immunized with microneedle flu vaccines showed higher hemagglutination inhibition (HAI) titers.

4.2 Human Trials

- Phase I and II trials have confirmed the safety, tolerability, and immunogenicity of microneedle flu vaccines.
- **Example**: A study conducted by Georgia Institute of Technology and Emory University reported robust immune responses and high patient satisfaction with microneedle patches.

4.3 Manufacturing

- Advances in microfabrication technologies have enabled large-scale, cost-effective production of microneedle patches.

5. Case Study: Micron Biomedical's Flu Vaccine Patch

- **Technology**: Dissolvable microneedles containing influenza antigens.
- **Clinical Outcomes**: Demonstrated comparable or superior immunogenicity to traditional injections in Phase I trials.
- **Patient Feedback**: Over 90% of participants preferred the microneedle patch due to its pain-free and convenient application.
- **Global Impact**: The heat-stable nature of the patch made it a viable option for deployment in regions with limited cold-chain infrastructure.

6. Challenges and Limitations
6.1 Regulatory Approvals

- Regulatory pathways for microneedle systems remain complex due to the novelty of the technology.

6.2 Production Scalability

- Large-scale production of microneedles with consistent quality poses technical challenges.

6.3 Cost Concerns

- Initial manufacturing costs are higher compared to traditional syringes and needles.

6.4 Skin Variability

- Differences in skin thickness and sensitivity across populations may influence vaccine efficacy.

7. Broader Implications for Vaccine Delivery
7.1 Pandemic Preparedness

- The ease of administration and distribution makes microneedle systems ideal for rapid vaccination during pandemics.

7.2 Expansion to Other Diseases

- Research is underway to adapt microneedle technology for vaccines against diseases like measles, rubella, and hepatitis B.

7.3 Integration with mRNA Platforms

- Combining microneedles with mRNA vaccines could revolutionize immunization strategies for infectious diseases and cancer.

8. Future Directions
8.1 Optimizing Formulations

- Developing microneedle flu vaccines with broader strain coverage or universal flu vaccines.

8.2 Reducing Costs

- Innovations in manufacturing processes to make microneedle vaccines affordable for low- and middle-income countries.

8.3 Enhancing Stability

- Improving the heat stability of microneedle formulations to eliminate cold-chain dependence entirely.

12.2 Challenges in Implementation
12.2.1 Scaling Up Production
Scaling up vaccine production to meet global demand is a critical challenge in the implementation of new vaccine technologies. Whether addressing seasonal influenza, pandemic outbreaks like COVID-19, or the deployment of innovative platforms like mRNA vaccines or microneedles, expanding production capacity involves overcoming significant scientific, technical, logistical, and regulatory hurdles. Successful scale-up requires collaboration between academia, industry, and governments, along with

strategic investments in infrastructure, workforce training, and supply chain resilience.

1. Factors Influencing Vaccine Production
1.1 Complexity of Vaccine Manufacturing

- Vaccine production involves multiple precise steps, including:

  - Antigen generation (e.g., live virus, recombinant proteins, or mRNA synthesis).
  - Purification, formulation, and quality control.

- Strict compliance with **Good Manufacturing Practices (GMP)** is required, ensuring safety and consistency.

1.2 Specialized Infrastructure

- Production facilities require high-containment environments, bioreactors, and sophisticated equipment.
- Example: mRNA vaccines require lipid nanoparticle (LNP) encapsulation technology, a specialized and resource-intensive process.

1.3 Diverse Vaccine Platforms

- Each platform (e.g., inactivated virus, recombinant protein, or mRNA) presents unique challenges for scaling up:

  - Traditional platforms like egg-based flu vaccines are labor-intensive and slow.
  - Advanced platforms like mRNA allow rapid design but require novel manufacturing setups.

2. Challenges in Scaling Up Vaccine Production
2.1 Limited Manufacturing Capacity

- Global vaccine production is concentrated in a few countries and facilities, creating bottlenecks during pandemics.
- **Case Study**: During the COVID-19 pandemic, countries like India (Serum Institute of India) became critical hubs for vaccine production but faced

raw material shortages.

2.2 Supply Chain Disruptions

- Dependencies on specific suppliers for critical components like adjuvants, lipid nanoparticles, and syringes can delay production.
- Example: During the early stages of COVID-19 vaccine production, shortages of glass vials impacted supply chains.

2.3 Regulatory and Quality Control

- Scaling up production requires rigorous testing at every stage to ensure quality and safety, slowing the process.
- Each country may have unique regulatory requirements, complicating large-scale distribution.

2.4 Workforce Limitations

- Vaccine production demands highly skilled personnel trained in GMP protocols.
- Shortages of qualified staff can hinder expansion, particularly in low-resource settings.

2.5 Cost and Investment Challenges

- High upfront costs for building new facilities or upgrading existing ones are prohibitive for many manufacturers.
- Example: Developing countries may lack the financial resources to invest in large-scale production.

3. Solutions for Scaling Up Production
3.1 Decentralizing Manufacturing

- Building regional production hubs reduces dependence on a few facilities and ensures equitable access.
- **Example**: WHO's mRNA technology transfer hub in South Africa aims to empower low- and middle-income countries to produce their own vaccines.

3.2 Leveraging Modular Facilities

- Modular, portable biomanufacturing units can rapidly scale production in response to outbreaks.
- **Example**: BioNTech's mobile mRNA production units for deployment in underserved regions.

3.3 Enhancing Supply Chains

- Diversifying suppliers and stockpiling critical materials can mitigate supply chain disruptions.
- Implementing **digital tools** for supply chain monitoring enhances transparency and efficiency.

3.4 Streamlining Regulatory Approvals

- Harmonizing international regulatory standards accelerates the approval of production processes and facilities.
- **Example**: Collaborative frameworks like WHO's prequalification program help streamline approvals in low-resource settings.

3.5 Public-Private Partnerships

- Governments and NGOs can fund infrastructure and provide incentives for scaling up production.
- **Case Study**: Operation Warp Speed (USA) provided funding and logistical support to companies scaling up COVID-19 vaccine production.

3.6 Workforce Development

- Investing in training programs for biomanufacturing professionals ensures an adequate skilled workforce.
- Example: Partnerships between universities and vaccine manufacturers to establish biotech training programs.

4. Case Studies
4.1 COVID-19 Vaccine Scale-Up

- **Challenge**: Scaling mRNA vaccine production required global collaboration and investment in new facilities.
- **Solution**: Pfizer-BioNTech and Moderna rapidly scaled manufacturing using partnerships, modular production units, and international supply chains.

4.2 Influenza Vaccine Production

- **Challenge**: Egg-based flu vaccine production is slow and limited in capacity.
- **Solution**: Transitioning to cell-based and recombinant technologies allows faster and more scalable production.

4.3 Ebola Vaccine Deployment

- **Challenge**: Scaling up production during outbreaks was difficult due to limited demand in non-outbreak periods.
- **Solution**: Advanced Market Commitments (AMCs) incentivized manufacturers to maintain production capacity.

5. Future Directions in Vaccine Production
5.1 Automation and AI Integration

- Using AI to optimize production processes and monitor quality control can increase efficiency.

5.2 mRNA and DNA Vaccine Platforms

- Expanding the use of flexible platforms like mRNA reduces time-to-market for future vaccines.

5.3 Global Collaboration

- Strengthening international frameworks for sharing technology, data, and resources fosters global production capacity.

5.4 Green Manufacturing

- Developing environmentally sustainable vaccine production methods reduces the ecological footprint of biomanufacturing.

12.2.2 Overcoming Logistic Barriers

Logistics play a pivotal role in the effective implementation of vaccination programs, particularly in reaching underserved populations during pandemics or routine immunization campaigns. Logistic barriers, such as inadequate infrastructure, cold-chain requirements, workforce shortages, and geopolitical challenges, can delay vaccine delivery and exacerbate health inequities. Overcoming these barriers requires a multifaceted approach involving technological innovation, strategic planning, and global collaboration.

1. Key Logistic Barriers in Vaccine Delivery
1.1 Cold-Chain Dependency

- Many vaccines require precise temperature control to maintain potency, with some, like mRNA vaccines, necessitating ultra-cold storage.
- **Challenge**: Inconsistent cold-chain infrastructure in low- and middle-income countries (LMICs).

1.2 Limited Transportation Networks

- Geographic barriers, such as remote locations or difficult terrains, hinder vaccine distribution.
- **Challenge**: Lack of accessible roads, vehicles, or transportation infrastructure.

1.3 Workforce Shortages

- Vaccine distribution and administration require trained personnel, which may be lacking in resource-constrained areas.
- **Challenge**: Limited numbers of healthcare workers to manage storage, transport, and immunization.

1.4 Supply Chain Disruptions

- Dependencies on single suppliers or insufficient stockpiles lead to delays during high-demand periods.

- **Challenge**: Bottlenecks in manufacturing and delays in raw material procurement.

1.5 Political and Economic Factors

- Conflicts, trade restrictions, and economic instability can disrupt vaccine supply chains.
- **Challenge**: Export bans and sanctions during global crises hinder equitable distribution.

2. Strategies to Overcome Logistic Barriers
2.1 Strengthening Cold-Chain Systems

- **a. Cold-Chain Technology Innovations**

  - Solar-powered refrigerators and portable cooling units ensure temperature stability in remote regions.
  - Example: SolarChill refrigerators used in sub-Saharan Africa.

- **b. Thermal Packaging Solutions**

  - Advanced thermal insulation materials maintain vaccine potency during transport without refrigeration.

- **c. Vaccine Formulation Advances**

  - Developing heat-stable vaccines reduces dependence on cold chains.
  - Example: Lyophilized (freeze-dried) vaccines for reconstitution at the point of use.

2.2 Enhancing Transportation Networks

- **a. Drone Delivery Systems**

  - Drones provide rapid delivery to hard-to-reach areas, bypassing poor infrastructure.
  - Example: Zipline drones in Rwanda and Ghana have successfully delivered vaccines to remote clinics.

- **b. Community-Based Distribution Models**

  - Leveraging local transport options (e.g., motorbikes, boats) ensures last-mile delivery.

- **c. Geographic Information Systems (GIS)**

  - Mapping tools optimize delivery routes and identify logistical bottlenecks.

2.3 Workforce Development

- **a. Training Programs**

  - Investing in healthcare worker training for vaccine handling, storage, and administration.

- **b. Task Shifting**

  - Utilizing non-traditional workers, such as community health volunteers, to support vaccine delivery.

- **c. Mobile Immunization Teams**

  - Deploying specialized teams for mass immunization drives in underserved areas.

2.4 Strengthening Supply Chains

- **a. Diversifying Suppliers**

  - Reducing reliance on single sources for raw materials and critical components.

- **b. Real-Time Monitoring Systems**

  - IoT-based sensors track vaccine shipments, providing data on temperature, location, and potential delays.

- **c. Strategic Stockpiles**

  - Establishing regional vaccine reserves ensures readiness for emergencies.

2.5 Addressing Political and Economic Challenges

- **a. International Agreements**

  - Initiatives like COVAX promote equitable vaccine access by coordinating global procurement and distribution.

- **b. Humanitarian Corridors**

  - Establishing neutral zones for vaccine delivery during conflicts ensures uninterrupted immunization.

- **c. Financial Support**

  - Subsidies and funding from international organizations (e.g., WHO, GAVI) support vaccine distribution in economically unstable regions.

3. Case Studies
3.1 COVID-19 Vaccine Rollout in Rural India

- **Challenge**: Geographic barriers and limited cold-chain infrastructure in remote villages.
- **Solution**: Mobile vaccination units equipped with portable refrigerators and community health workers conducted door-to-door campaigns, significantly increasing coverage.

3.2 Drone Vaccine Delivery in Rwanda

- **Challenge**: Remote regions lacked reliable roads, delaying access to vaccines.
- **Solution**: Zipline drones delivered vaccines and medical supplies within hours, ensuring timely immunization.

3.3 Polio Vaccine Distribution in Nigeria

- **Challenge**: Political instability and distrust in vaccination programs hampered outreach.
- **Solution**: Community engagement, combined with the use of boats and motorbikes for delivery, facilitated immunization in conflict-affected areas.

4. Technological Innovations
4.1 Blockchain for Supply Chain Transparency

- Blockchain technology ensures real-time tracking and tamper-proof records of vaccine shipments, improving accountability.

4.2 AI for Demand Forecasting

- Predictive analytics optimize inventory management, reducing wastage and ensuring timely replenishment.

4.3 Mobile Cold-Chain Units

- Portable cooling devices powered by renewable energy expand cold-chain access in underserved regions.